IMAGES
of America

TOWN OF WALLKILL

I0812714

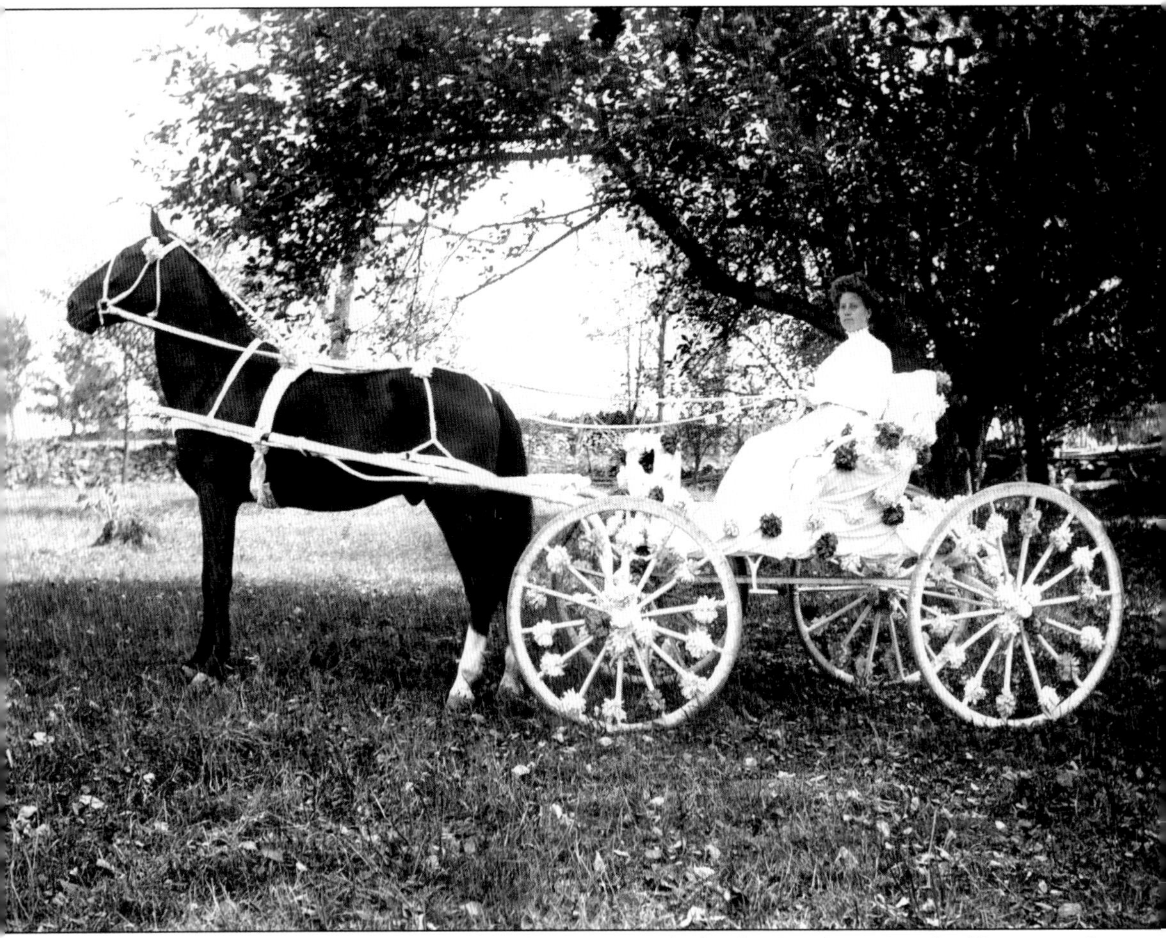

Lillian Hoyt Beyea poses in her decorated carriage, ready for the Coaching Parade. (Courtesy of the Paul Weisshaar collection.)

On the cover: The Orange County Agricultural Society has sponsored the annual Orange County Fair since 1841. Greatly enlarged since this 1920s photograph, the fair still combines traditional farm-related events with modern amusements.

IMAGES

of America

TOWN OF WALLKILL

Dorothy Hunt-Ingrassia

ARCADIA
PUBLISHING

Copyright © 2005 by Dorothy Hunt-Ingrassia
ISBN 978-0-7385-3941-6

Published by Arcadia Publishing
Charleston, South Carolina

Printed in the United States of America

Library of Congress Catalog Card Number: 2005933166

For all general information contact Arcadia Publishing at:
Telephone 843-853-2070
Fax 843-853-0044
E-mail sales@arcadiapublishing.com
For customer service and orders:
Toll-Free 1-888-313-2665

Visit us on the Internet at www.arcadiapublishing.com

This book is proudly dedicated to my grandchildren in the hope that it will encourage them to preserve the history of their own times.

CONTENTS

ACKNOWLEDGMENTS

Special thanks go to Gwen Deserto for her untiring dedication to the compilation of the history of our beloved Town of Wallkill. Our gratitude and thanks go to Marvin Cohen, who inspired us, and gave us endless guidance in this endeavor.

Sincere appreciation goes to all our family and friends for their support and encouragement in this preservation of the town's history. Last but not least, we owe a debt of gratitude to the many people and organizations who have shared their memories and photographs. This book would not have been possible without their support.

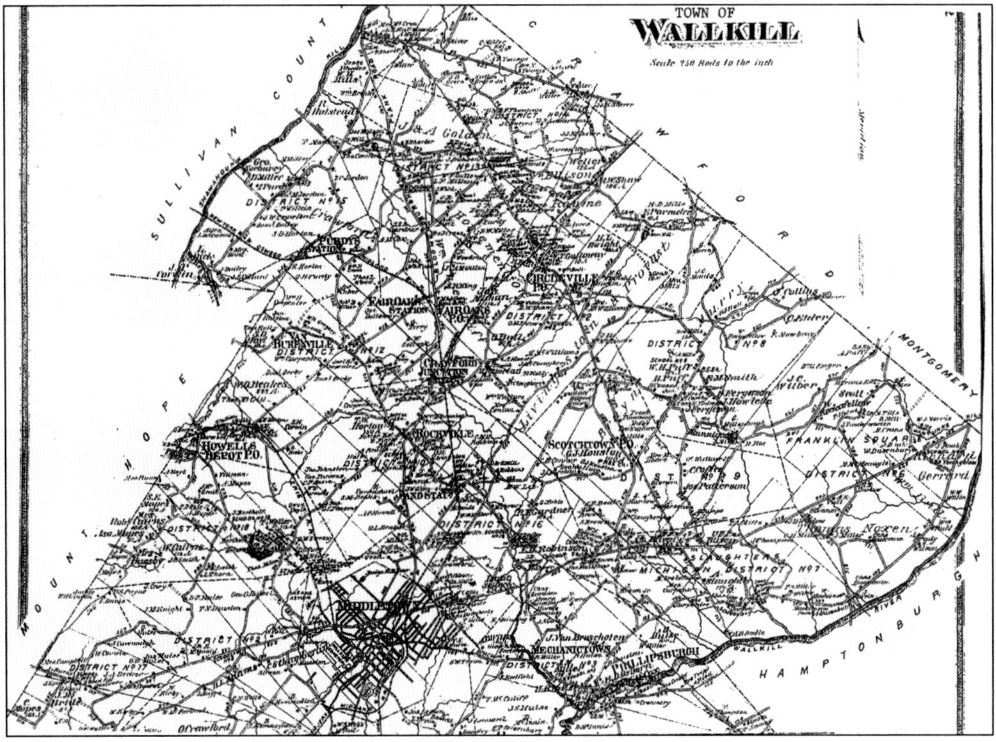

This map of the Town of Wallkill is dated 1875.

Introduction

The Town of Wallkill, a site of phenomenal growth, is located in the heart of Orange County, New York, midway between the Hudson River on the east and the Delaware River on the west, sixty miles north of New York City.

The original Wallkill Precinct (of which the present town is a successor), was created by an act of the Colonial Legislature on December 17, 1743, and was divided into two sections, the John Evans Patent and the Minisink Angle, extending into Ulster County. The original area was much larger than the present size and was peeled away gradually until the town arrived at its present day boundaries. The first town meeting of the new Town of Wallkill was held at the home of Samuel Watkins on April 7, 1772. William Dunn was elected supervisor and town clerk.

Wallkill's claim to fame during the Revolutionary War was when residents Henry Wisner and Moses Phillips produced much of the gunpowder used by American troops in their Phillipsburgh and Craigville factories. Wisner was a delegate to the Continental Congress in 1776, but he did not sign the Declaration of Independence. He was so intent on fulfilling his gunpowder contracts with the government that he hastened back to Orange County before the historic event took place.

In the early 1820s, George F. Reeve, a prominent Town of Wallkill resident, designed an invention that would relieve many housewives of the back-breaking chore of churning butter. A trained dog on a treadmill provided both dog power and amusement for a large number of Wallkill families.

Hamlets sprang up around the early churches, namely; Mechanicstown (deriving its name from the fact that it was a settlement of "industrious mechanics"), Scotchtown, Circleville, Phillipsburgh, Howells Depot, Van Burenville, Fair Oaks, Rockville, Bull Hack, Millsburgh, Brimstone Hill, Michigan Corners, Davistown, LaGrange, Honey-Pot, Guinea, Crawford Junction, Purdy's Station, and Lockwood's (the last three being trackside stopping places on the New York, Ontario and Western Railway). Van Burenville, so named by Christian Shons in honor of the newly elected President Martin Van Buren, was doomed when it was by-passed by the coming of the railroad to Howells Depot. The post office at Van Burenville was moved to Howells in the late 1840s.

The area between the present hamlet of Howells and Mount Hope was known for many years as Mapestown because of the dense population of families with that name.

With its magnificent water power and government contracts for powder during the Revolutionary War, Phillipsburgh had every prospect of advanced growth. People from the vicinity of what is now Middletown went to Phillipsburgh to do their shopping. However, the growth of Middletown, as an important railway village, dwarfed Phillipsburgh. When the Erie Railroad began daily service for passengers and freight in 1843, the village of Middletown became the end of the line and an important rail center.

As the Civil War era approached, Middletown and Wallkill together supplied no less than six companies and regiments to fight for the Union.

The Town of Wallkill, pursuant to the legislative act of 1856, sent children to district schools and at present still has no school districts of its own.

The town is served by seven volunteer fire companies, the earliest of which is Howells Fire Company (1924), followed by Mechanicstown Engine and Chemical Company No. 1, Circleville Volunteer Fire Company, Washington Heights Volunteer Fire Company, Silver Lake Volunteer Fire Company, and Pocatello Volunteer Fire Company. Bloomingburg Fire Company also covers a northern portion of the town.

In the early 1960s, the town began to feel the impact of development as new highways put it within driving distance of New York City and New Jersey. The opening of Route 17 and Interstate 84 and the placement of interchanges in the town changed the complexion of the area. In 1960, the census reported 8,000 people, and by 2000, it had grown to 24,659. Today, the town boasts having 12 parks and recreational areas and its own golf club.

Along with its commercial development, Wallkill remains a town with beautiful scenic roadways, neighborhood hamlets, and a rural atmosphere.

One

EARLY HOMESTEADS

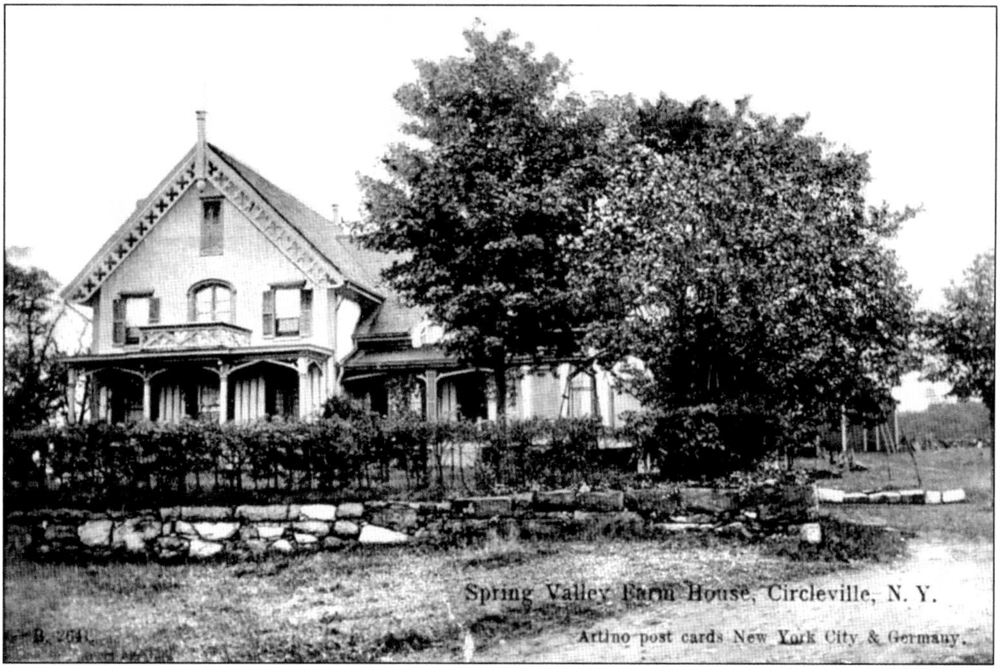

In 1854, Nathan D. Mills had this home built as a wedding present for his daughter. The Spring Valley Farmhouse became a northern tobacco plantation, and mulberry trees were also grown there. The last residents to occupy this Victorian house, with board and batten siding, were Isabelle and William Vincent Weber. This charming home is located near Circleville on the Goshen Turnpike. (Photograph courtesy of Leona Trimmer, information courtesy of James and Isabelle Townsend.)

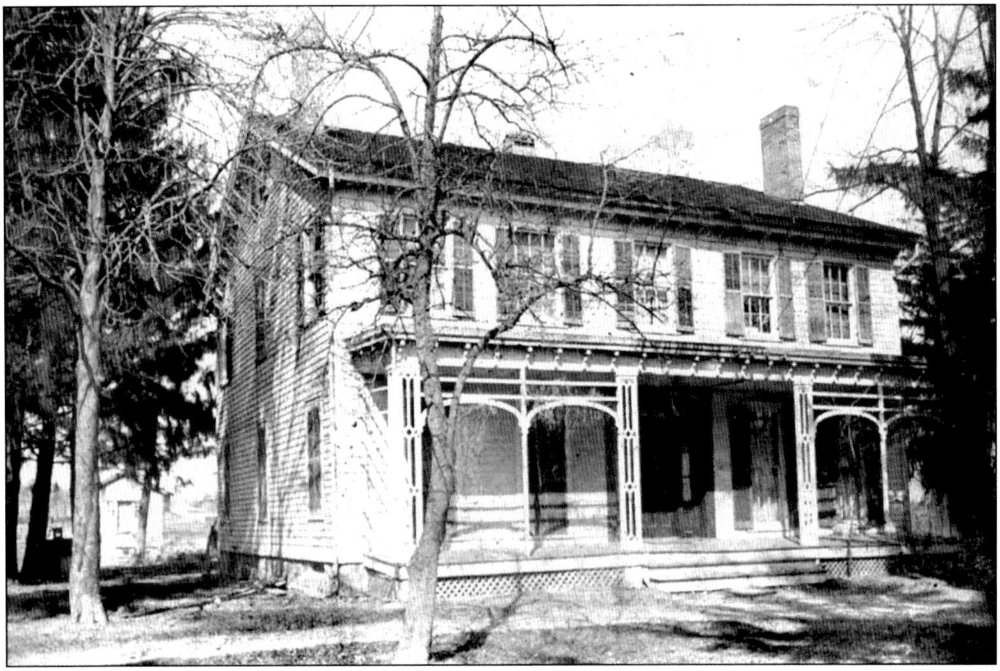

Capt. Thomas Everson Hulse erected this country home in 1855. Located on East Main Street in Mechanicstown, the Capt. Thomas Everson Hulse home later became the Pine Grove Inn. Hulse was a captain on steamships on the Hudson River, one of which he named after himself, the *Thomas E. Hulse.* (Courtesy of the Historical Society of Middletown and the Wallkill Precinct.)

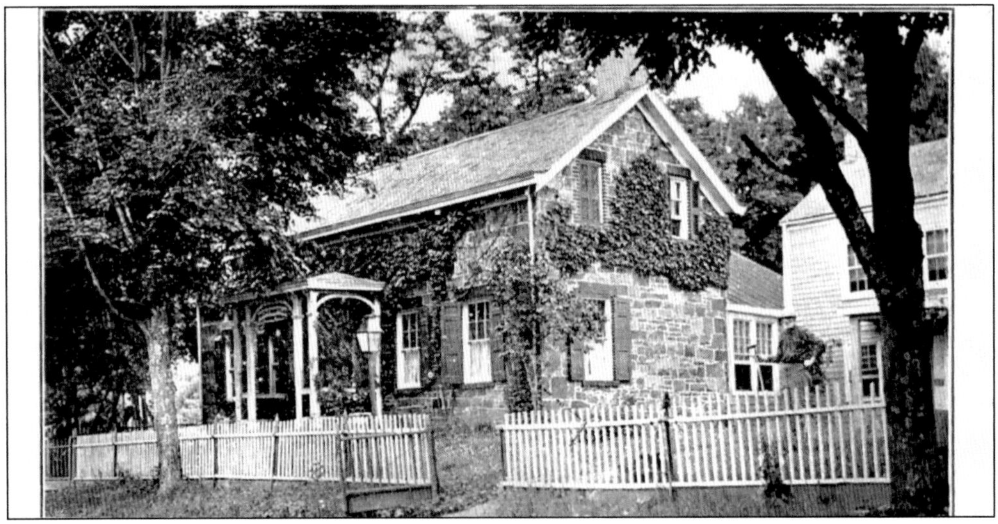

Samuel Bull, a great-grandson of William and Sarah Bull, built this house in Circleville in 1831. But Circleville was not in existence then, and the new house stood in a sparsely settled area known as Bull Hack. Mary Osborn Bull, sure their crossroads would become a thriving center, said it must have a name, and at a November 1841 meeting at the Samuel Bull Homestead, the company adopted her suggestion that it be called Circleville. She had heard about a town in Ohio with that name and thought it would be a pleasant title. Partitions as well as the exterior of this home are of stone. The frame structure in which the Bulls lived during the completion of the stone house was finished off to serve as a wing of the stone structure. (Courtesy of Leona Trimmer.)

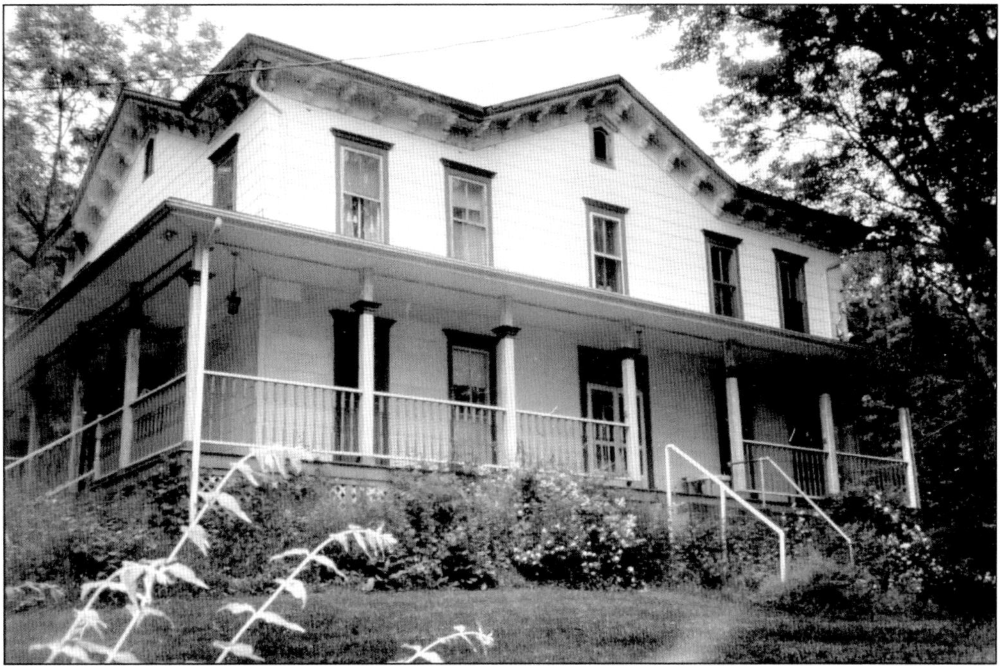

At the end of East Main Street in Phillipsburgh was the beautiful country home of Henry B. Hulse, built in the early 1800s. Across the road from his Rosedale Farm was his gristmill, alongside the Wallkill River. In 2005, the Henry B. Hulse home was torn down after it was purchased by the Orange Regional Medical Center for its new complex.

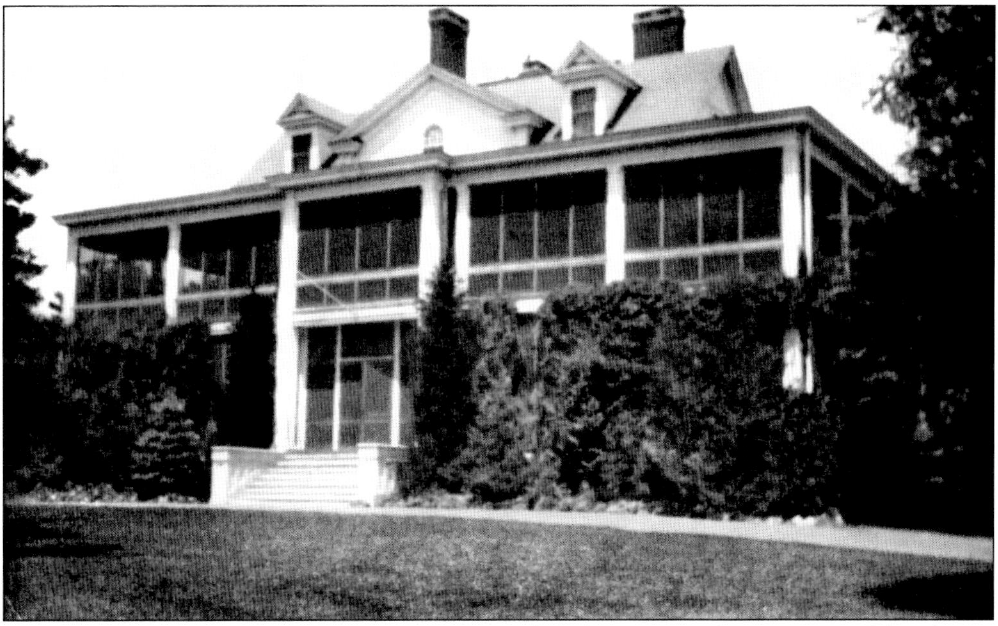

Located on Hufcut Road, the Hume Homestead included 12 rooms. The main part of this elegant home was built in 1856 by Mary Shorter. The back portion of the house is older. (Courtesy of the Hume Family.)

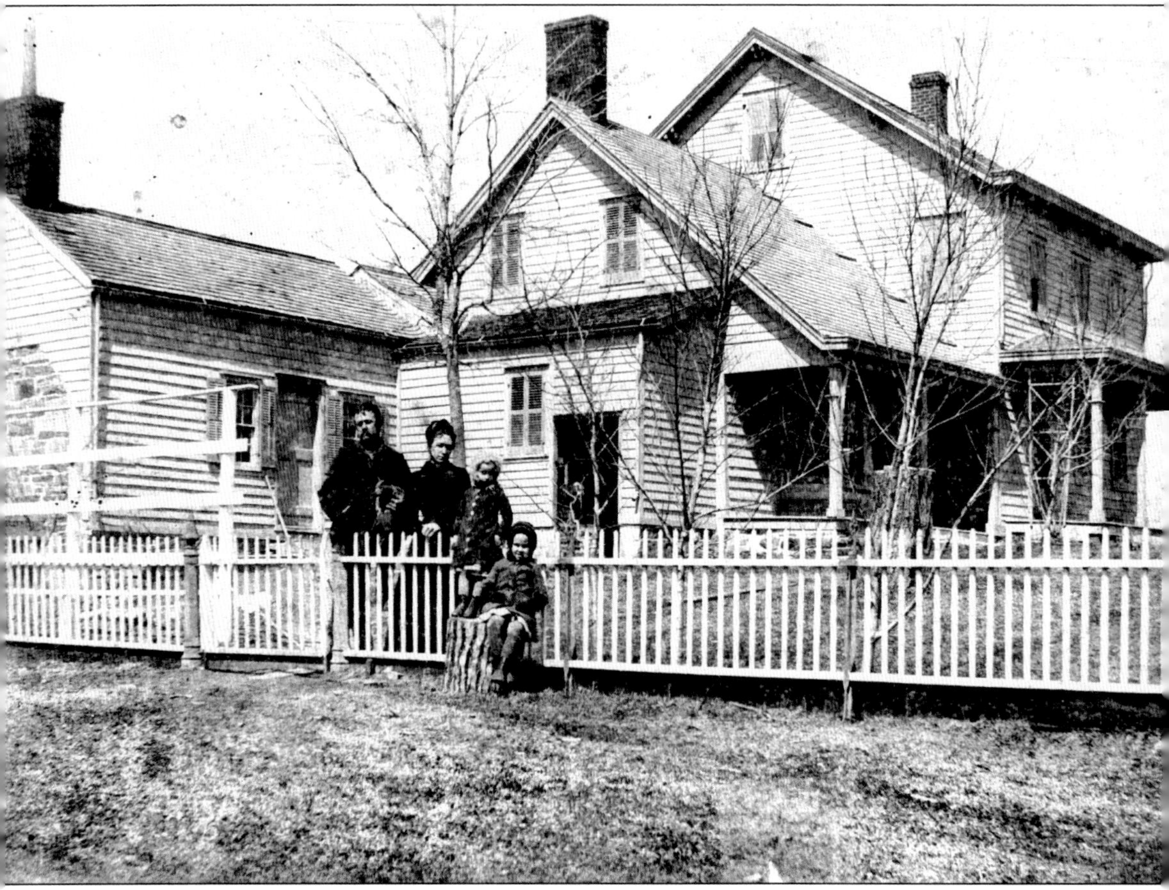

Pictured in front of the late-1800s David Ayres home in Circleville are, from left to right, David Ayres, Mary Ayres, Bertha Ayres, and unidentified. The house was demolished in order to build the Circleville elementary school. (Courtesy of the Paul Weisshaar collection.)

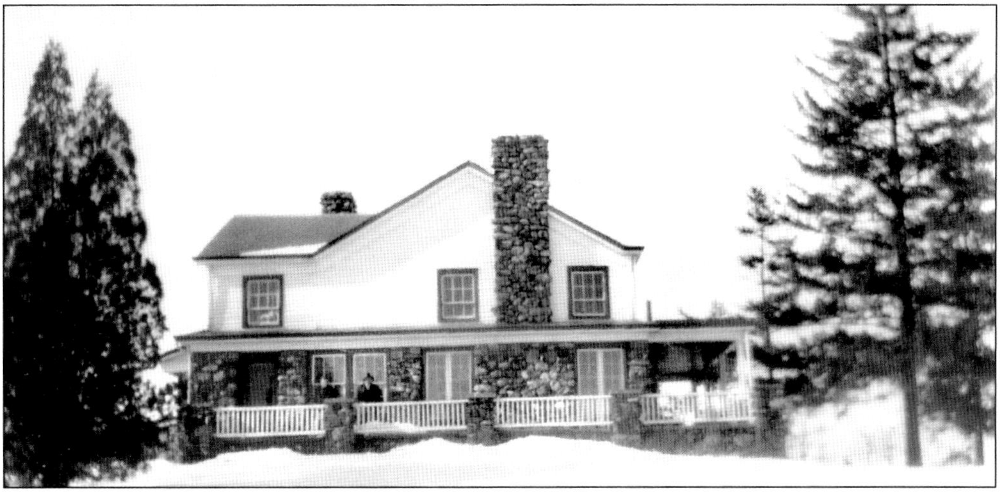

This early home, with its inviting front porch and stone chimney, was built by Horace Henry Dunning. The Dunning family resided in this charming home for many years. In 1978, Park Manor was built on a part of the property. Later, the house was purchased by Price Chopper, demolished, and a store was built. Dunning Road was named for this well-known family. (Courtesy of Marjorie Stewart.)

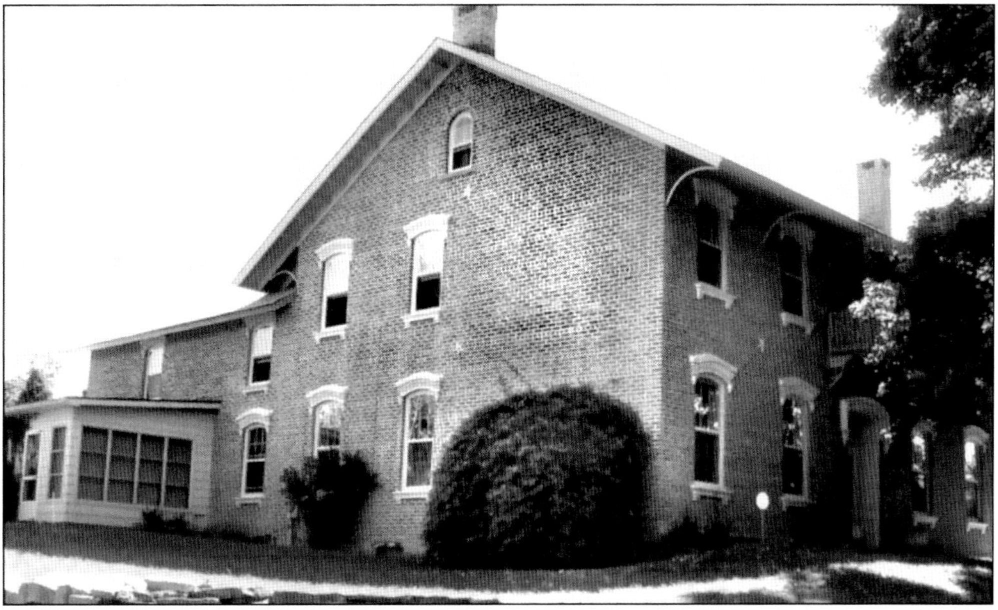

Samuel Callendar Howell purchased 57 acres of land from George Bell in 1845. The Erie Railroad route cut across the property soon afterward. The Erie Railroad did not have funds to build at this intersection, so Howell himself built a station, vast freight sheds for housing bulk materials, a hotel, and several dwellings. A population center was created, and Howells Depot was the natural name. Samuel Howell built his home, and in 1869, the housewarming was to also celebrate the marriages of their two sons Henry and James. Recognizing a fire hazard, the Samuel Howell Home was built of brick, and the shutters were fireproof, made of massive panels of iron. As the home was on a bluff above the station, Howell could look down on his humming hamlet and his wife, Sally Jane Beakes, could watch her farmer sons come each day to the creamery. The name of the hamlet was later shortened to Howells.

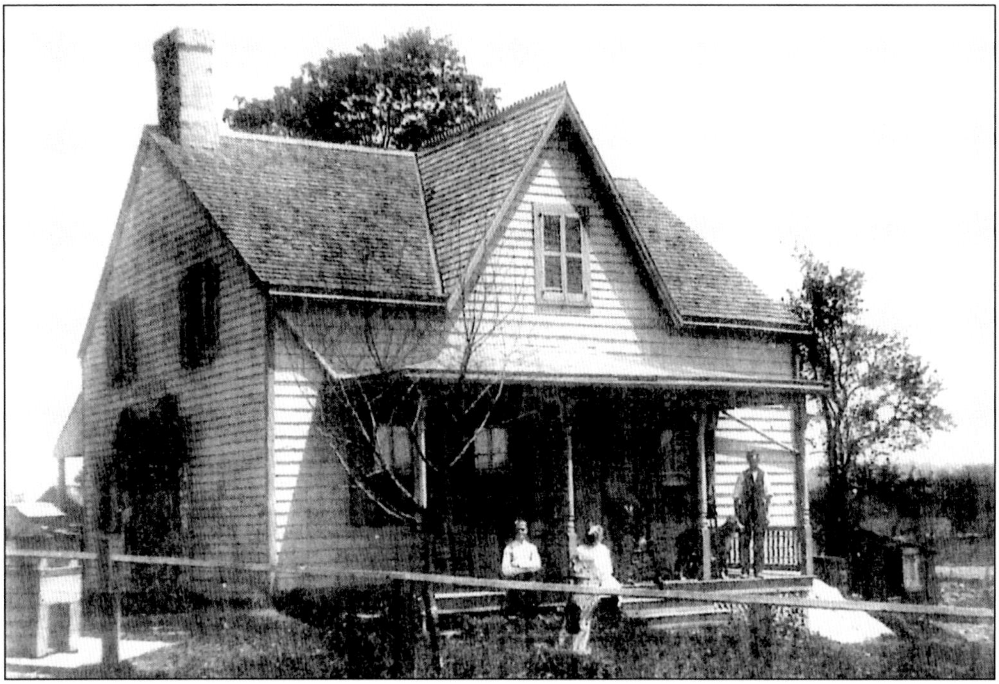

The Olver Home belonged to Frank and Gladys Olver and their four children. Formerly known as the Roger House, it possibly was one of the original houses of the Smith Livingston family. Gladys Olver was a descendent of Smith H. Livingston. In this 1918 photograph, family members stand in front of the Olver Home, located on Maples Road in the Town of Wallkill. (Courtesy of the Olver family.)

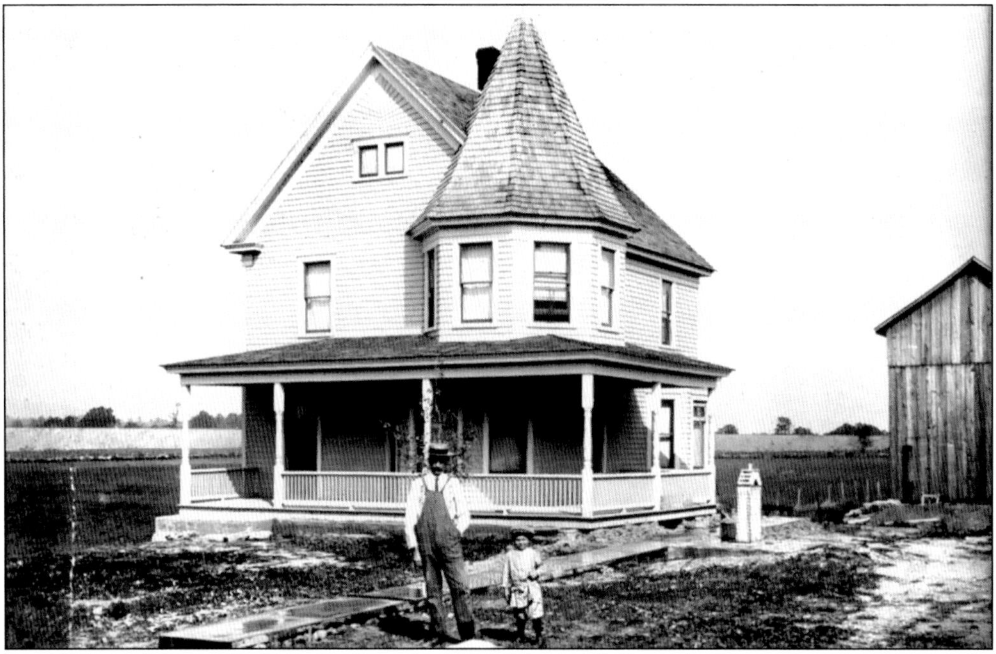

This Victorian home, built by the Townsend family in 1901, is located on Elm Street in Howells. The historical Townsend House is still used as a residence. (Courtesy of Larry and Linda Weyant.)

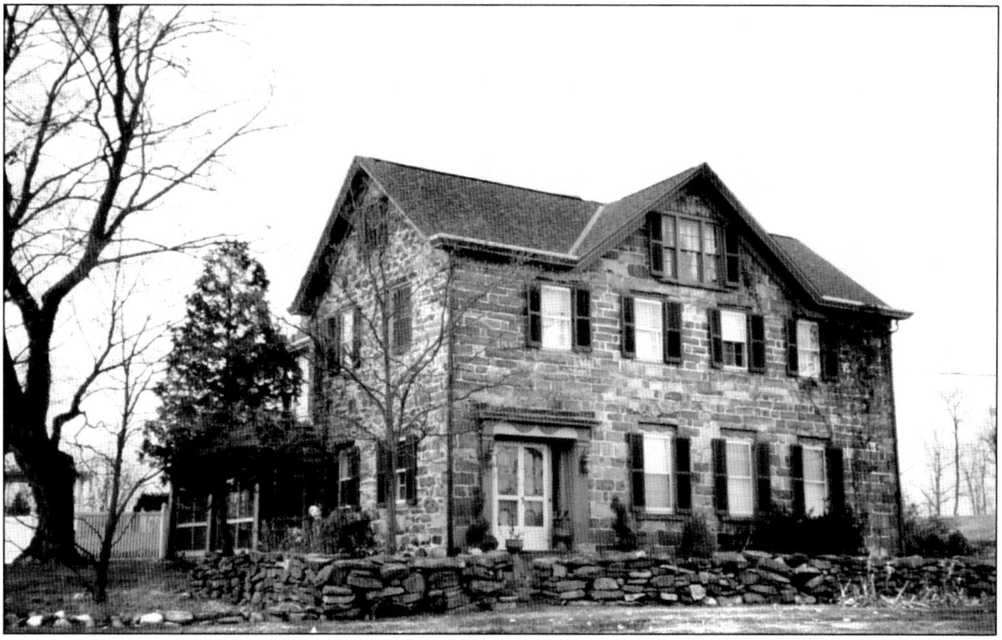

In 1791, Jacob Mills built this home on a large uncleared tract in Wallkill. It is said the stones used for this home were excavated on the farm. He occupied the stone house until 1807, when he built a large frame dwelling near the Scotchtown Church. Due to the large number of Mills families that resided in the immediate area, the hamlet was named Millsburgh. The historical Jacob Mills House is still used as a residence.

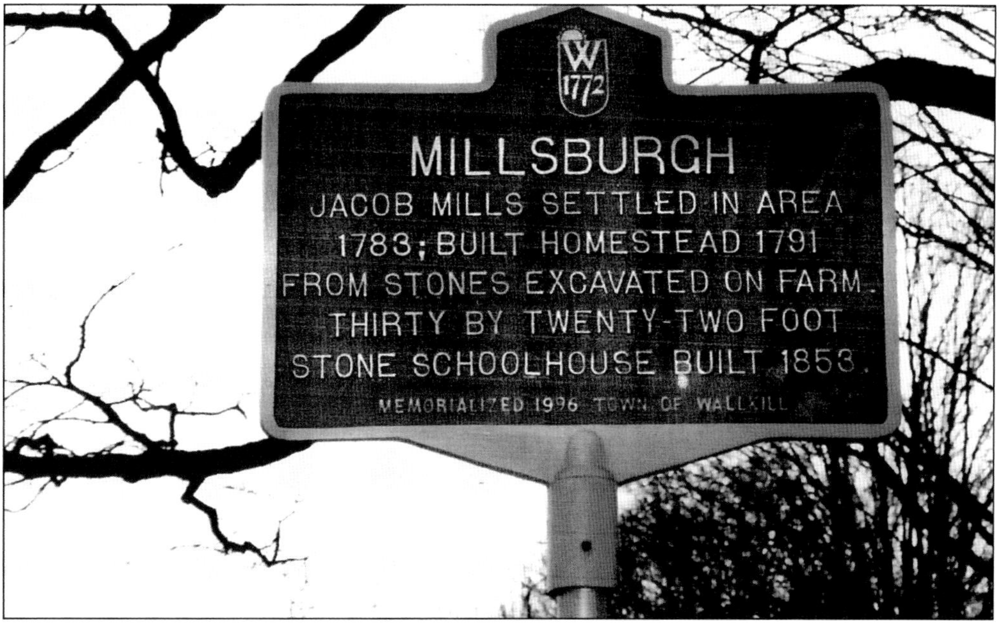

Shown is one of the New York State historic markers.

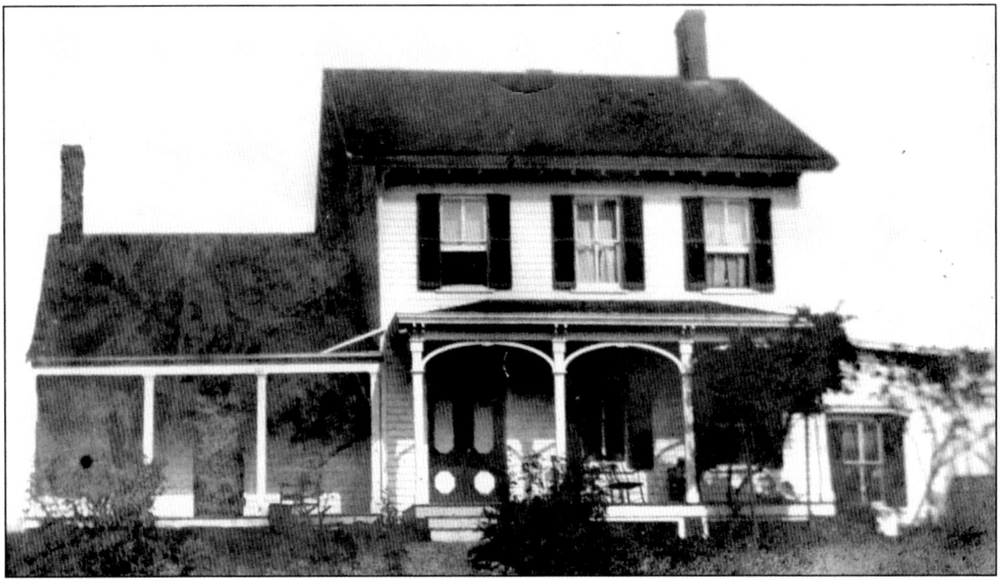

This property was conveyed by Benjamin Tuthill to William Lockwood in 1796. From 1853 to 1908, the Lockwood Home was in the possession of Allan Lockwood and his heirs. During this period there was a railroad station on the New York, Ontario and Western Railway called Lockwood's. The property was sold to Adeline Simpson in 1908, and she ran a boardinghouse at that site. During World War I, she boarded soldiers who were assigned to guard the railroad trestle. She sold the property to George M. Miller who, in 1930, sold it to Raymond Dolfini.

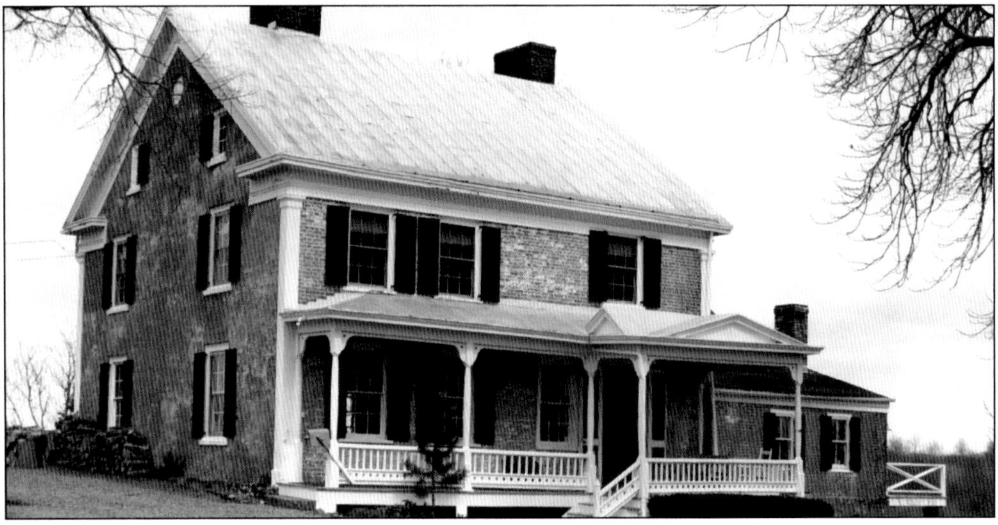

The Bull Home on Bart Bull Road is unique among early Bull houses in Orange County since it was made of brick instead of stone. William Bull, grandson of William and Sarah, who had been promoted to captain in the Continental forces at Valley Forge, undertook the construction of the home for himself and his father's family immediately upon returning from the war in 1780. Debris from the log hut that had served as a home until then is still found in the field across from the house. Bricks were used not only for the outer walls, four bricks thick and three stories high at the gable ends, but also for every partition in the 15-room house. The total cost was $800. Five generations of the Bull family have lived in this spectacular home, including Orange County's well-known educator, Amy Bull Crist.

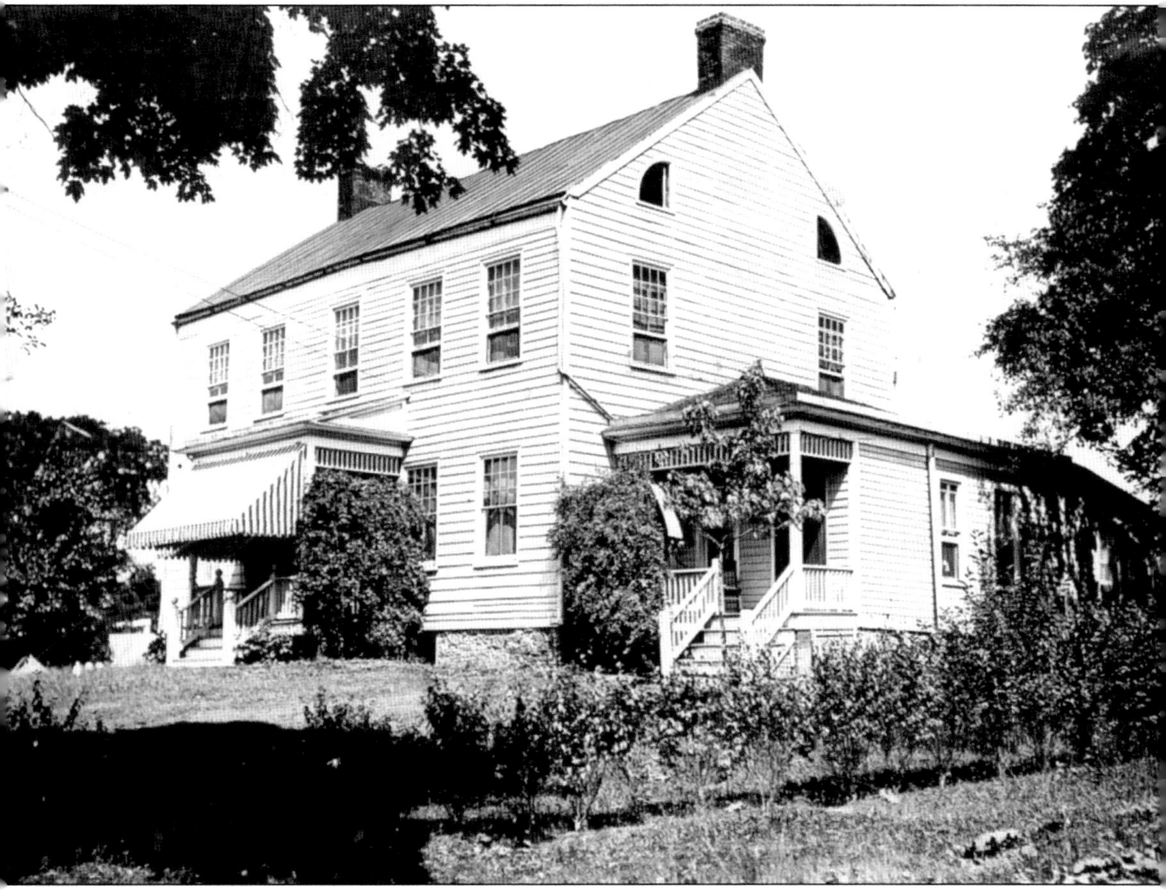

William Otis built this house around 1814, when he married Clarissa Gale, a neighbor's daughter. However, the activities of his younger half-brother, Issac, and who stayed only a couple of years at Mechanicstown, will be remembered longest. Isaac Jr. came in 1816 with his father, a veteran of the Revolution. From descendants of the Otises it is revealed that, in a small shop beside the busy brook, the Otises made the first cut nails in this region. Isaac, who had taken over William's house, discontinued the tavern there and turned over a large upper room for Masonic purposes. He became junior warden of the lodge, founded in the fall of 1818 and named the Hoffman Masonic Lodge for Martin Hoffman, deputy grand master. (Courtesy of the Historical Society of Middletown and the Wallkill Precinct.)

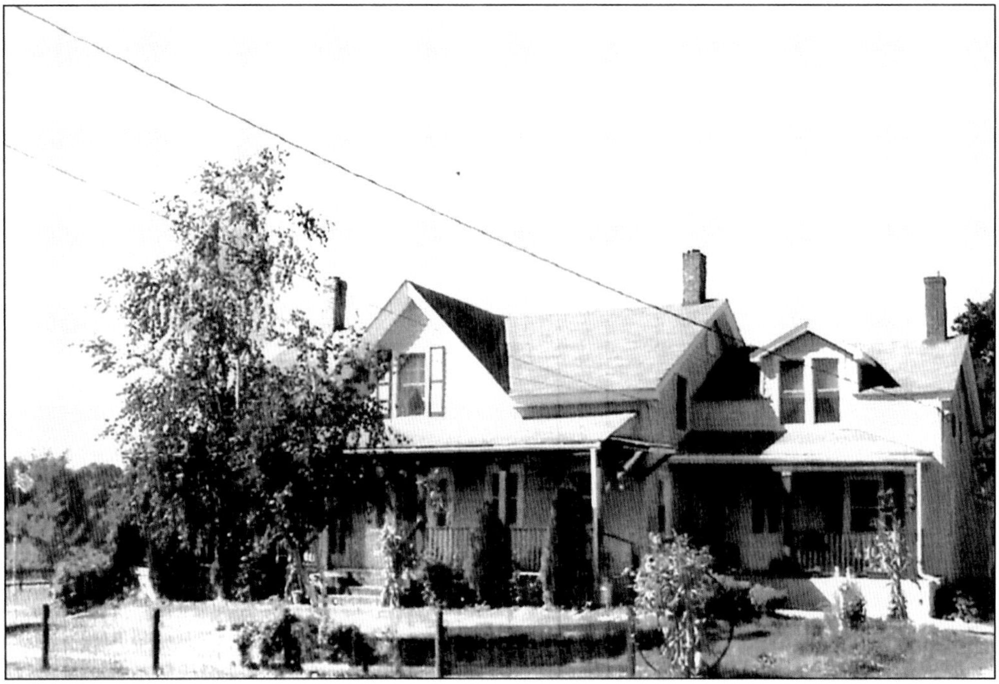

The Smith H. and Katherine Livingston tract of land was a very large parcel with three houses, which ran from Samuel Wilkinson's cradle factory, to Phillipsburgh, to land of Jeremiah Cox, and to land of Hiram S. Dunning, dating to before 1870. In 1870, Isaac Livingston conveyed land to the New York and Oswego Midland Railway, and the Livingstons built a railroad station on this line at the Sands Station location (now known as Maples Road). The land was acquired by Arthur Heimbach and his wife, Sofie, on February 28, 1945. The Livingston Home still serves as a residence.

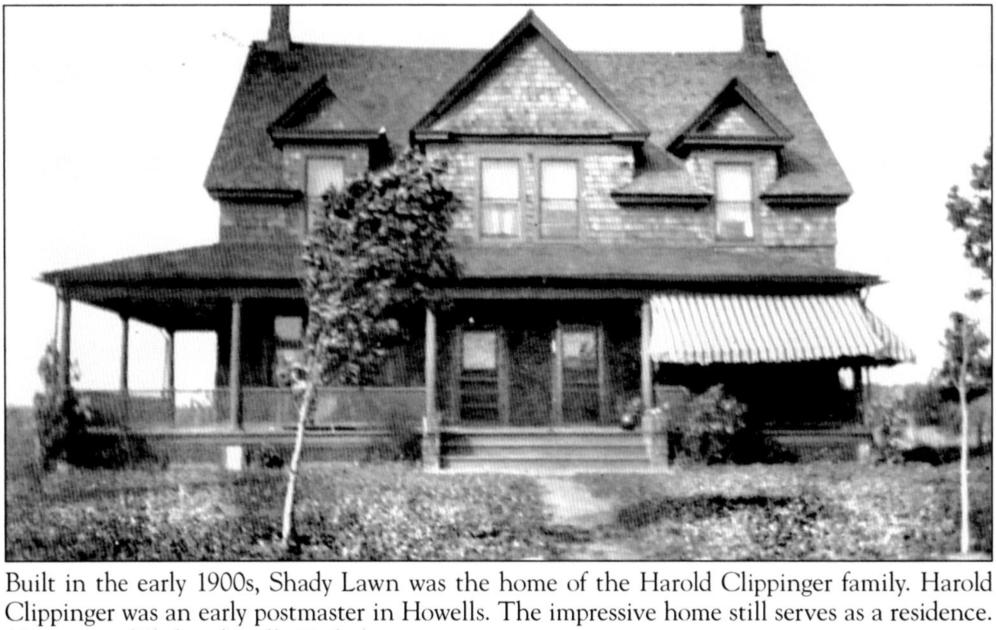

Built in the early 1900s, Shady Lawn was the home of the Harold Clippinger family. Harold Clippinger was an early postmaster in Howells. The impressive home still serves as a residence. (Courtesy of Phil and Stella Higby.)

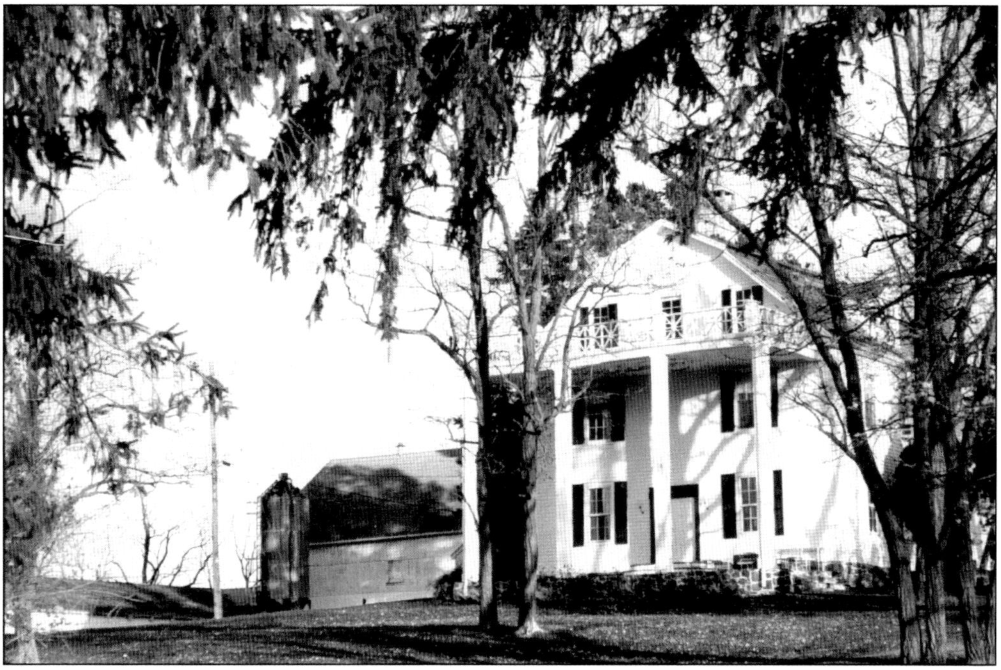

The Blue Sky Polo Club is located on Bart Bull Road in the Town of Wallkill. Days of yore are recalled with the restoration of this beautiful home, built in 1812. (Courtesy of Charles Elmes, Jr.)

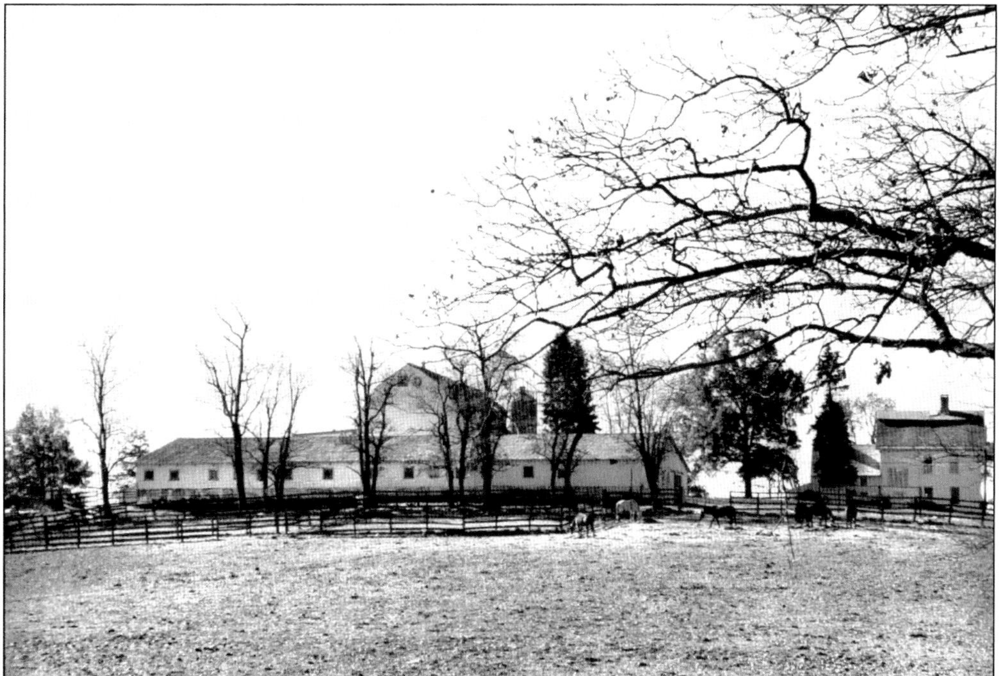

The barns and the large house are settled on the ridge. Fences, horses, and dogs greet visitors in the long driveway.

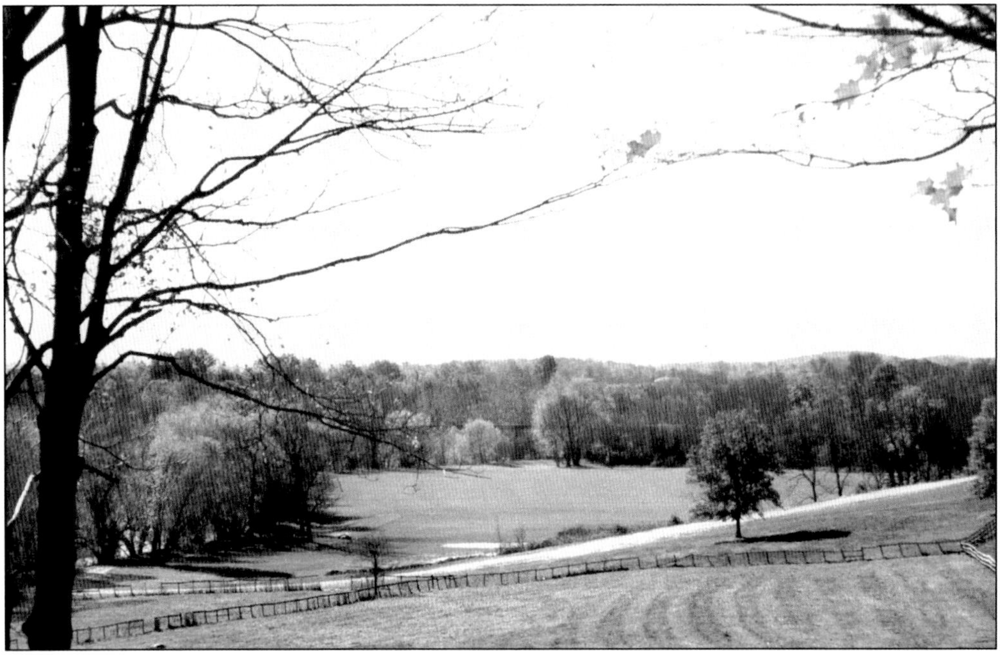

Polo games are played on a very large polo field, next to the Wallkill River. Large old trees line the river's edge, and fences enclose the horse fields.

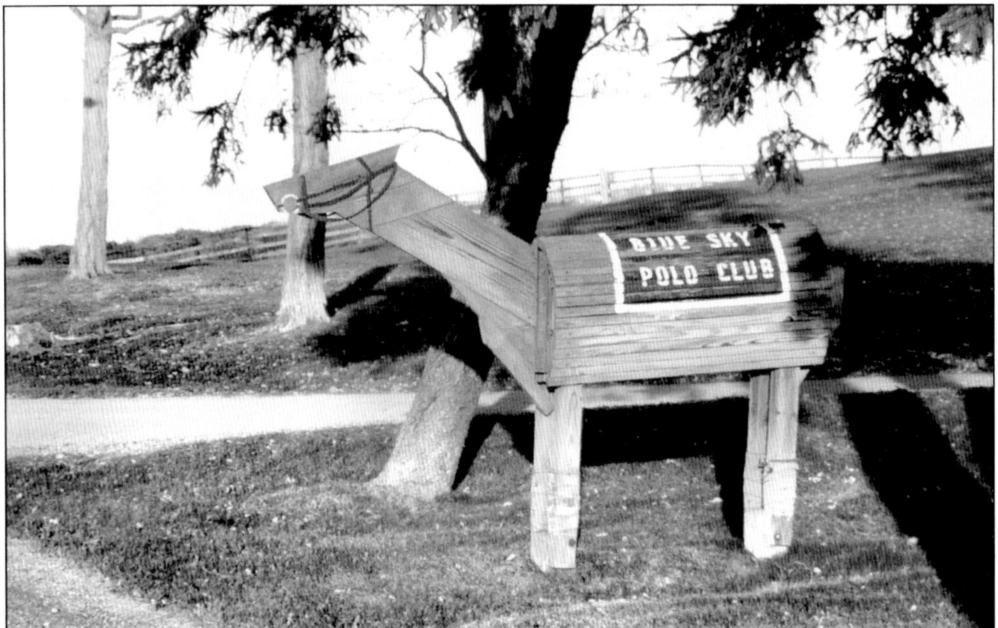

This unique sign serves as a welcome to the Blue Sky Polo Club.

Two

FARMS

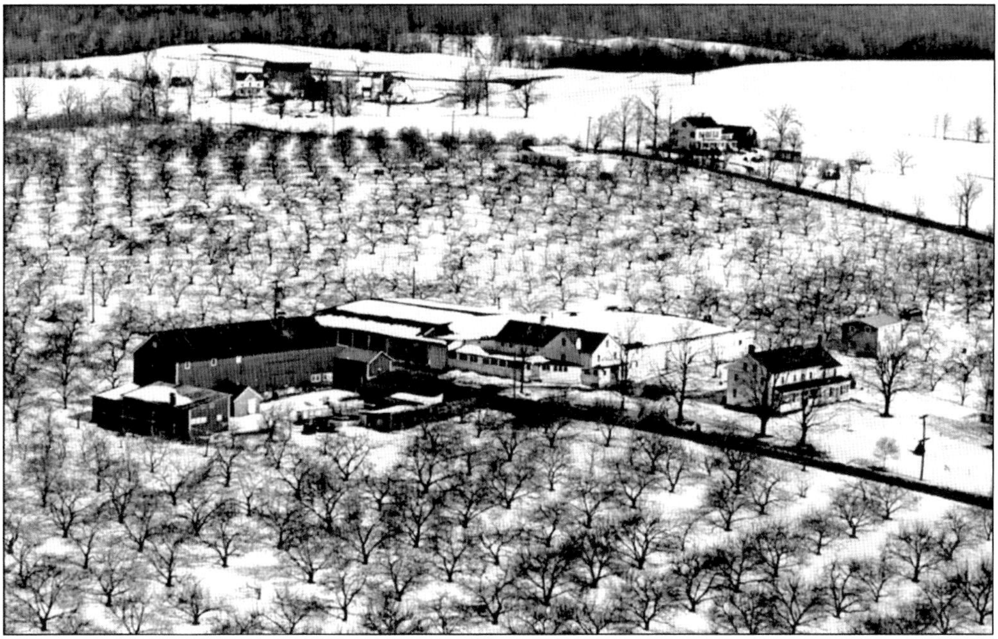

The Mills brothers, Howard Mills Sr. and Jacob Mills, planted the first fruit trees in 1925 on an old dairy farm. The Scotchtown section of the Town of Wallkill became a large orchard, the sixth largest in the Hudson Valley, with apple, pear, peach, and prune plum trees on 150 acres. Apples from Mills Brothers Orchards were sent across the East Coast and even overseas to Germany and England. The farm had cold storage space for 200,000 bushels. The packinghouse was one of the largest in the Hudson Valley. Then, in July 1959, a hailstorm ravaged the area and the crop was lost. Howard Mills Jr. and John E. Mills, sons of Howard Mills Sr., then started construction of homes on the land. Today, the remnants of the past linger with some well-tended fruit trees on area lawns. (Information courtesy of John E. Mills.)

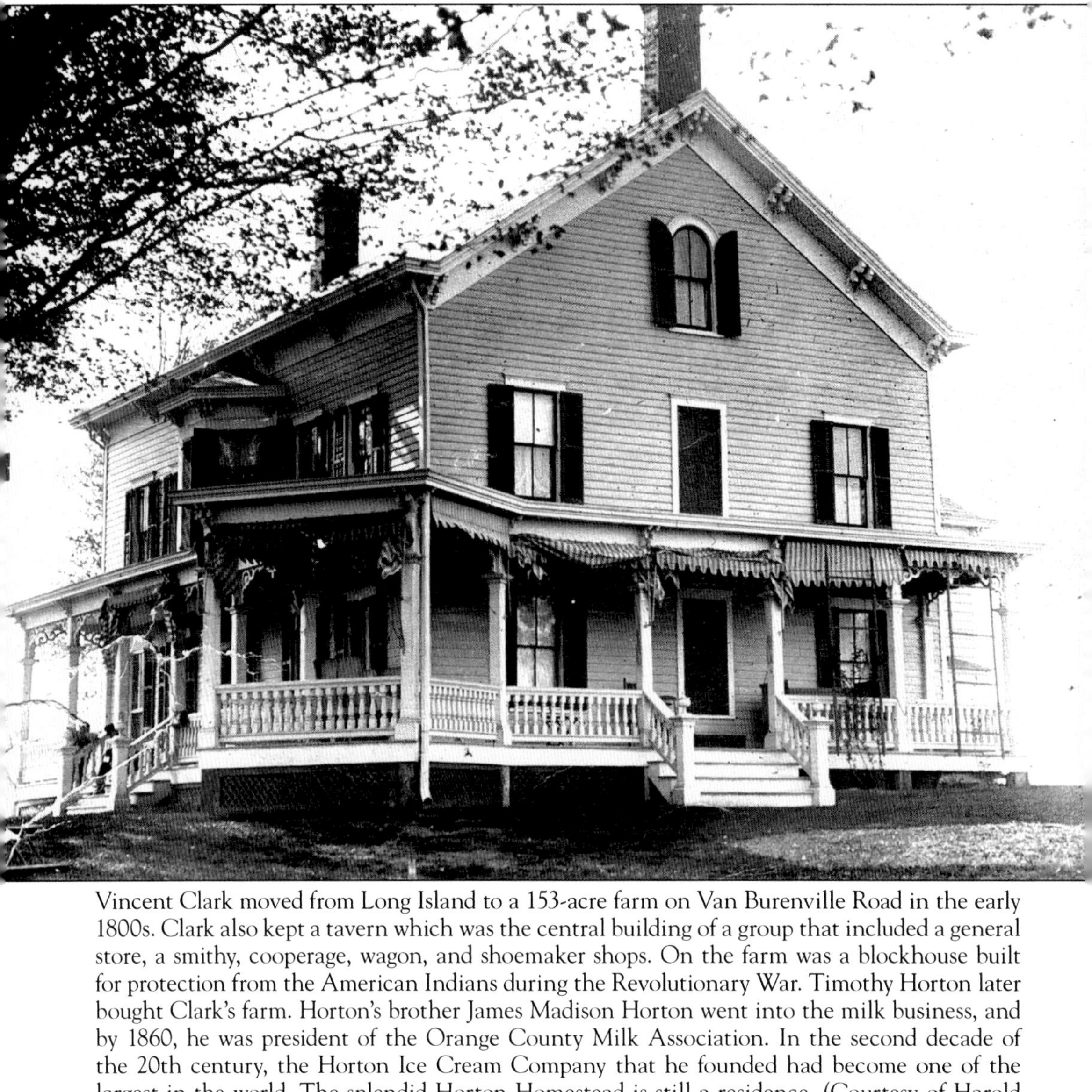

Vincent Clark moved from Long Island to a 153-acre farm on Van Burenville Road in the early 1800s. Clark also kept a tavern which was the central building of a group that included a general store, a smithy, cooperage, wagon, and shoemaker shops. On the farm was a blockhouse built for protection from the American Indians during the Revolutionary War. Timothy Horton later bought Clark's farm. Horton's brother James Madison Horton went into the milk business, and by 1860, he was president of the Orange County Milk Association. In the second decade of the 20th century, the Horton Ice Cream Company that he founded had become one of the largest in the world. The splendid Horton Homestead is still a residence. (Courtesy of Harold and Kathleen Card.)

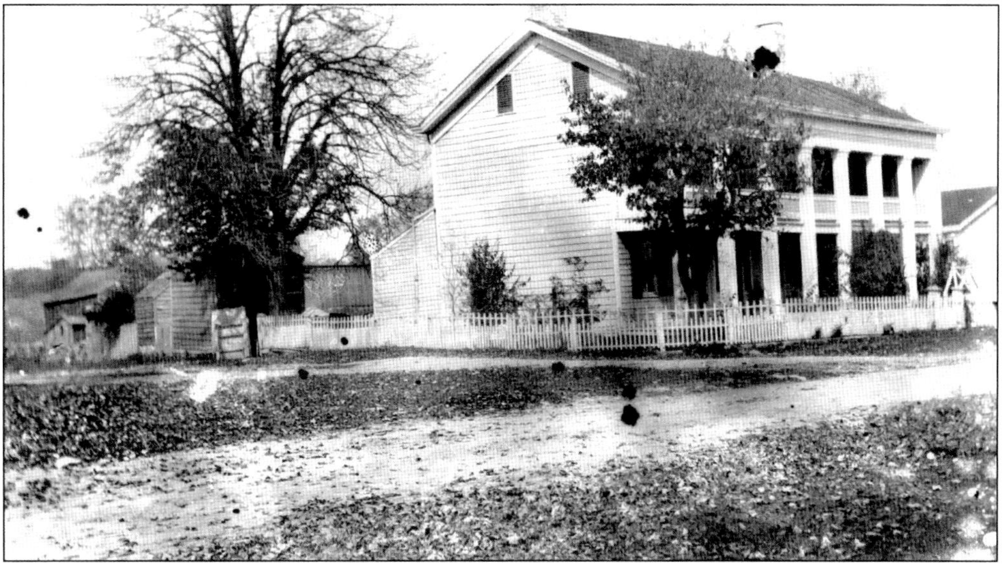

In the center of Scotchtown is a home owned from 1787 to 1920 by the Houston family. John Houston, son of George Houston, the first Houston there, enlarged the family home into a hospitable 19th-century tavern when the turnpike from Goshen to Bloomingburg was developed. There was a ballroom on the second floor and full length verandas at both floor levels. In 1920, the Houston Homestead became the John B. Hasbrouck family home and farm.

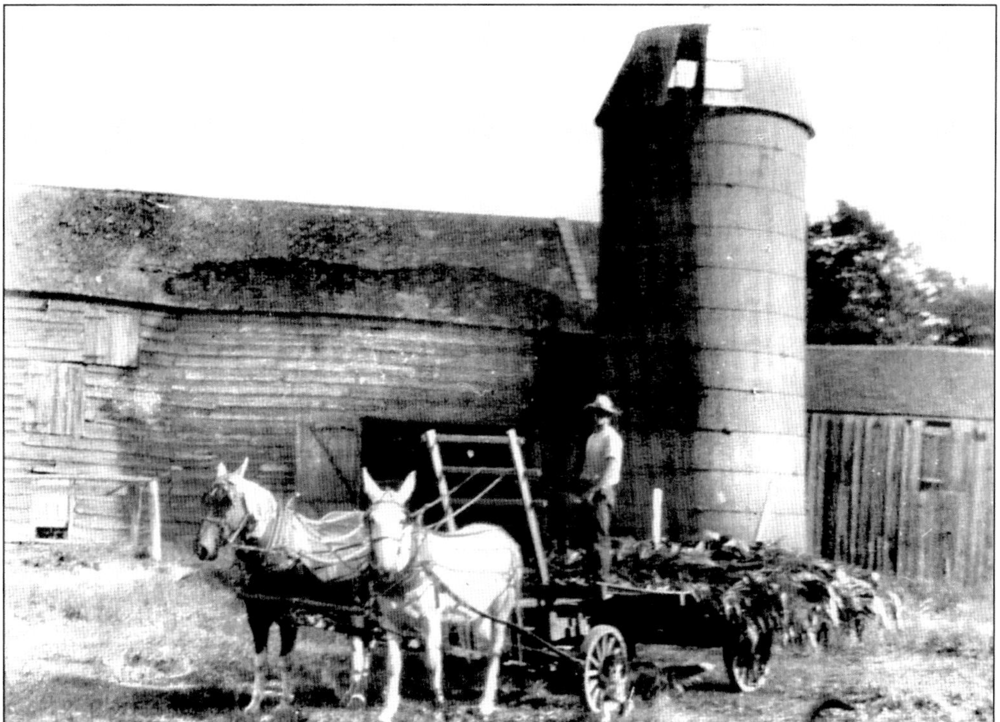

John B. Hasbrouck is pictured on his wagon in front of his barn.

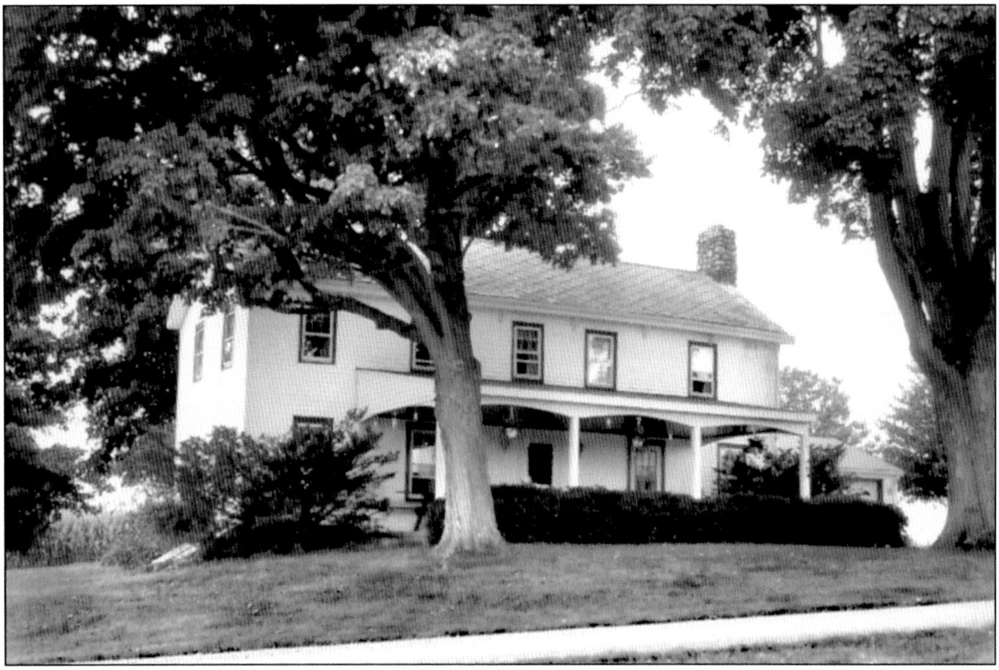

One of the few remaining working farms in the town is the Smiley Farm, located on Stage Road. The Erie Railroad and Interstate 84 are dividers of the original farm. The farm is a pleasant sight from Interstate 84, with its colorful fields, farm setting, and tall silos. The property was owned in 1895 by the Noah and Phebe Stage family and the road was named after this early family. In 1959, it was purchased by William and Winifred Smiley and is being operated by them and their son Russell Smiley. (Information courtesy of the Smiley family.)

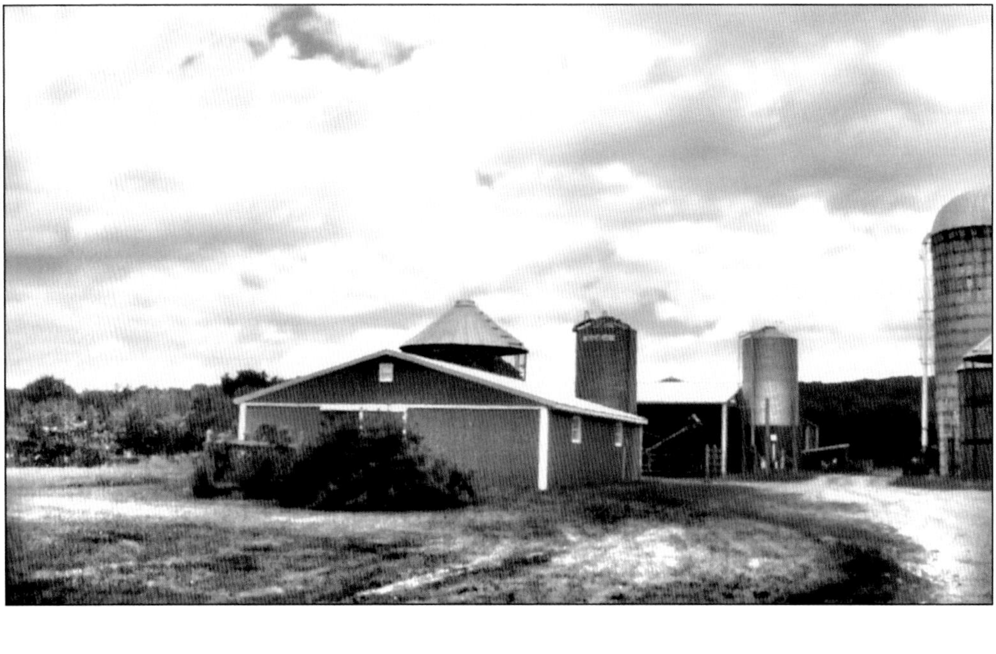

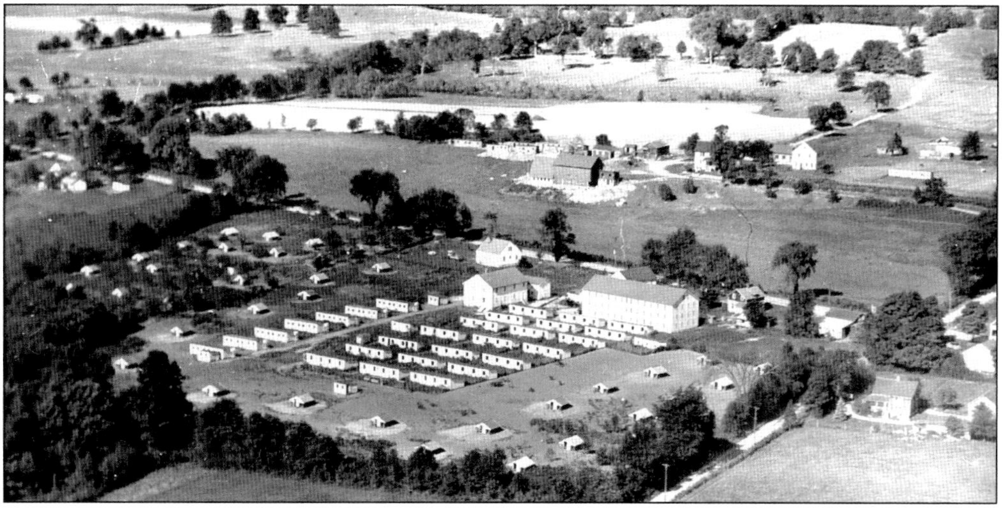

In 1926, James C. Smith, with his wife, Grace, one son, and two stepdaughters, settled on 8.49 acres of land on Montgomery Road (now Route 211 East). The first structure they built was a chicken coop, which became the family's home until their new house was built nearby. While Smith worked in town, his wife cared for the chickens, hand-carrying buckets of water and feed daily. In 1933, Smith decided to devote all of his time raising poultry. His son, James W. Smith, became interested and entered into the family business in 1937 at age 18. In 1947, the business was flourishing. Additional land had been acquired and about 100 buildings of various sizes had been erected. The business became Wayside Farm, named for the Wayside strain of Rhode Island Reds developed by Smith, which won acclaim as superior egg producers. Some 3,000 of these layers were housed in a large four-story building that incorporated the latest technology in the poultry business; newest ventilation, overhead feeding, automatic watering systems, and labor-saving methods of sanitary cleaning. (All photographs courtesy of the Smith family.)

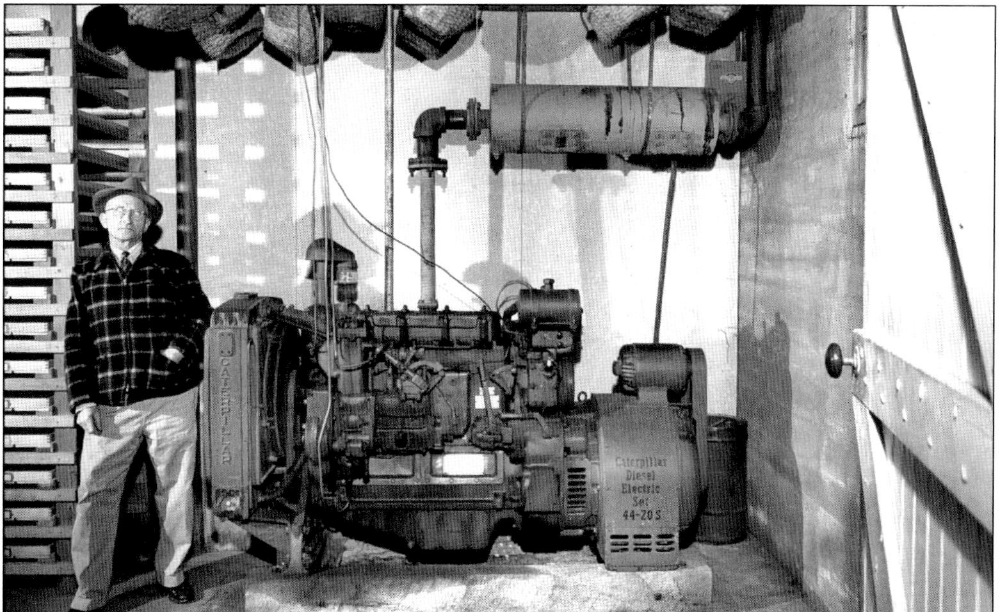

James C. Smith poses next to a Caterpillar D4400 diesel electric generator set that provided standby power for operations at the hatchery should there be a power failure.

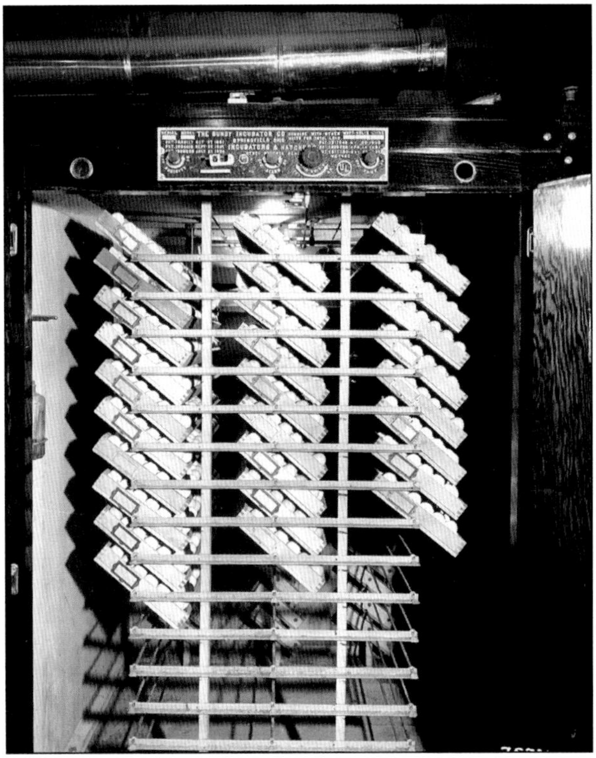

These are egg crates inside incubators and the electric incubators. Eggs were hatched in 21 days and were kept warm by being placed near electric heat lamps called brooders until time for shipment, mainly to farms within a 30-mile radius. Fresh eggs and chickens were sold at Wayside Farm and wholesale to markets in New York City. The up-to-date equipment had a capacity of 70,000 eggs per hatching cycle.

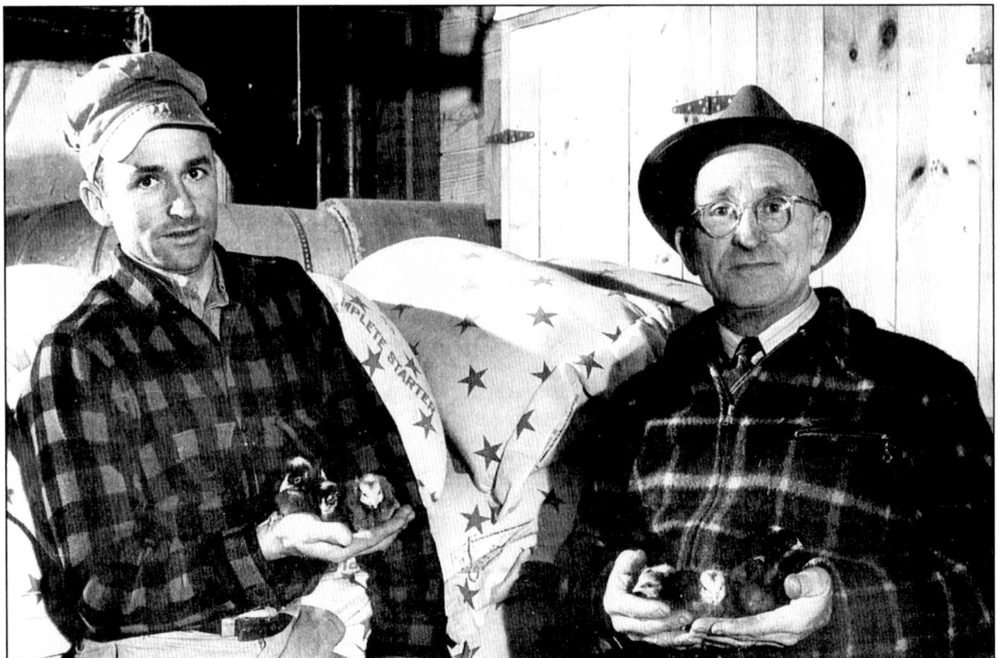

James W. Smith (left) and his father, James C. Smith, hold baby chicks. Some 15,000 chicks a week were hatched at this farm. In 1963, the business was discontinued due to competition from huge poultry firms that were being established.

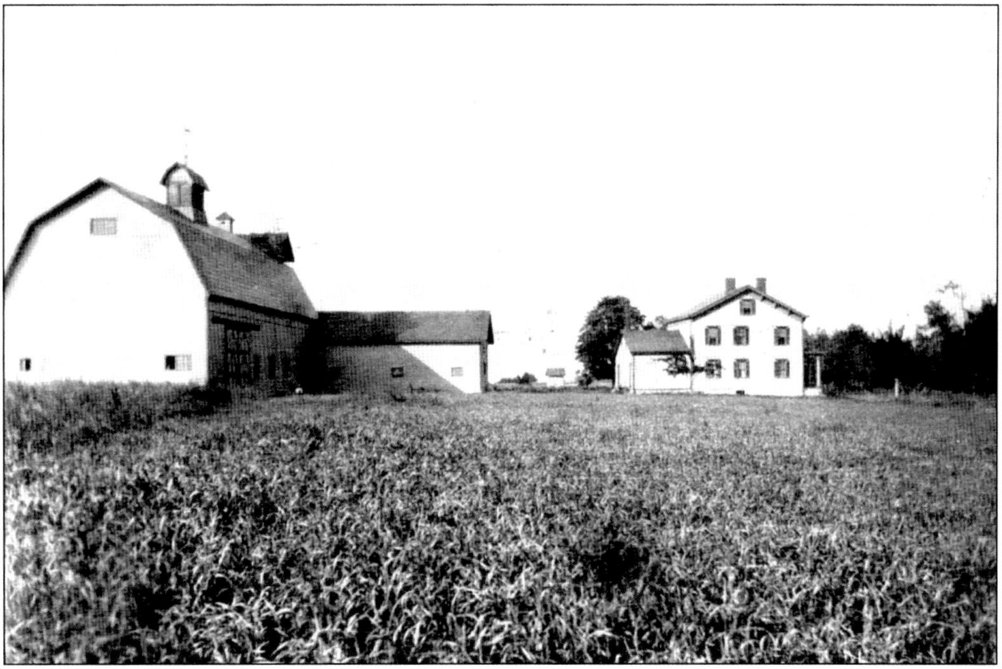

Bellevernon Farm was purchased in 1920 by Harry C. Schutt and his brother Louis E. Schutt.

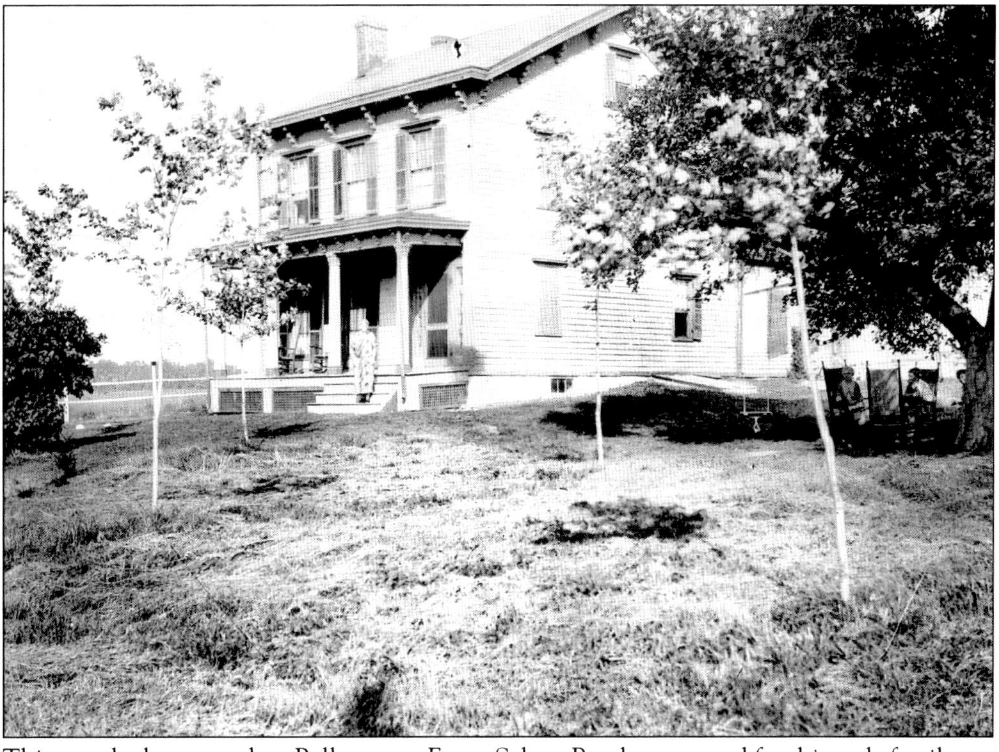

This was the homestead on Bellevernon Farm. Schutt Road was named for this early family.

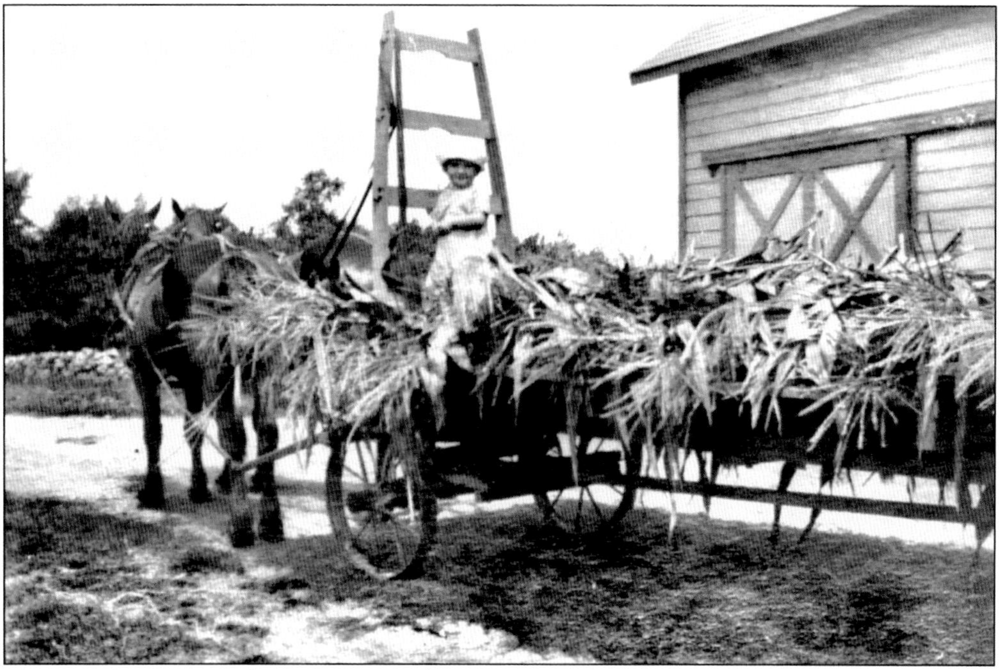

The son of Harry C. Schutt, A. Louis Schutt, is pictured on a wagon in the 1920s. As an adult, he was director of the Orange County Fair Association for 53 years. He was also superintendent of the poultry and livestock divisions of the fair for many years.

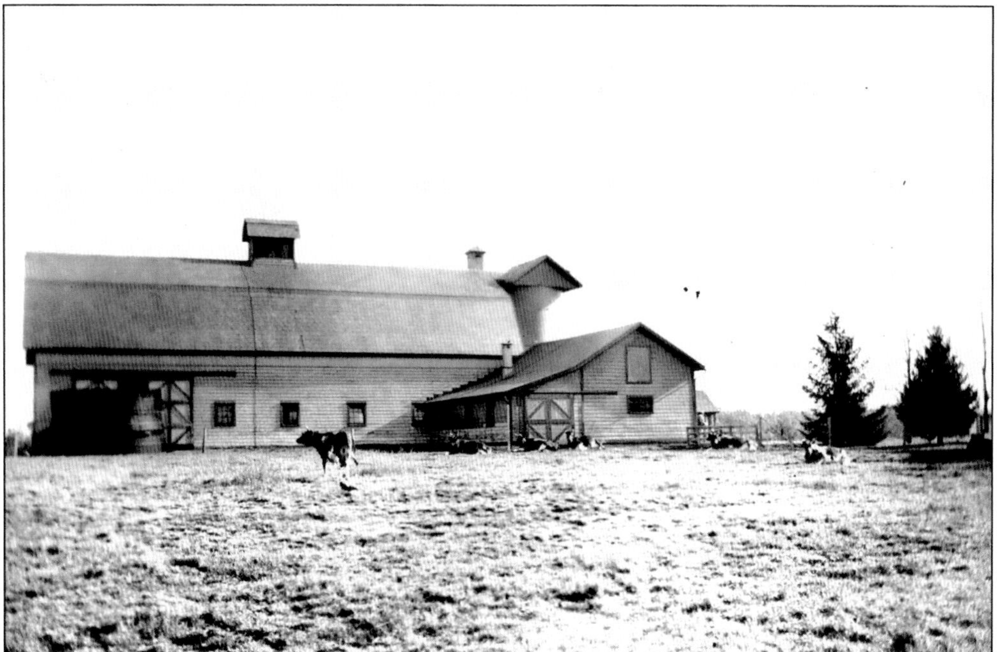

Shown is the Bellevernon barn on the former Schutt family homestead. When the farm was sold to the Meadows Development, the barn was renovated to serve as recreation center and office. (All Bellevernon photographs courtesy of Linda Schutt Martin.)

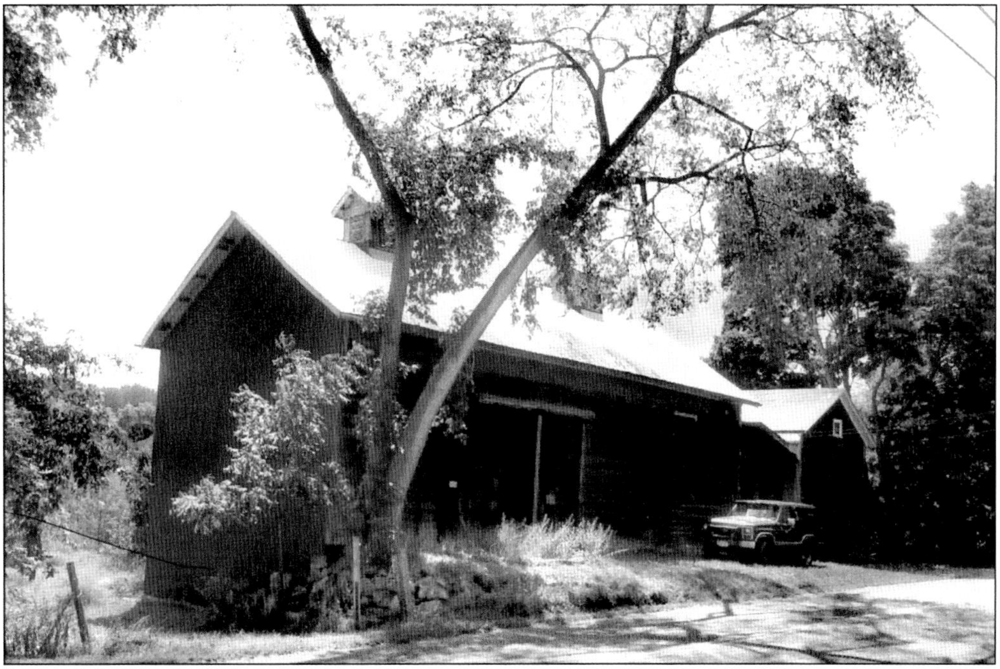

This *c.* 1800 Borgmann Farm was purchased by August Borgmann in 1936. With its 129 acres, the farm is located on Midland Lake Road. The home is across the road, nestled among a group of trees. It is still owned by members of the family. (Information courtesy of Brent Borgmann.)

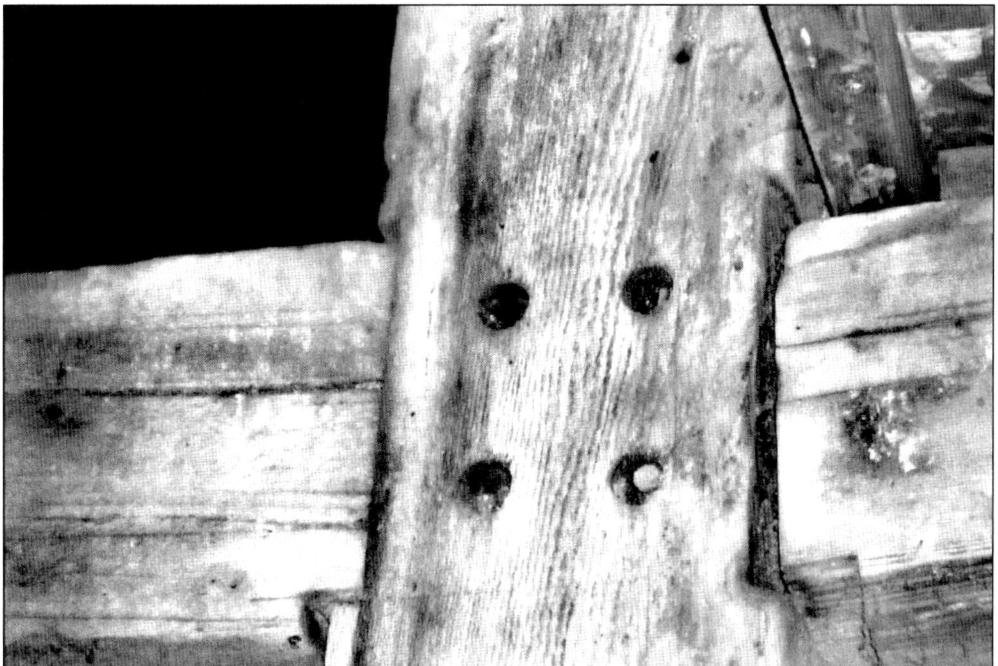

The Borgmann barn is built with wooden pegs that hold the beams together.

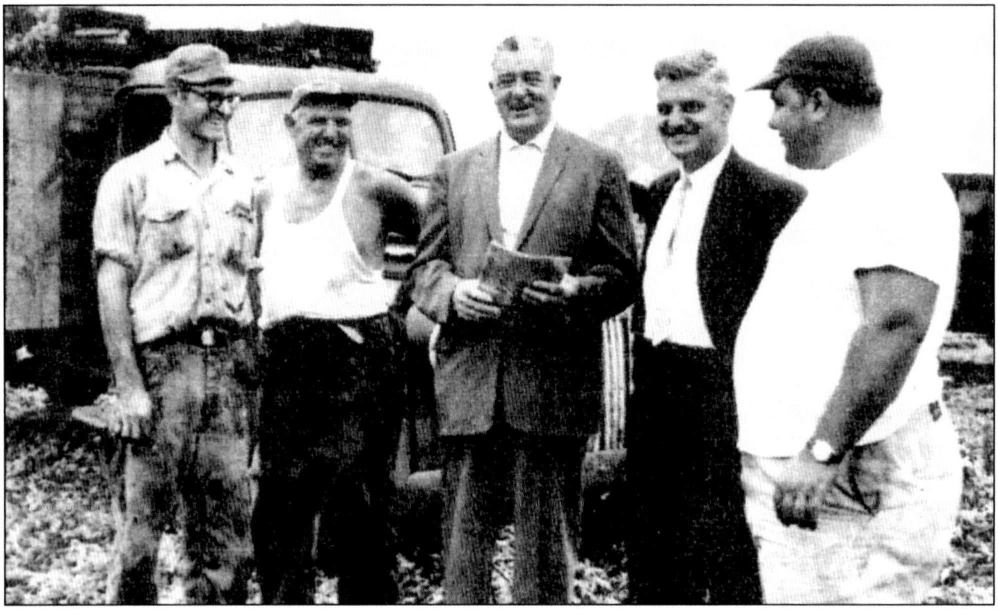

"Black gold" was neither coal nor oil to the Ingrassia and LaScala families of the Town of Wallkill. It is that vein of black muck land that swoops and swirls its way over the land maps of central New York. In 1909, it thrilled these Italian families, who first put their roots down here after leaving the overworked European soil. Standing in front of the harvest truck are, from left to right, Joseph Ingrassia Jr., Frank Ingrassia, Barney Cohen (an Esso distributor), Carl Reischel (a salesman), and Louis Ingrassia. (Courtesy of the Ingrassia family.)

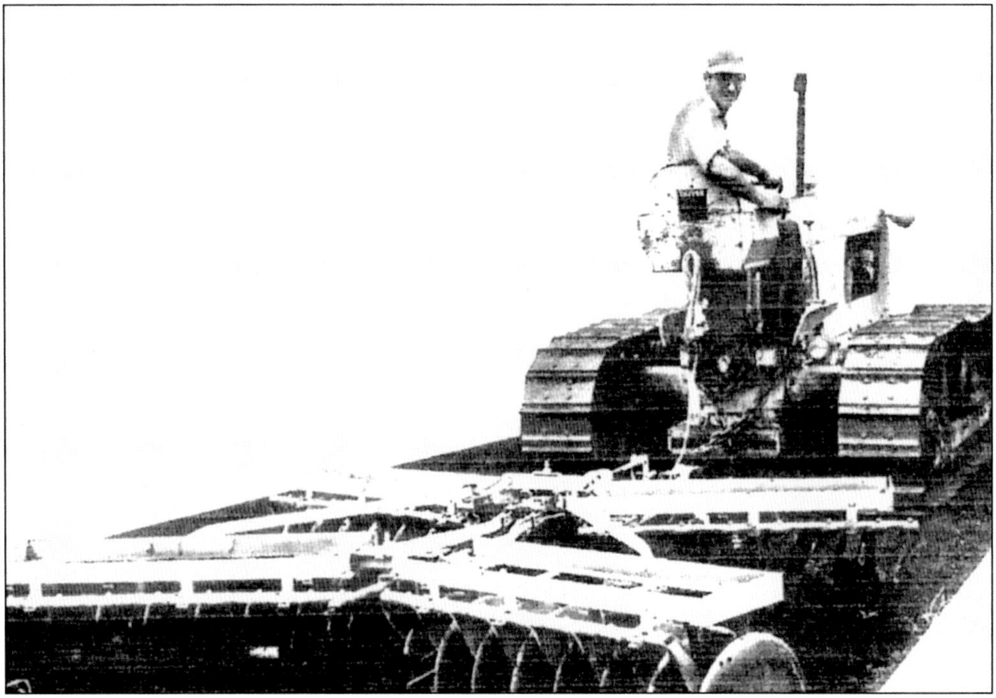

Joseph Ingrassia Jr., the author's husband, tills the "black gold" of the farm's 110 acres—45 of them planted with celery.

Jane Ingrassia poses in front of the onion fields.

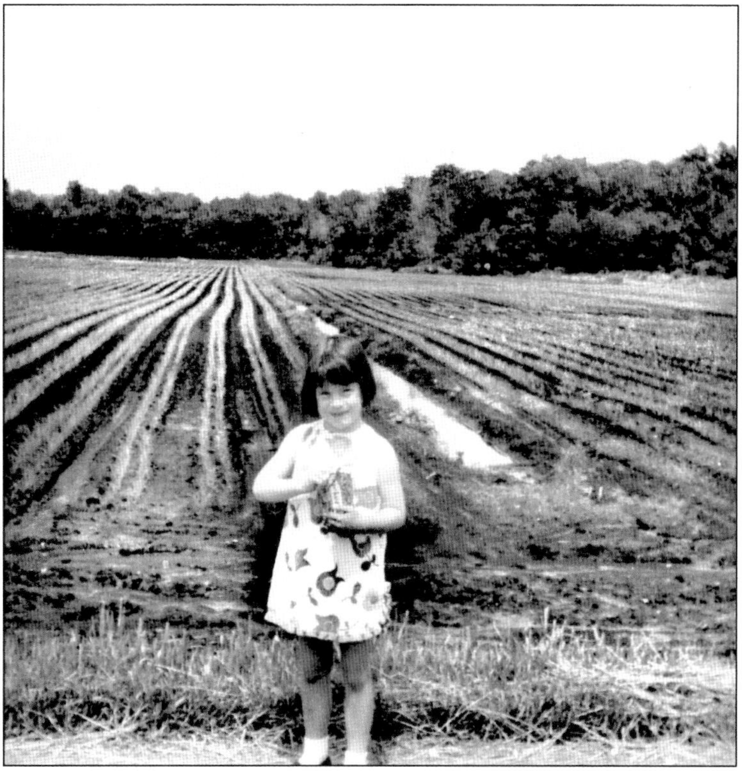

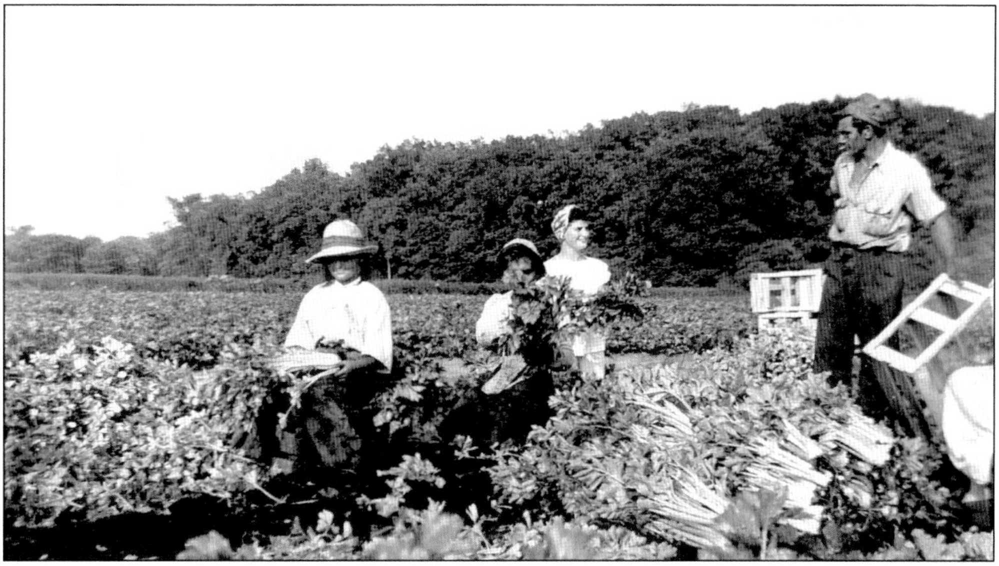

Harvesting the celery are, from left to right, Marion (Ingrassia) Smith, unidentified, Grace (Ingrassia) Costanzo, and Kenny Krull.

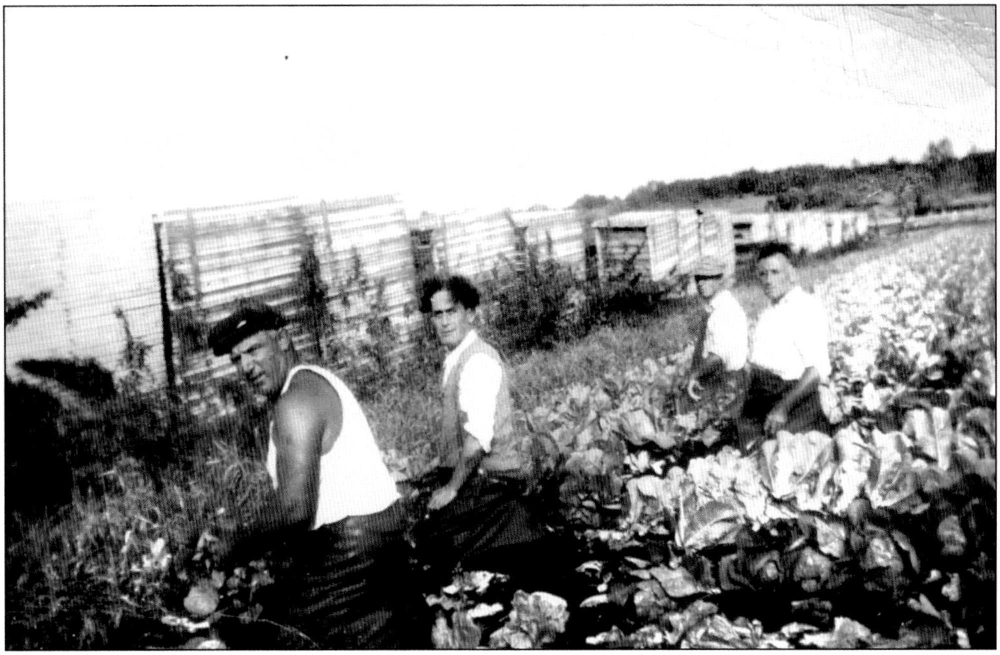

Harvesting the lettuce are, from left to right, Frank Ingrassia, Joe Fontana, Sam LaScala, and Joseph Ingrassia Sr.

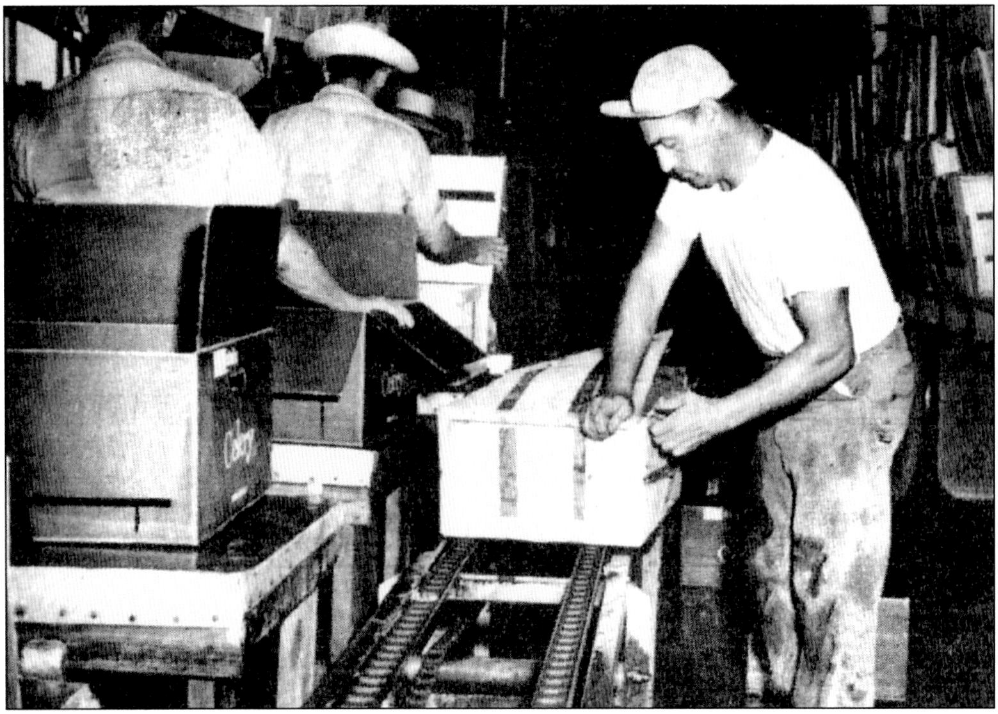

Freshly washed celery is packed in a modern assembly line plant, under the supervision of Tony LaScala (right).

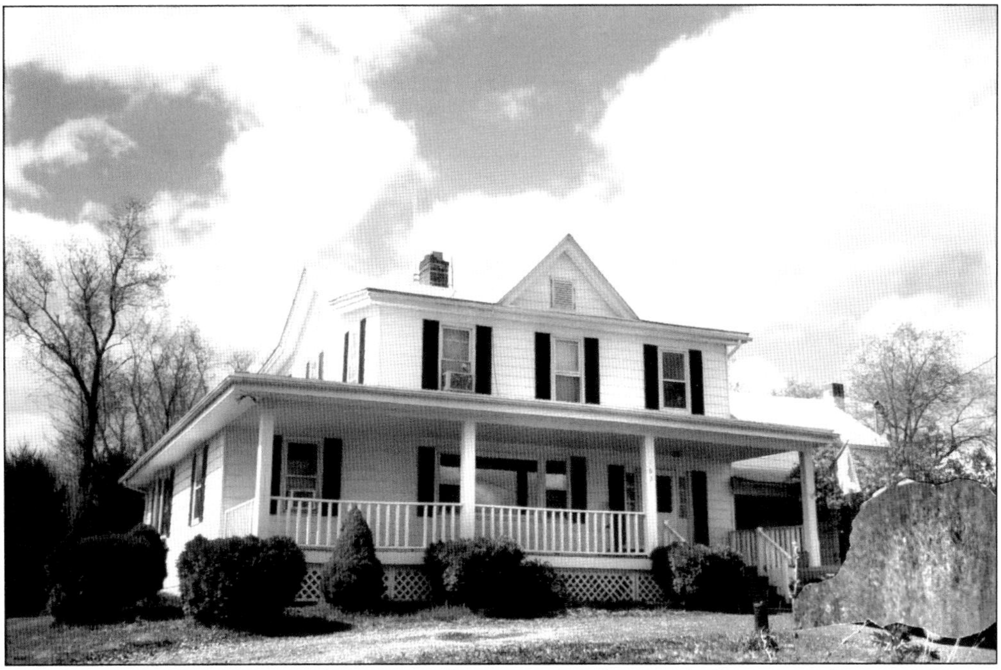

In payment for seven years of service with George Washington's Continental army, Thomas Gillen was granted 238 acres of land on what is now Gillen Road. Seven generations of the Gillen family have resided in this home, built on a portion of the large farm. (Courtesy of Gwen Deserto.)

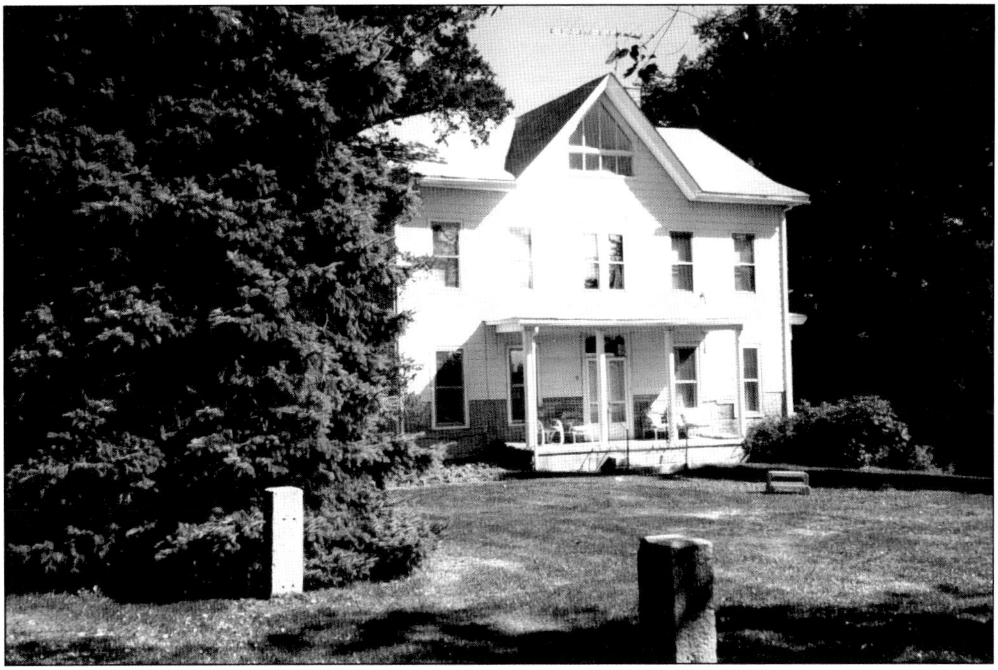

This majestic 17-room home is on a gravel way known as Slaughter Road. Built in 1876, it originally had pillars around the front. The farm originally included more than 100 acres. (Information courtesy of Terry Gillian.)

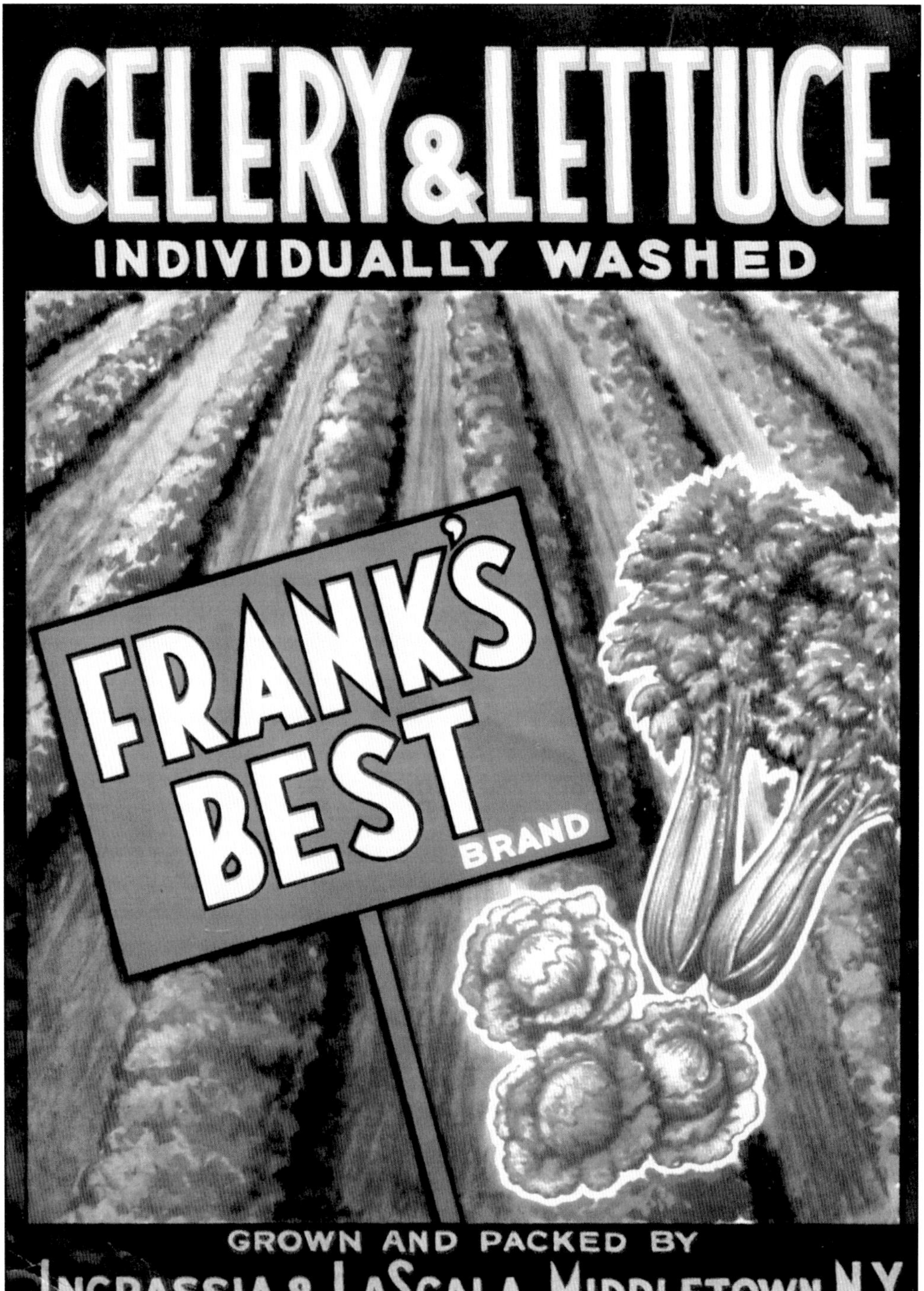

This label is from a farm crate.

Three

BUSINESS

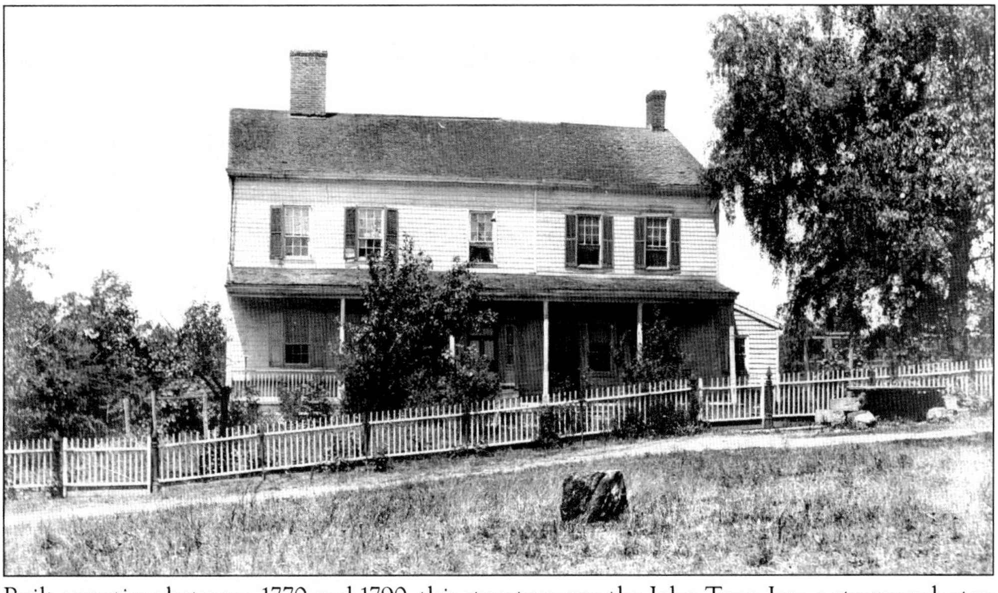

Built sometime between 1770 and 1790, this structure was the John Tears Inn, a stagecoach stop on the toll road between Bloomingburg and Goshen (now the Goshen Turnpike). The stepping stone used by stagecoach passengers, still in its original location, can be seen at the far right of the photograph. The original inn sign was found in the attic. The wooden sign, printed on both sides with a version of the seal of the United States, had been cut to fit a fireplace opening. The sign was wallpapered on one side and protected with a sheet of tin on the other side. Thus, it was preserved unnoticed until 1974. The eagle's head was lost in the cutting, but the "J. Tears Inn" lettering and the widespread wings and shield still retain their color. The former inn is listed on the National Register of Historic Places and, for the past 70 years, has served as a private residence. (Courtesy of Leona Trimmer.)

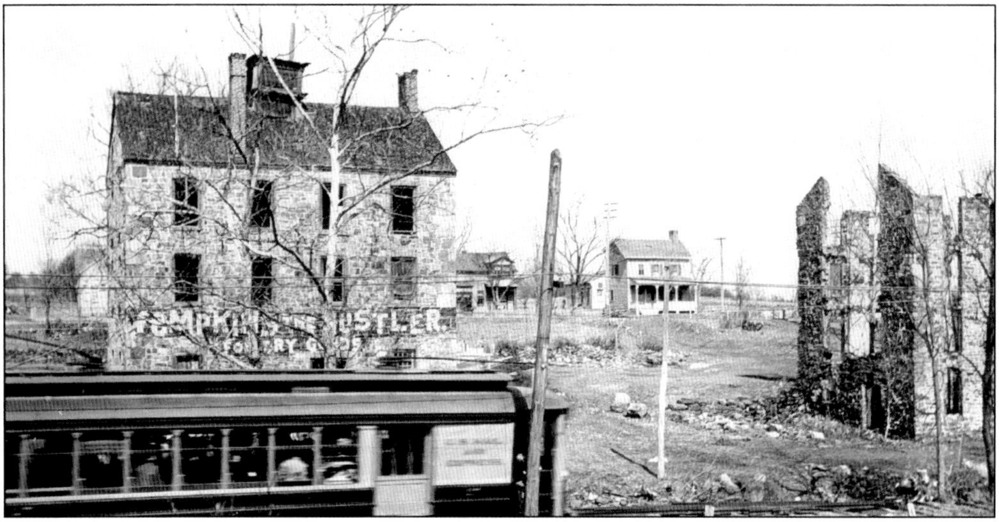

The hamlets of Mechanicstown and Phillipsburgh were located on East Main Extension in the Town of Wallkill. This road was part of the ancient Minisink Trail used by Native Americans and their white successors. There was a hotel at Mechanicstown, a glove manufactory, and a feed mill. The Phillips family set up a trip-hammer mill, where gun flints, spearheads, and bayonets were manufactured. William Phillips, Moses Phillips's son, built the Mechanicstown Woolen Mills in 1835. During the Civil War, the mills produced large yellow blankets for the government. Early in the 19th century, the cadet gray that has ever since been the official uniform color at West Point was developed at a Mechanicstown woolen mill. (Courtesy of the Historical Society of Middletown and the Wallkill Precinct.)

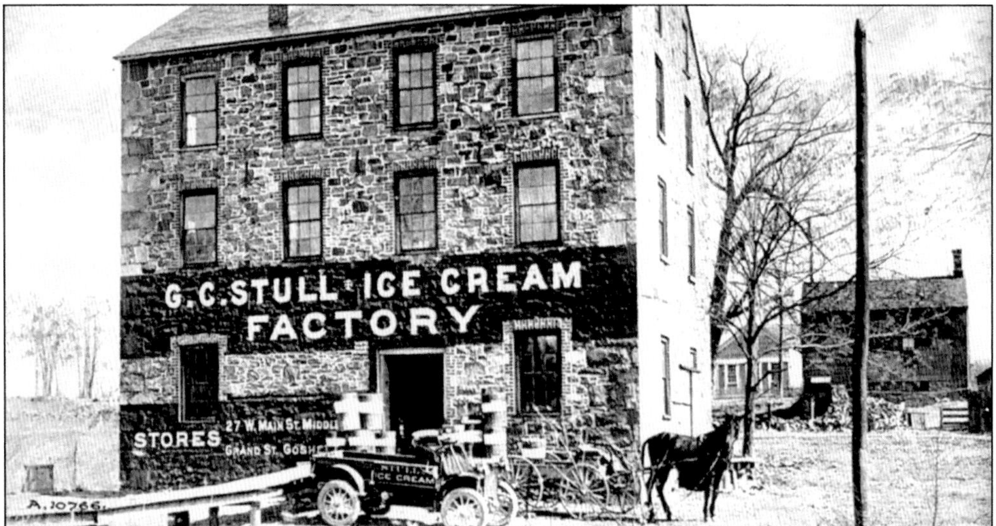

When the woolen mills became a thing of the past, one of the buildings, which was not destroyed by fire, became the home of the G. C. Stull Ice Cream Factory. The trolley from Midway Park passed by the back of the Stull building, and the ads were placed there for the trolley passengers to read. Ice cream was very reasonable: ice pops for 5¢ and cups of ice cream for 10¢. Three young men who worked at Stull's in the summer were Robert Maxwell, Robert Truex, and Floyd Truex. They worked from 7:00 a.m. to 5:00 p.m., and their wages were $1 per day. (Photograph courtesy of William Maxwell and information courtesy of H. Jean Truex.)

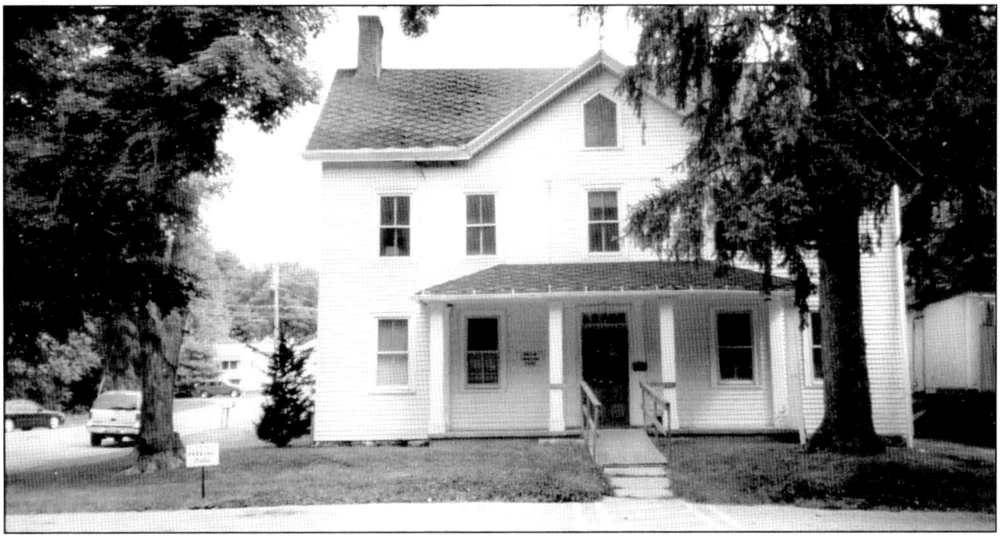

About 1767, Henry Wisner of Phillipsburgh, knowing the advantages of waterpower at this point on the Wallkill River, built a dam and employed Moses Phillips to put up a gristmill. People came, some from long distances, by twos and threes for safety, on horseback with their bags of grain and camped around the mill waiting for their grist. In March 1769, Henry Wisner deeded 175 acres at Phillipsburgh to "Moses Phillips, carpenter, and my daughter, Sarah, his wife" who had married January 1768. During the Revolutionary War, the first powder mill, owned by Henry Wisner, was built in this area and the powder was stored in a hillside magazine across from the Moses Phillips home until it was delivered to the army.

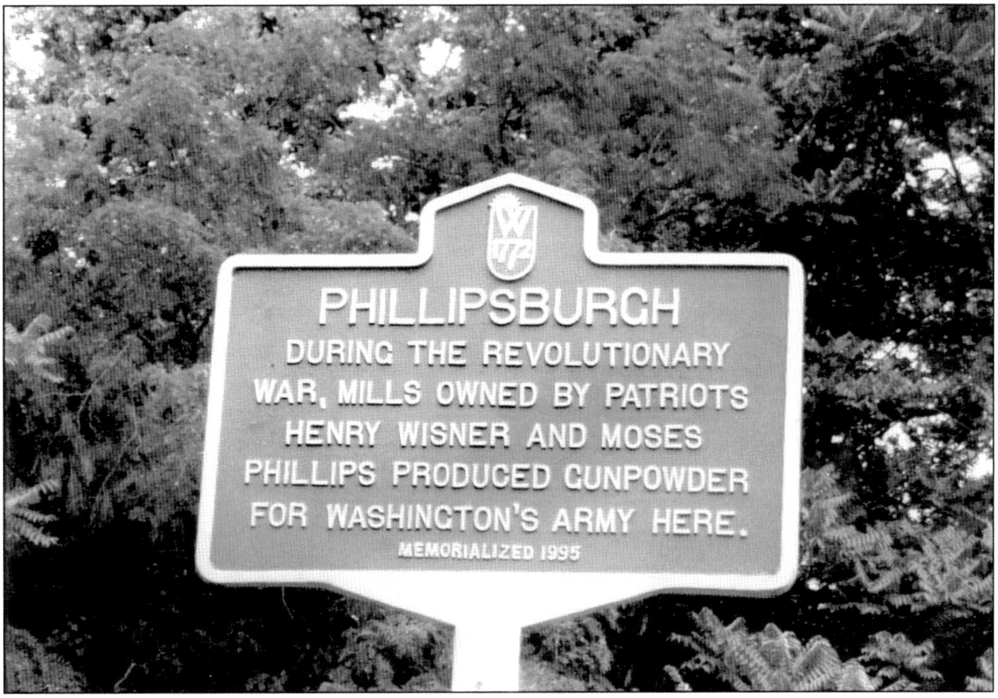

Shown is the state historic marker placed at the former home of Moses Phillips.

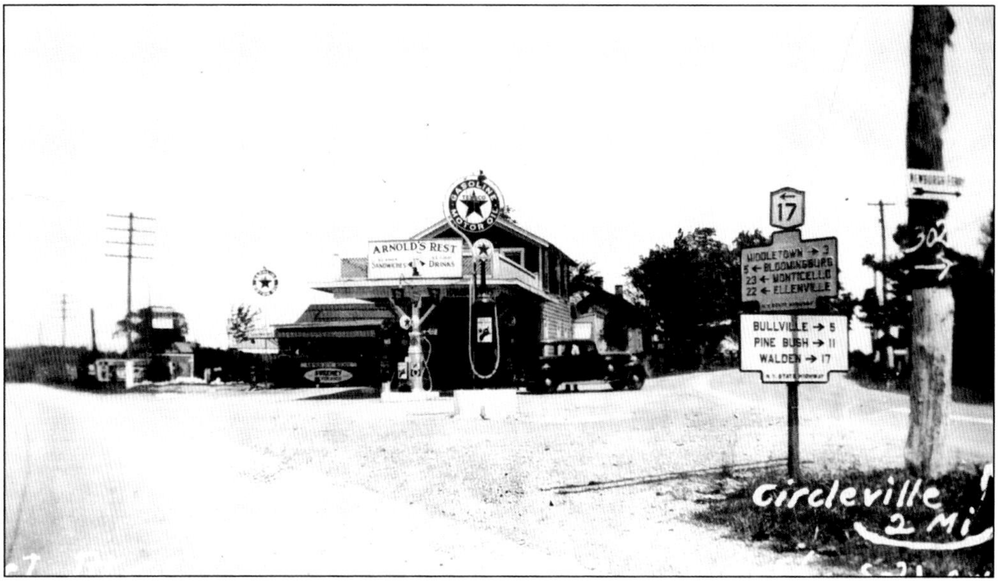

An early business in the outlying area was Arnold's Rest gasoline station at the intersection of Routes 302 and 17M, two miles from Circleville. They also served sandwiches and cold drinks. (Courtesy of the Paul Weisshaar collection.)

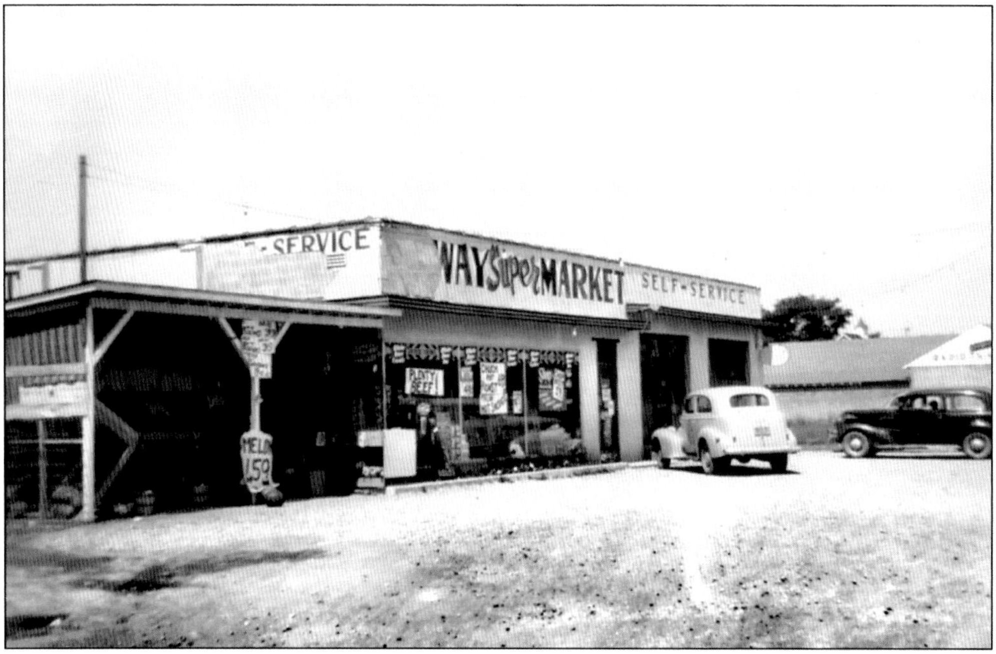

This building was originally built to house the Tucker Automobile Agency, which never opened. Barberio's opened a highway market, located on Route 84 (now Route 211 E) just before the Silver Lake area. This early self-service market advertised chuck pot roast for 69¢ a pound. (Courtesy of the Historical Society of Middletown and the Wallkill Precinct.)

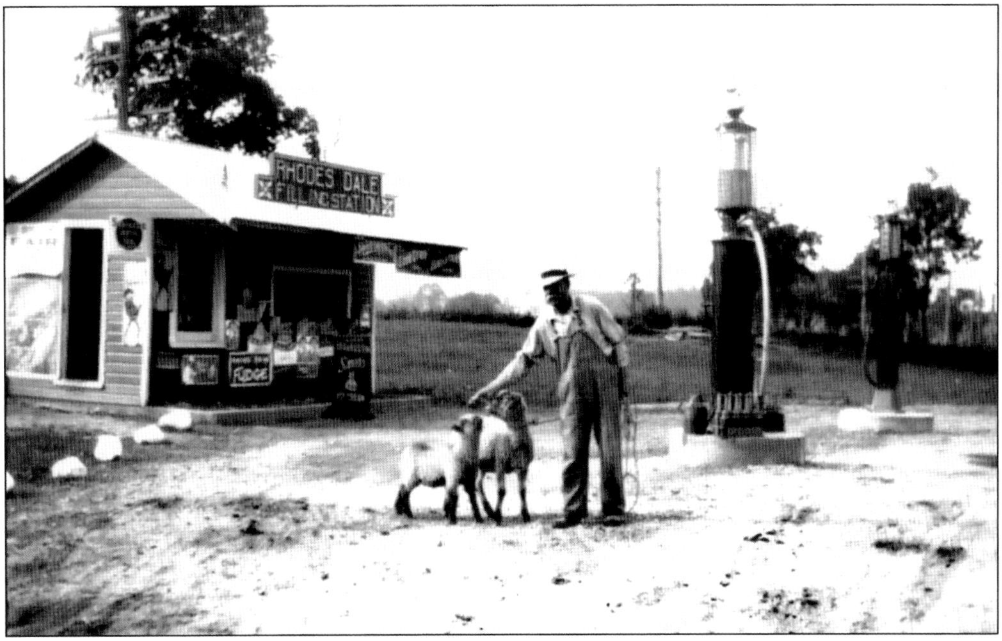

Walter Rhodes stands in front of his Rhodes Dale Filling Station with his goats. The station was located across the road from what is now the Middletown Auction Pavilion on Route 17M. Rhodes sold gasoline and goat's milk at this location, along with homemade fudge and other refreshments, according to the sign in front of his establishment. (Courtesy of Wes and Gary LaBagh.)

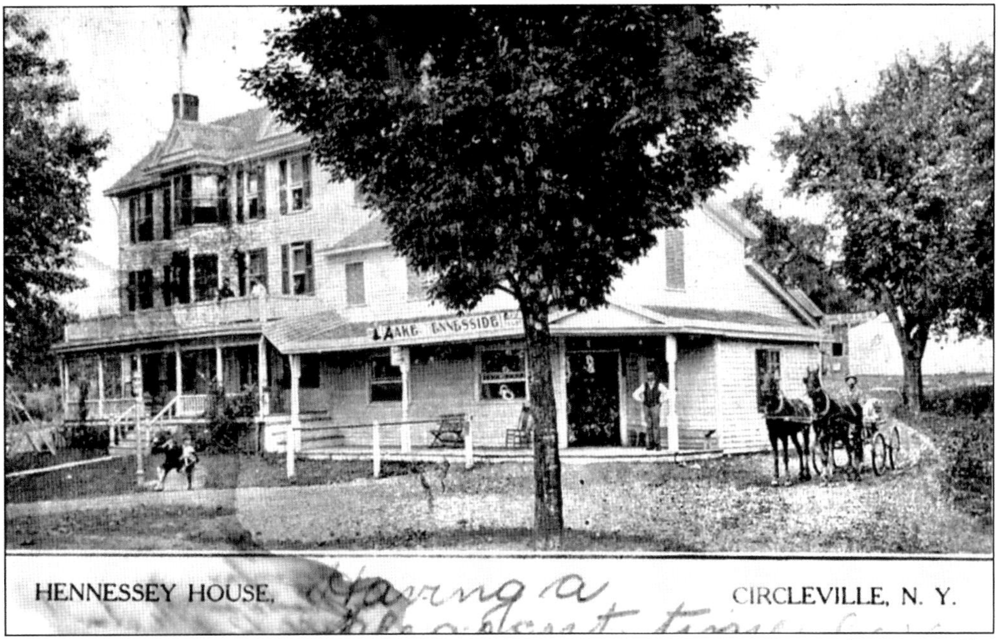

Located in Circleville, near Lake Hennesside, the Hennessey House was a popular resort. The name was later changed to Hotel Brome and, in recent years, to the Circleville Inn. The lake, now called Circleville Lake, is part of the C. Hudson Thompson Memorial Park. (Courtesy of Leona Trimmer.)

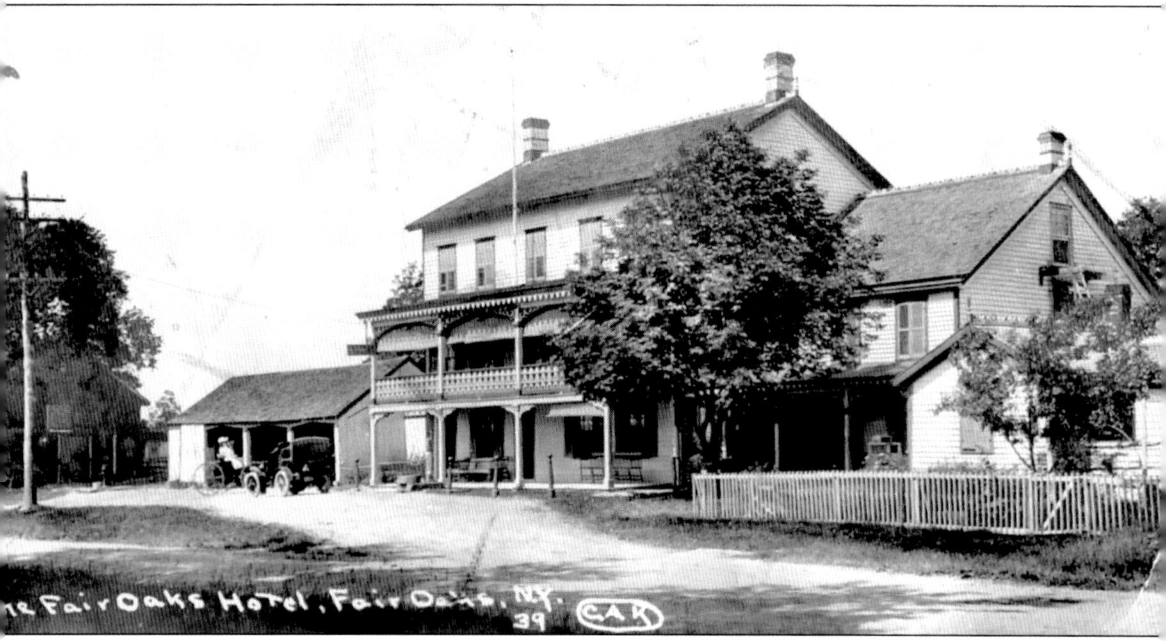

The builder of the Fair Oaks Inn, a three-story hotel that was once known as the Half-Way House because of its location on the Bloomingburg road, is unknown. Matthew S. Askew Sr. first became its proprietor at the end of its first decade in 1871 and the property remained in the family until the state took it over in 1949 for highway purposes. The hotel ceased to operate as such with Prohibition in 1919 but remained a residence for the Askew family. The main building was begun in 1861 and was completed by the next spring. The hotel, according to Ruttenber and Clark in their Orange County history, "was built and opened for business the day the battle of Fair Oaks, Va. was fought in the late war. In a conversation that day over the name, Fair Oaks, then in everybody's mind, was suggested and speedily adopted." The Fair Oaks battle, also known as the Battle of Seven Pines, occurred on May 31 and June 1, 1862, and was declared a victory for McClellan's Army of the Potomac. Residents recall the brighter days of the old building's past when they would stop their horse-drawn carriages at the Askew Half-Way House for refreshments on their way to Bloomingburg. Other travelers bound for more distant destinations found rest within its walls. (Information courtesy of the *Times Herald Record*, 1950.)

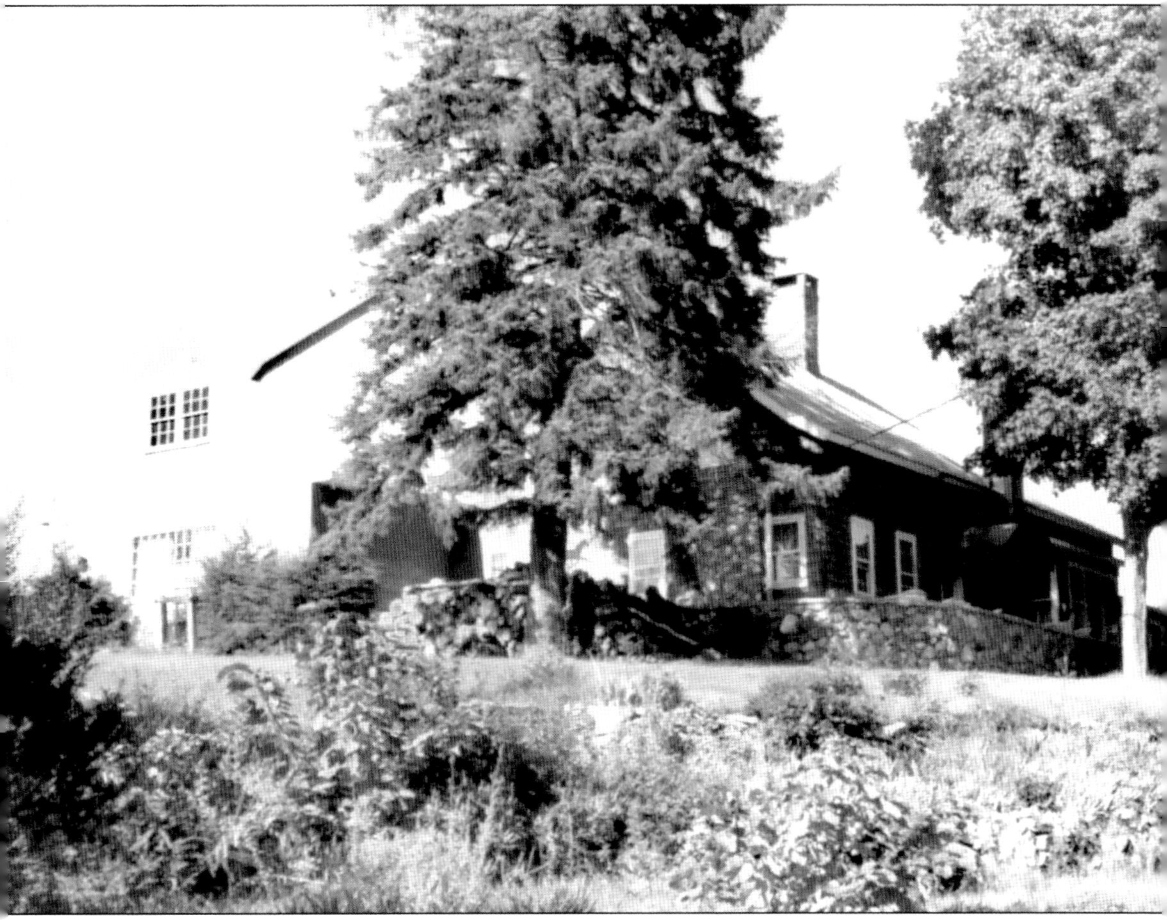

In 1620, Peregrine White, the first white child born in New England, was born on the *Mayflower* as it lay in Provincetown Harbor. The little boy's father died during the first year of the Pilgrims' settlement, and his mother later married Gov. Edward Winslow. The builder and original owner of this home was John White, a direct descendant of Peregrine White, and himself a major in the Revolutionary War. His descendants continued to live in and build onto this Colonial house for five generations. The Barberio family, Archie, Ann, Ernie and Joseph, acquired this historic home around 1970, naming it Archie's Inn. With its inviting New England décor, the huge fireplaces, hand hewn beams, wide plank flooring and delicious food, it became a well-known restaurant in the area. Archie's Inn was destroyed by fire on May 19, 1991.

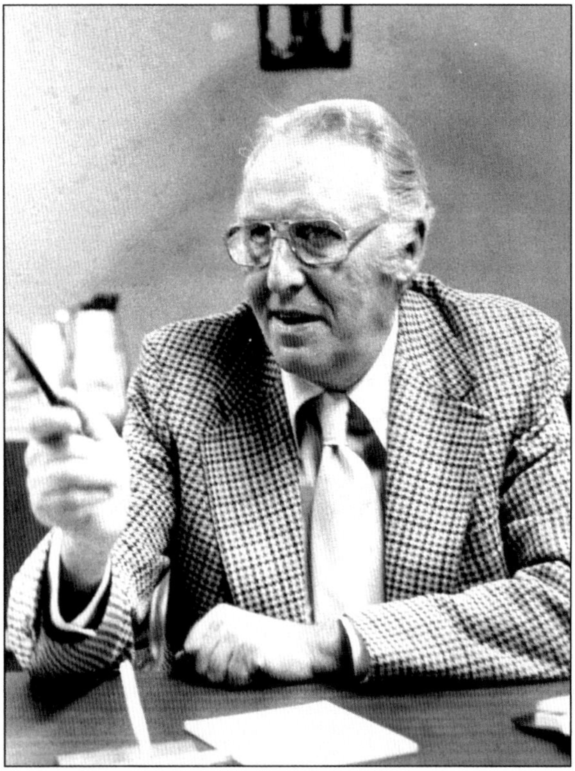

In 1950, legendary businessman Edmund S. Lloyd built a supercenter in a cow pasture beside a two-lane country road, Route 84 (now Route 211), in Wallkill. During the 1960s, Route 211 became the region's major retail strip and was christened the Miracle Mile, and Lloyd was the miracle worker. Today, Route 211 is a six-lane highway. (Photographs not otherwise identified, courtesy of Edward Konefal, a former Lloyd's employee.)

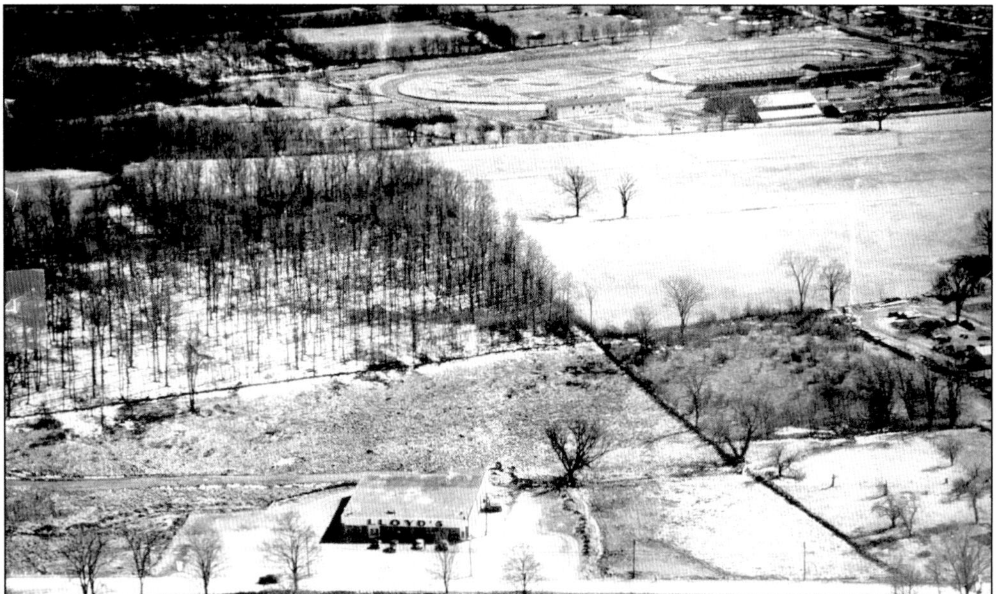

Unable to obtain financing from banks for this concept of "all under one roof," Edmund S. Lloyd sold bonds directly to the working-class community and revolutionized the retail industry. Lloyd's was the first grocery store in New York state to sell prepackaged meat. When he added a pharmacy to his grocery store—the first in the state—lawmakers had to pass a special bill to allow it.

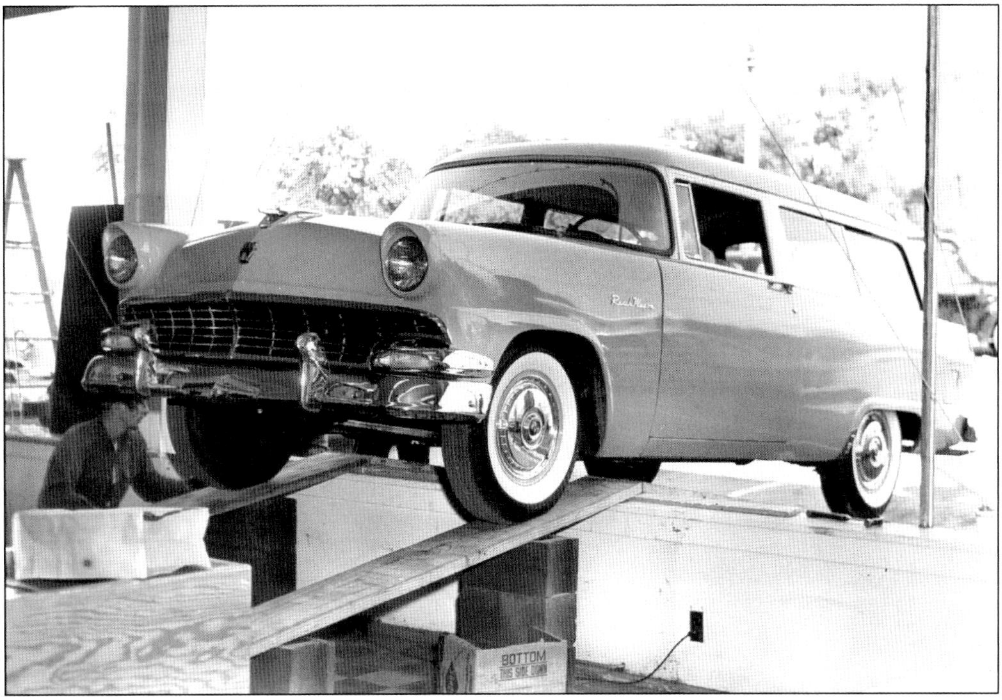

Each year Lloyd's gave away an automobile. A front window was removed, the car driven over the ramp into the store and the car was displayed until the drawing. The driver is Edward Konefal.

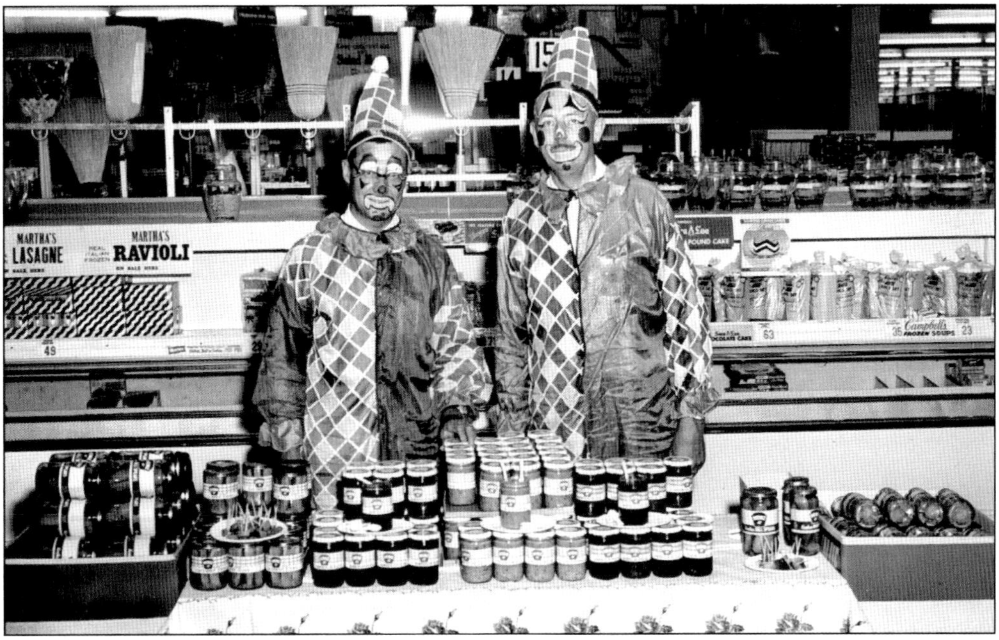

Lloyd's always had sales, and the customers loved them. Edmund S. Lloyd purchased railroad cars of sugar and truckloads of paper towels. Buying in such volume, there was no competition. Customers came from far away for bargains, and enjoyed the free coffee offered. Lloyd could be seen daily mingling with customers and listening to their comments.

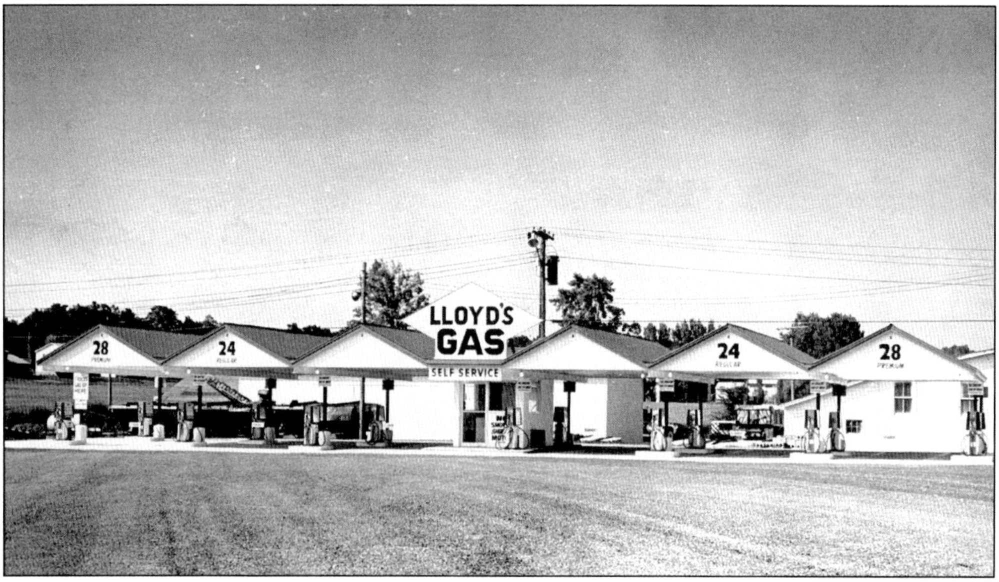

Lloyd's added car washes and gas stations to his supercenters. Gasoline was 24¢ a gallon for regular and 28¢ a gallon for premium.

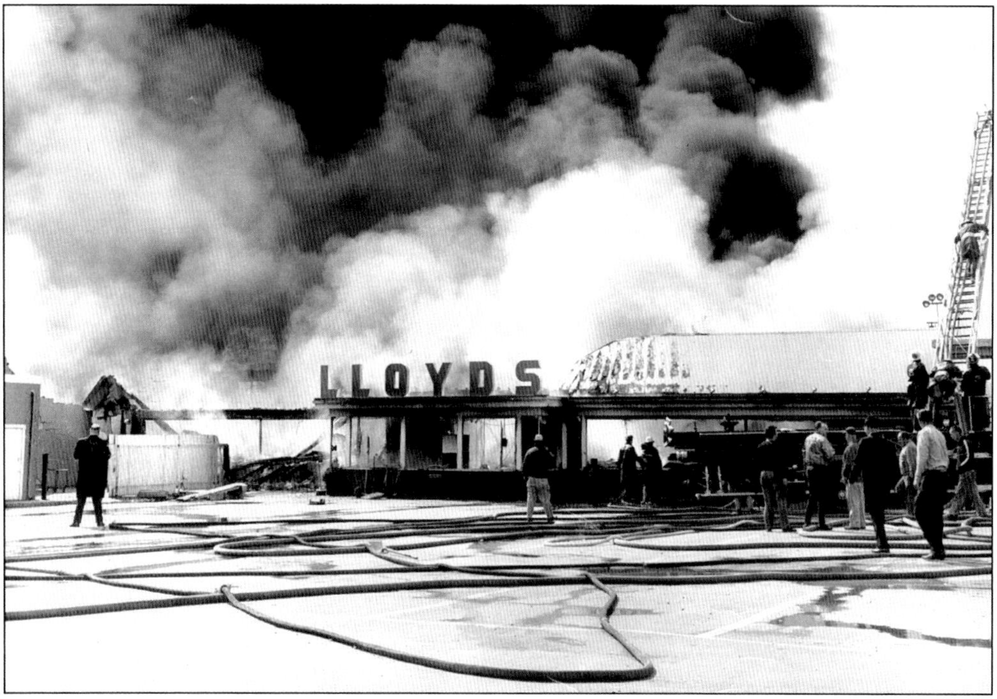

Lloyd's Middletown store was demolished by fire on May 12, 1968. Surviving that catastrophe, Edmund S. Lloyd rallied his supporters and built an even bigger and better store. However, time ran out for Lloyd's, as national chain stores moved into the area in the 1980s, and in the 1990s, he filed for bankruptcy. In 1996, a marquee in front of his Middletown store, which he authorized, said: "Thank you for 62 great years. Ed Lloyd." Lloyd's was the beginning of the evolution from farming to commercial establishments in the Town of Wallkill. (Photograph courtesy of Russell Thomas.)

Four

PEOPLE, PLACES, AND THINGS

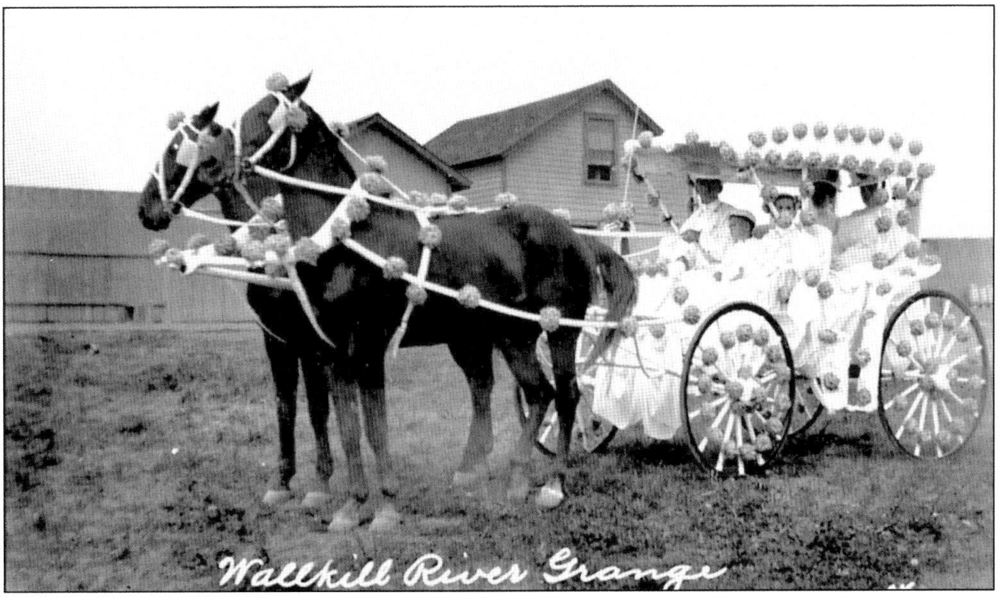

A special prize goes to Fairmont Farm's handsome horses, beautifully decorated carriage, and lovely ladies who participated in the Wallkill River Grange Parade, held September 22, 1908. The carriage was decorated by G. J. Skinner. (Photographs not otherwise identified, courtesy of the Historical Society of Middletown and the Wallkill Precinct.)

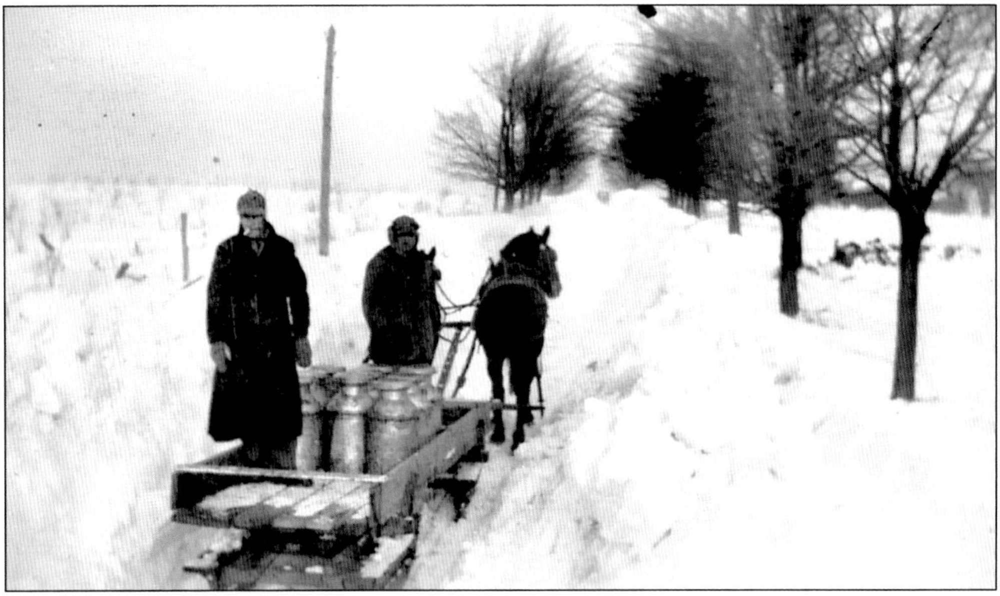

Roy Trimmer (left) takes milk to the creamery on a bobsled with a team of horses. (Courtesy of Leona Trimmer.)

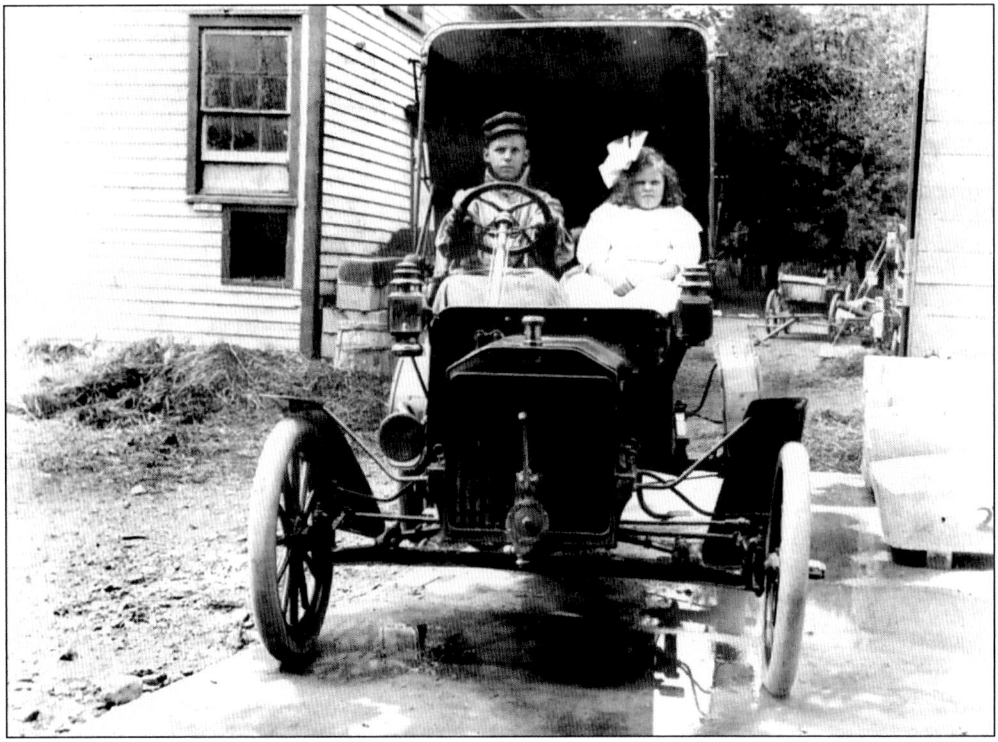

A handsome couple gets ready for a ride in a Ford Model T.

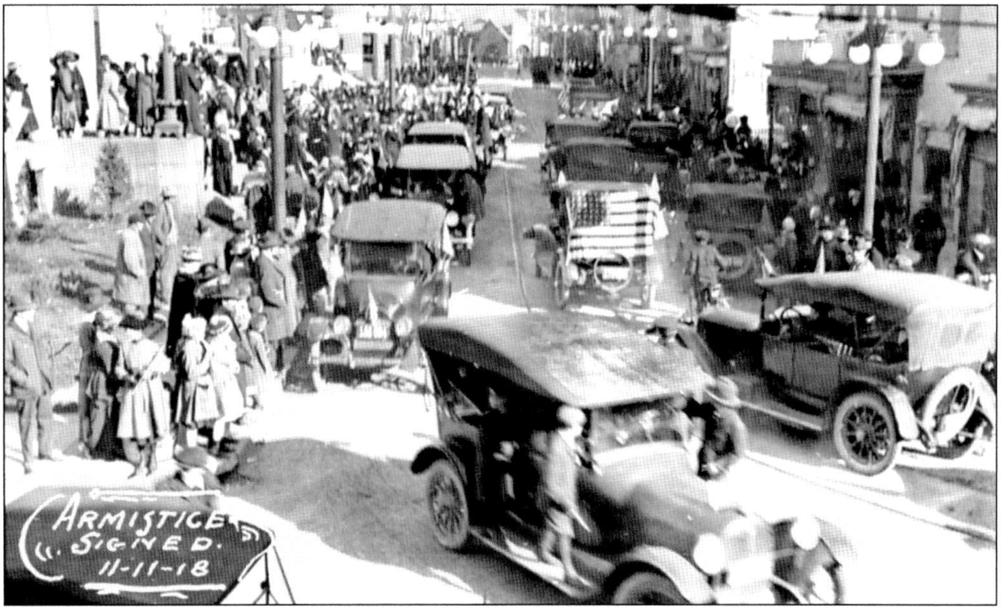

This is the celebration for the armistice that was signed on November 11, 1918.

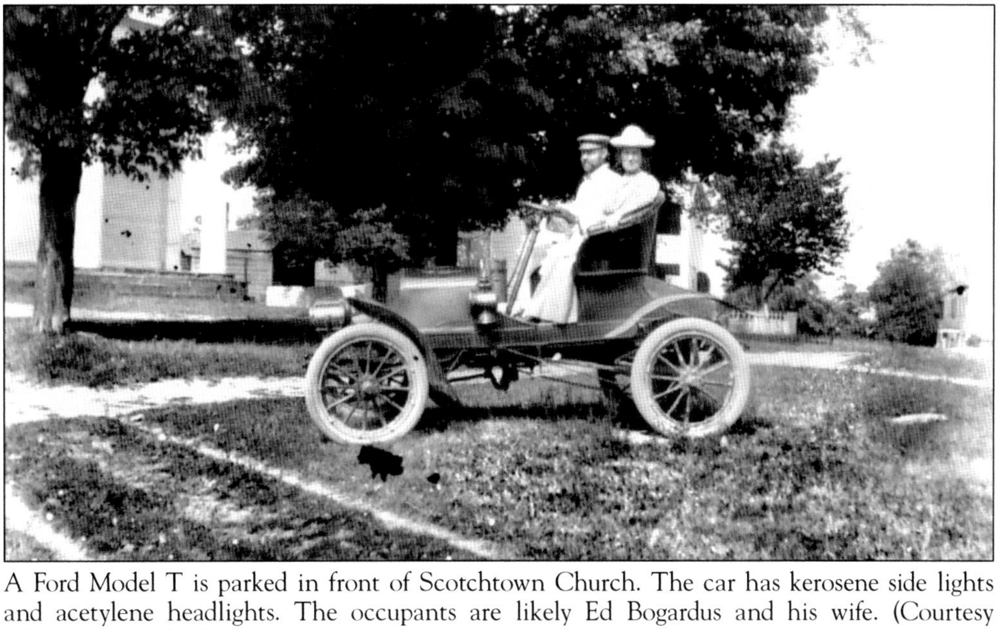

A Ford Model T is parked in front of Scotchtown Church. The car has kerosene side lights and acetylene headlights. The occupants are likely Ed Bogardus and his wife. (Courtesy of Milton Comfort.)

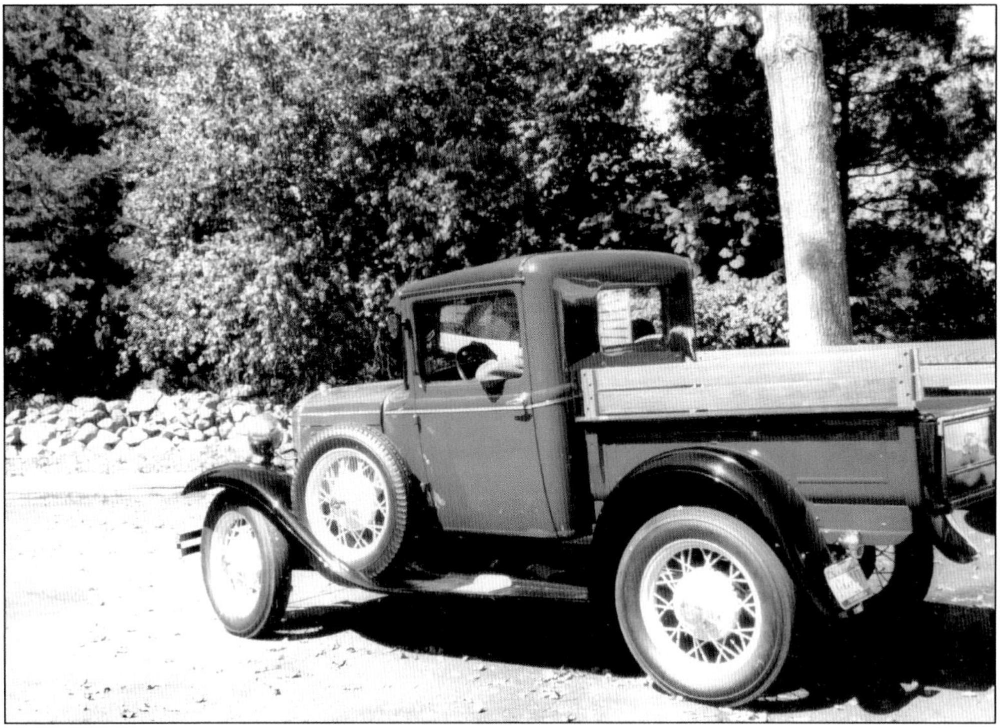

This 1931 Ford Model A pickup was owned by Richard Riker. (Courtesy of the Town of Wallkill Historian's collection.)

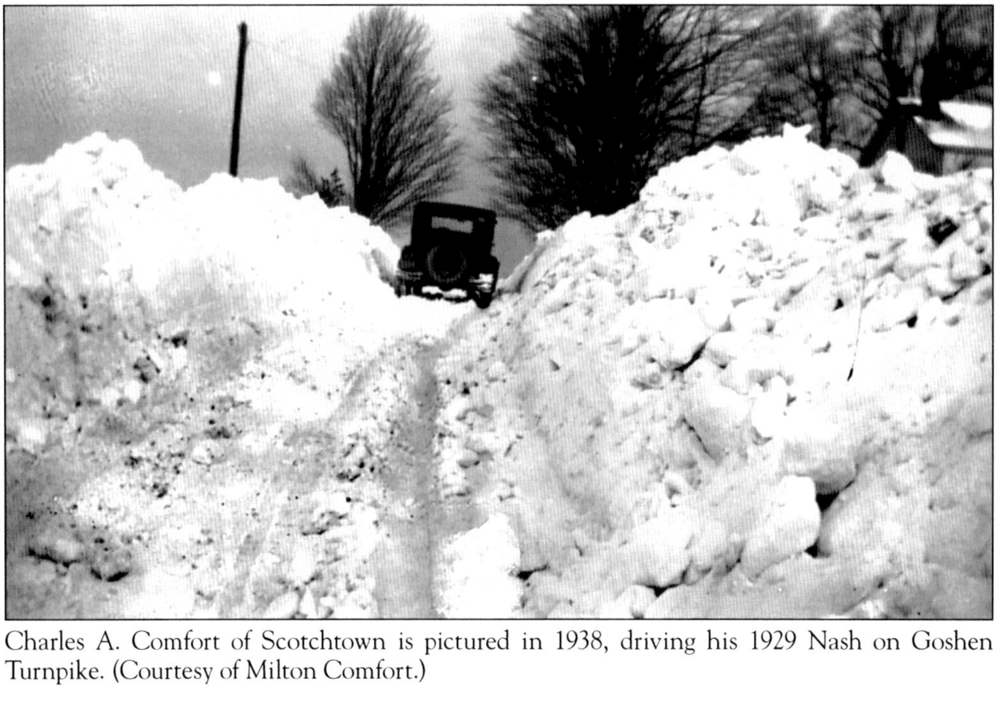

Charles A. Comfort of Scotchtown is pictured in 1938, driving his 1929 Nash on Goshen Turnpike. (Courtesy of Milton Comfort.)

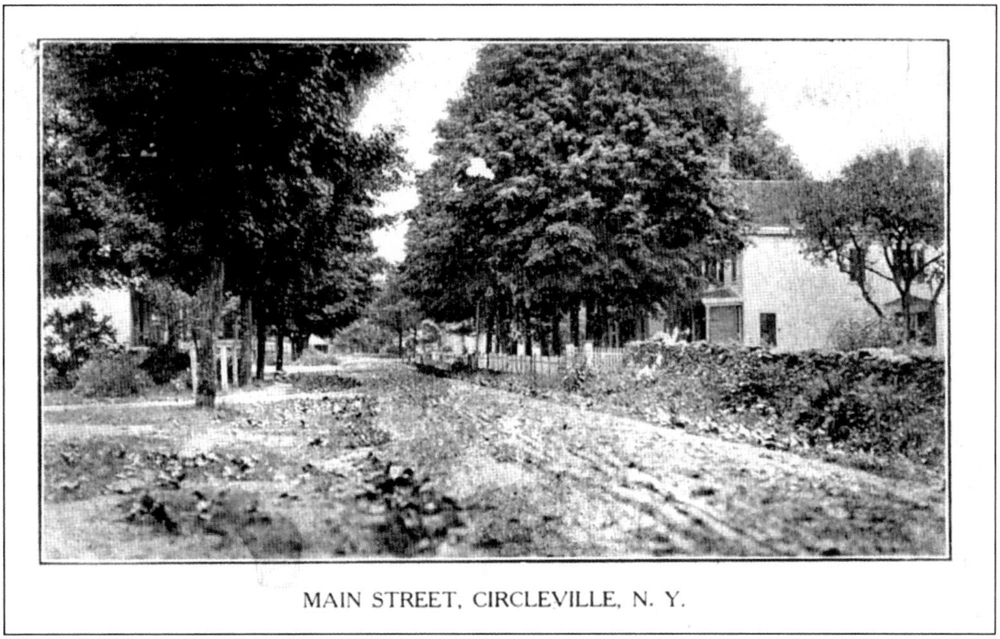

This early photograph shows an unpaved Main Street in Circleville. (Courtesy of Leona Trimmer.)

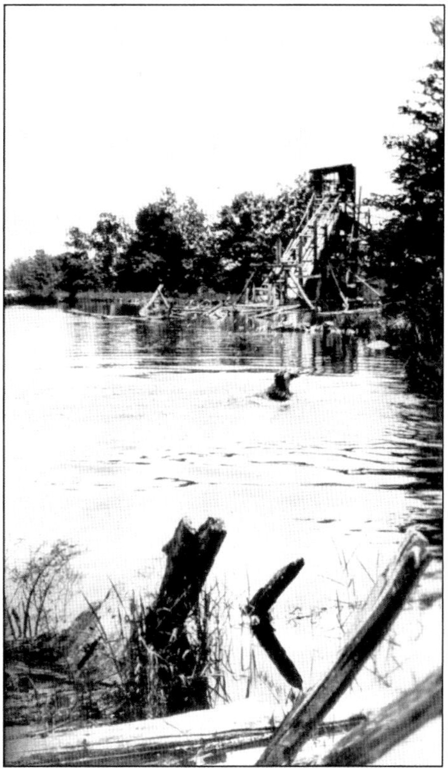

Pictured around 1910 at Lake Hennessey in Circleville is an ice conveyer.

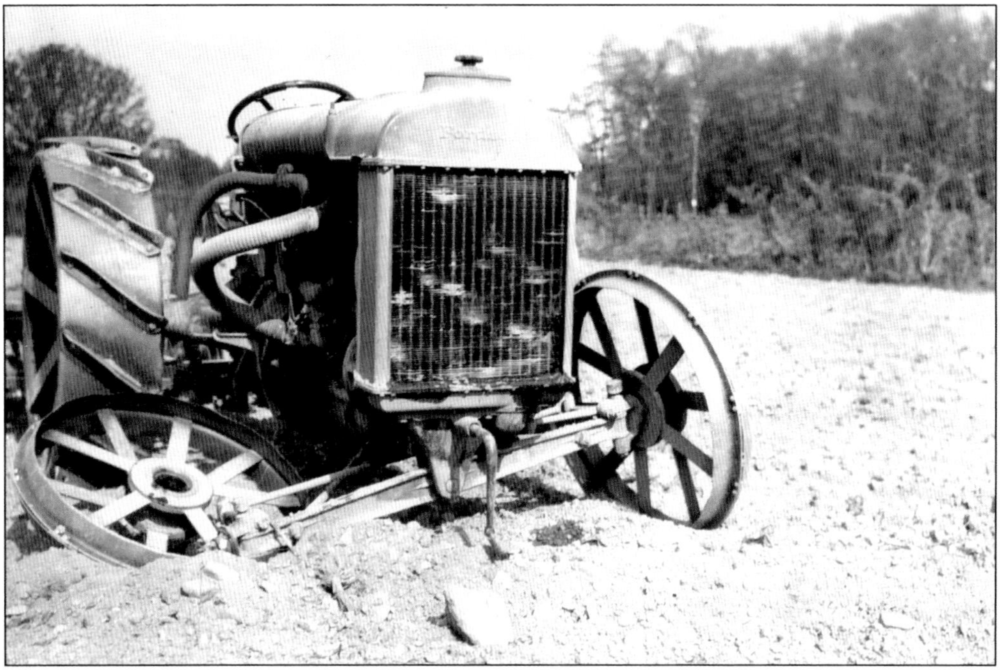

This Fordson tractor, on metal wheels, meets with a slight problem. (Courtesy of Glenn and Doris Hoyt.)

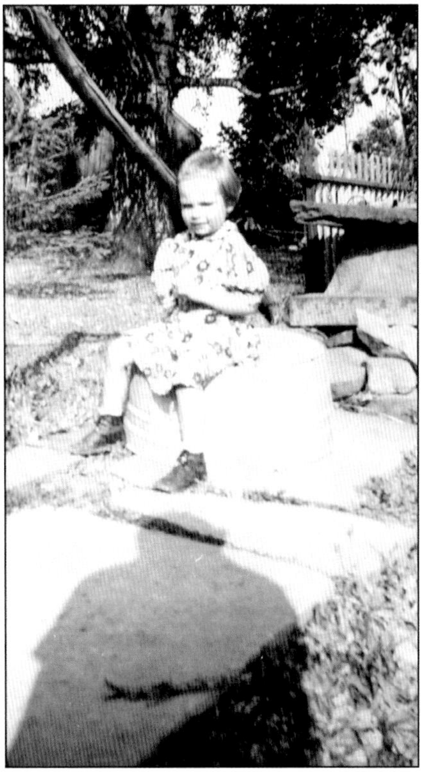

Next to the stagecoach stepping stone, Leona Trimmer sits on a bucket that was used to water the horses around 1940. (Courtesy of Leona Trimmer.)

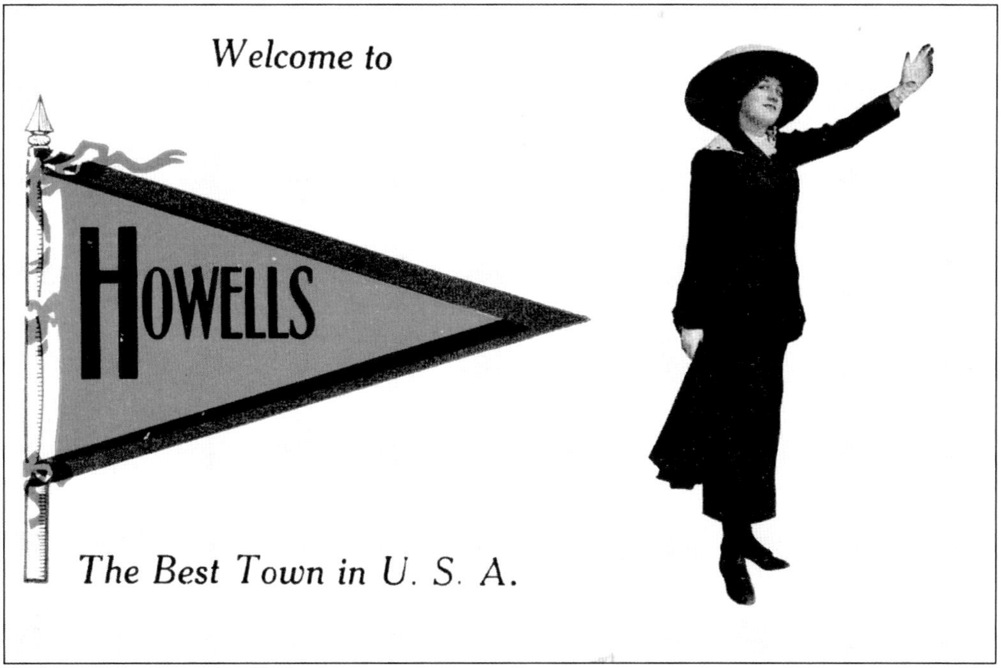

This early-1900s postcard reads, "Welcome to Howells!" (Courtesy of Phil and Stella Higby.)

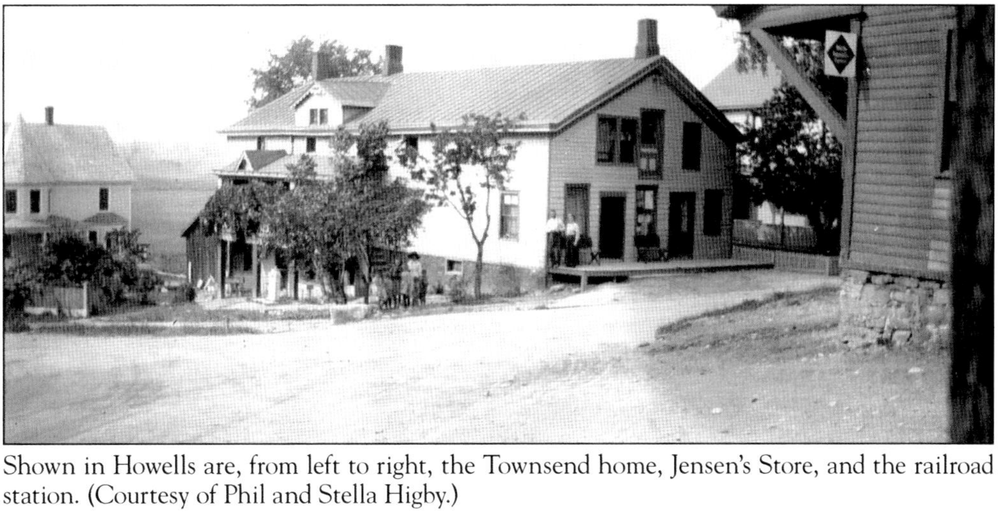

Shown in Howells are, from left to right, the Townsend home, Jensen's Store, and the railroad station. (Courtesy of Phil and Stella Higby.)

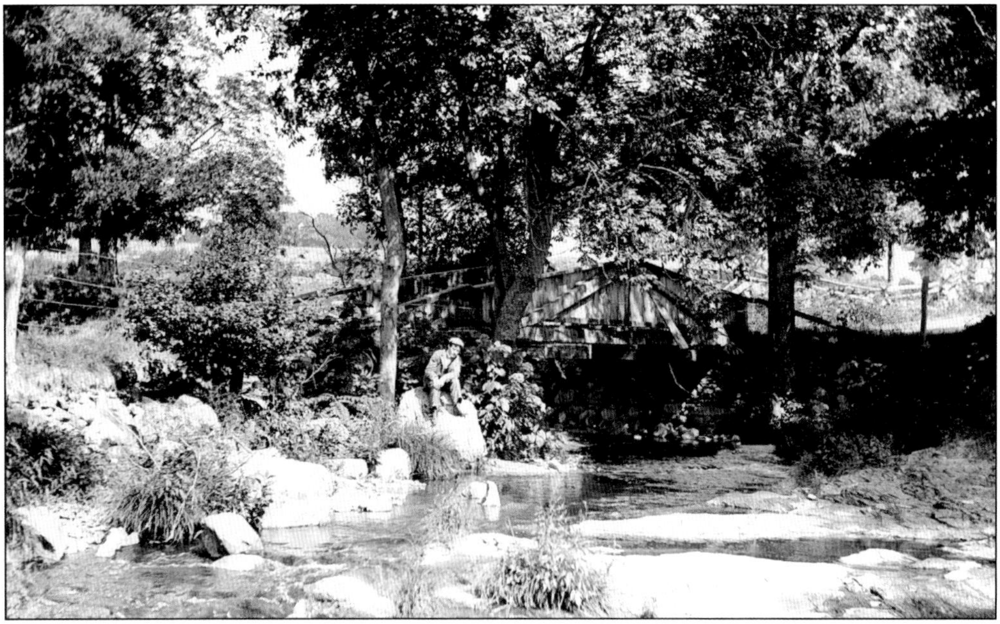

Phil Rorty sits on a rock at Masonic Creek near the Orange County Golf Club in 1895.

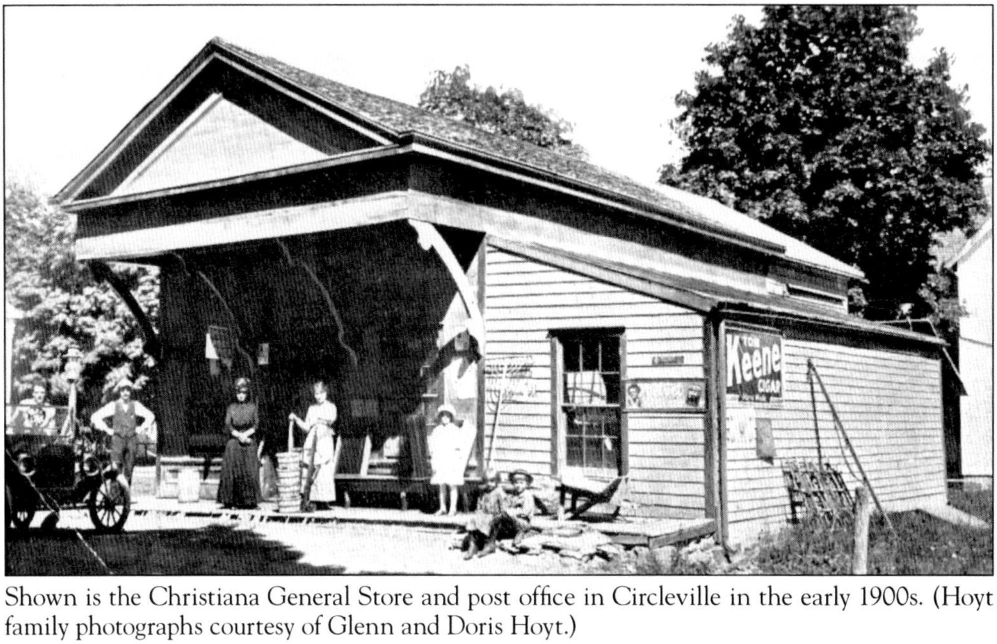

Shown is the Christiana General Store and post office in Circleville in the early 1900s. (Hoyt family photographs courtesy of Glenn and Doris Hoyt.)

Fredwood Christiana, owner of the Christiana General Store, was Doris (Travis) Hoyt's grandfather. He married Grace Markle, and their children were Millie, Laura (mother of Doris), Ruth, and Earl.

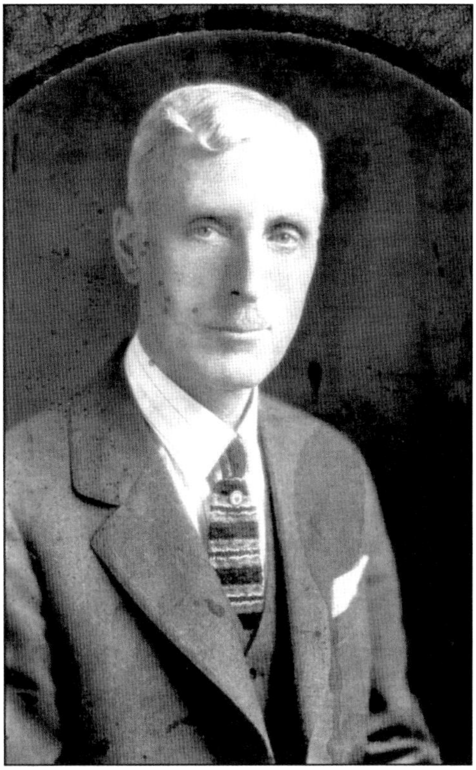

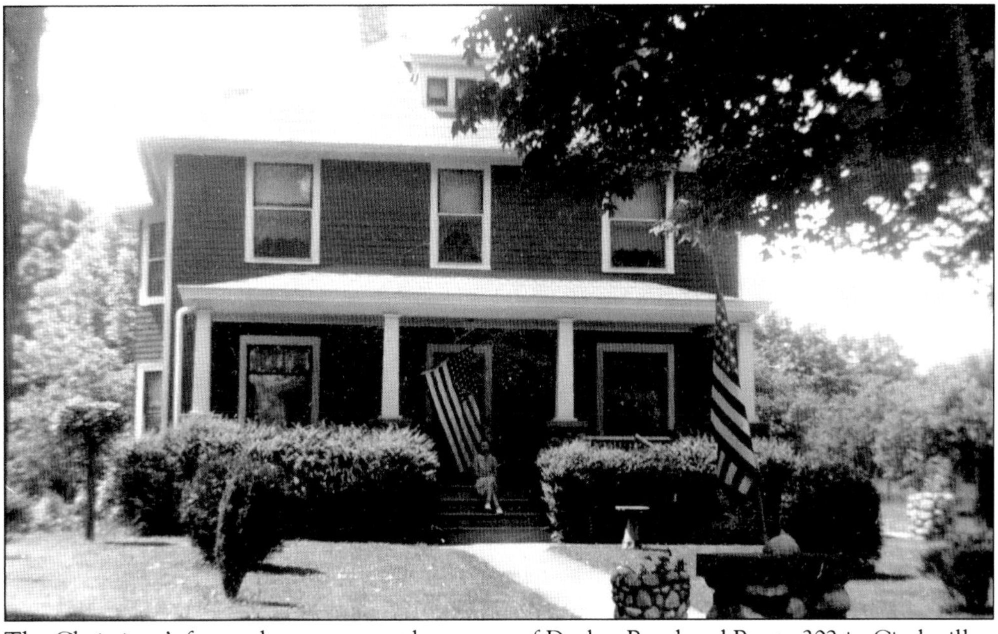

The Christiana's former home was on the corner of Decker Road and Route 302 in Circleville.

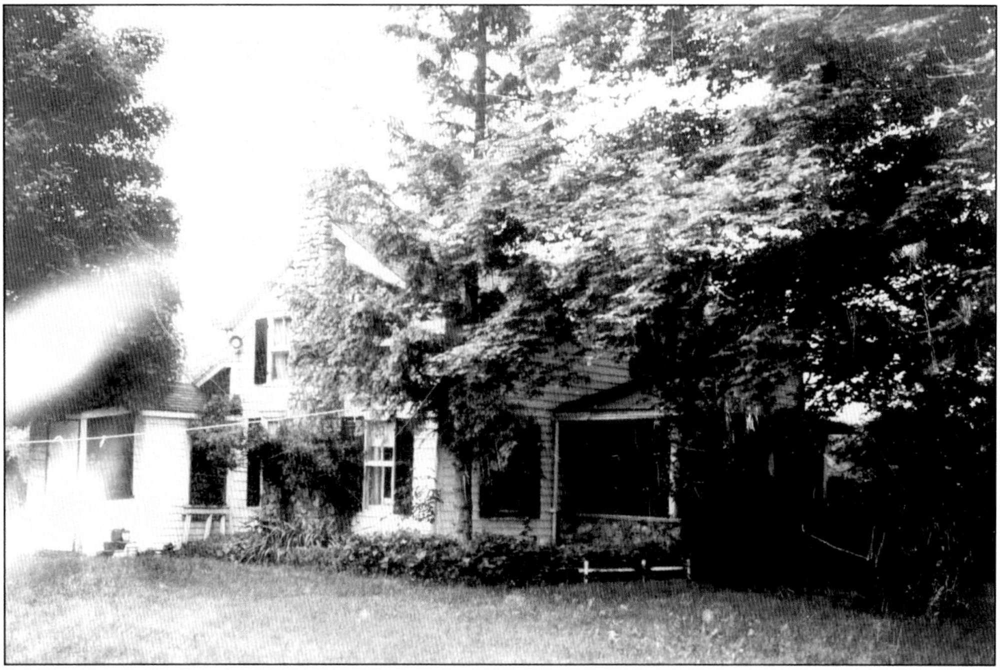

Laura Christiana married Melvin Travis, and the family resided on a farm on Van Burenville Road, where Doris was born.

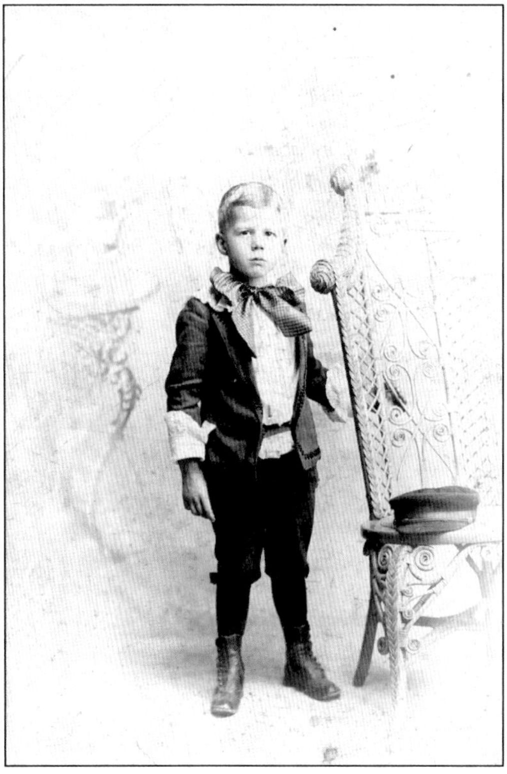

Harold Hoyt, Glenn Hoyt's father, poses for an early photograph.

Melvin Travis served in the army in World War I.

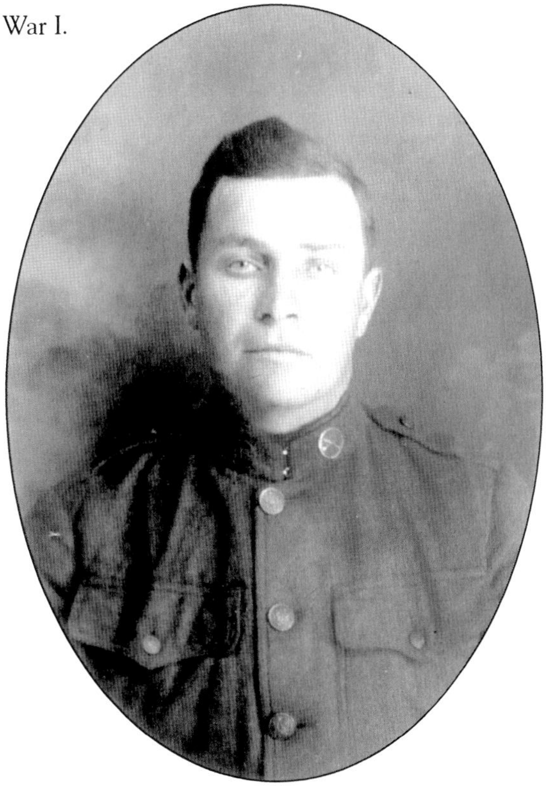

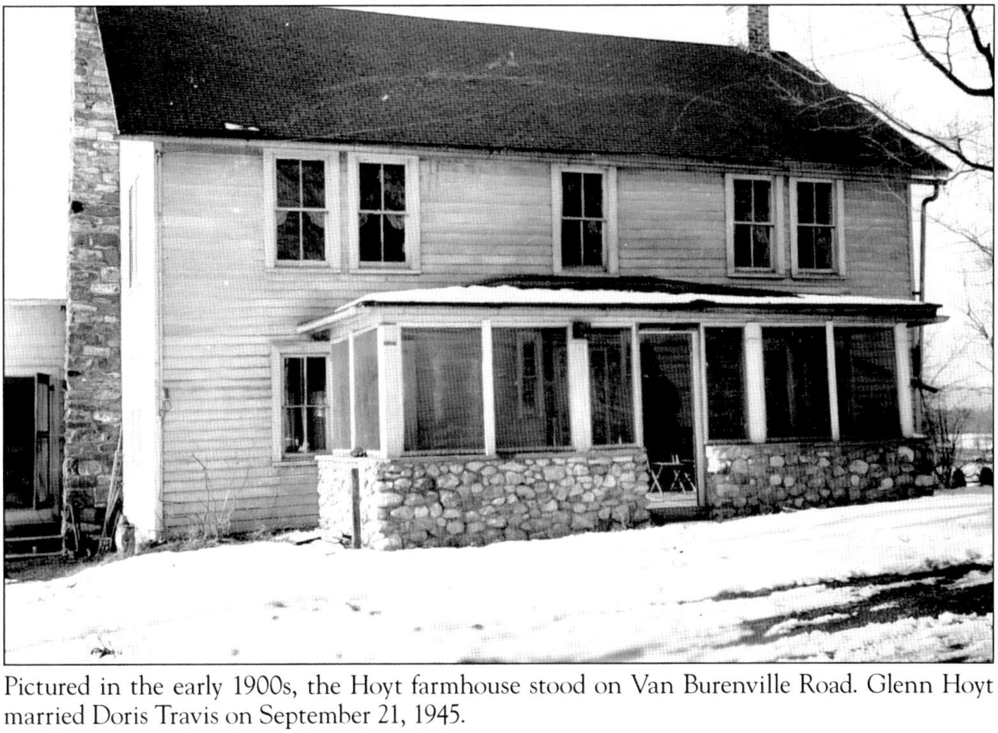

Pictured in the early 1900s, the Hoyt farmhouse stood on Van Burenville Road. Glenn Hoyt married Doris Travis on September 21, 1945.

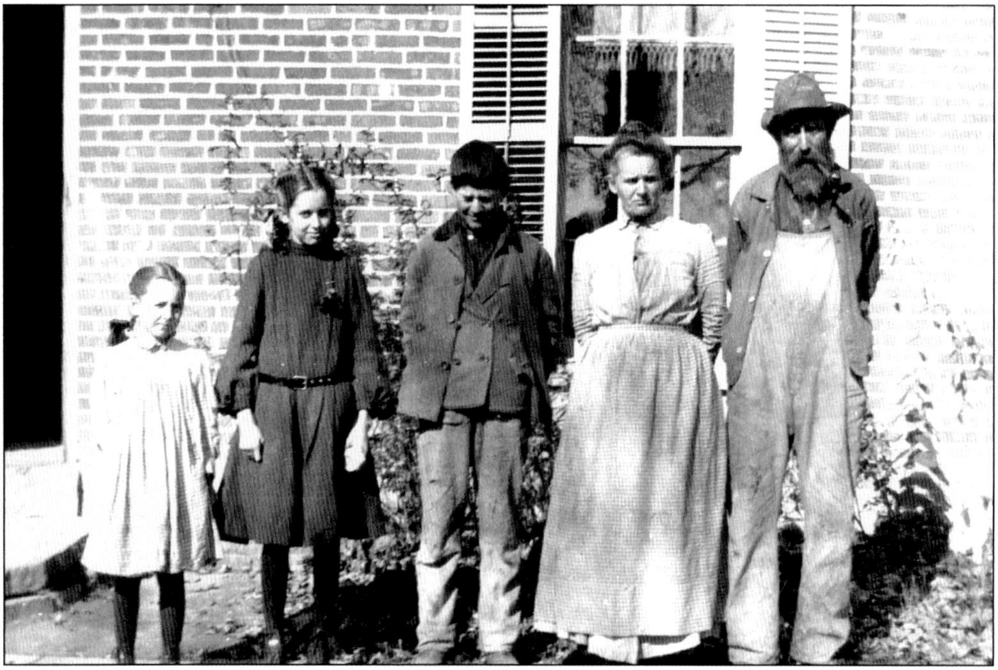

Glenn Hoyt's grandparents and family are, from left to right, Elizabeth Scott, Anna Suffern Hoyt, Nelson Suffern, "Gramma" Mary Suffern, and "Granpa" Simeon Suffern.

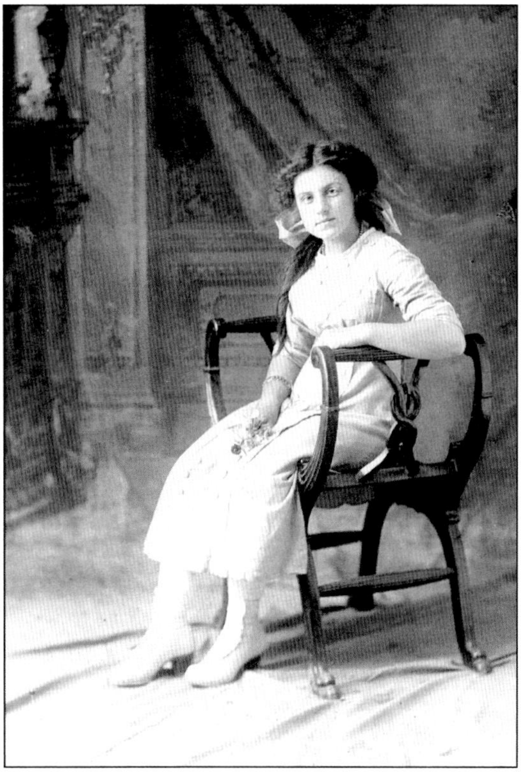

Shown is Julia Carpenter, Glenn Hoyt's cousin.

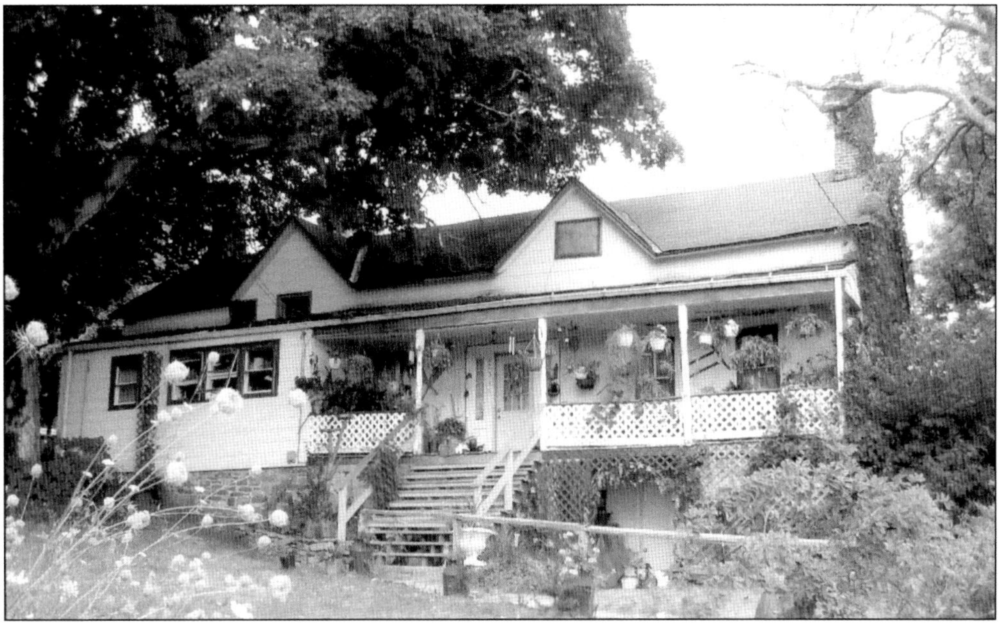

The *c.* 1800 home has been restored showing the open beam ceilings, the wide board flooring, and the large stone fireplace with stone mantle in the kitchen has been uncovered. An early owner was Dick Slee and the current owner is the Bonnie St. Clair family. A legend of the home is that on the bottom rail post of the cherry staircase railing there was a gold spike which signified the premises was mortgage free. (Information courtesy of Bonnie St. Clair.)

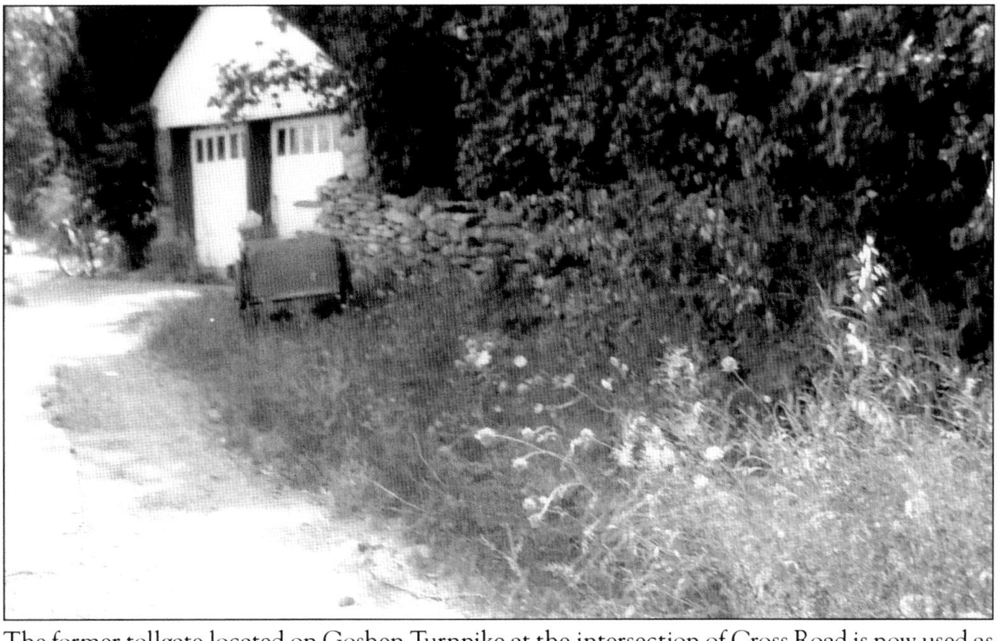

The former tollgate located on Goshen Turnpike at the intersection of Cross Road is now used as a garage. The tollgate was connected to the collector's home for easier access, and at this point in the road, Goshen Turnpike curved up in front of the tollgate. A stone in front with crude printing read, "From the boroughs [Bloomingburg] to the narrows [Scotchtown], toll 5 cents."

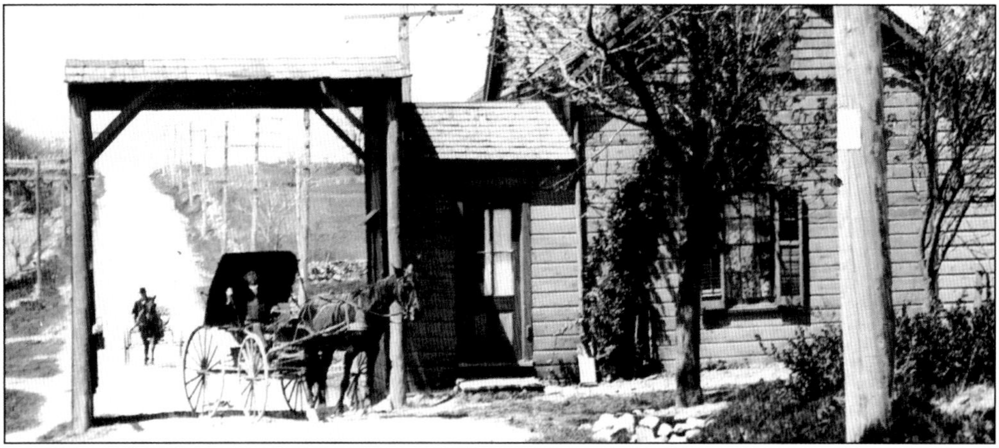

A horse and buggy pauses while the driver pays a few pennies at the Washington Heights tollgate of the Middletown and Wurtsboro Plank Road Company, where Judd Crane and his wife were collectors for many years. The road up the hill, now the well-populated Route 17M to Bloomingburg, became a town highway in 1910. The house was torn down in 1939. Irving J. Gibbs of Circleville, in a newspaper article, remembered the road was "all mud or all dust." When he drove his horse and wagon to high school in 1907–1909, he recalled that the planks that formed the road's base had rotted due to the increased traffic, and the pennies paid for the toll did not provide funds for upkeep of the road. Judd Crane was careful who passed over the road he represented, and an intoxicated man usually was taken into the house to sober up in order to avoid danger to himself and the highway. (Photograph courtesy of the Paul Weisshaar collection and information from *Times Herald Record* article of December 2, 1963.)

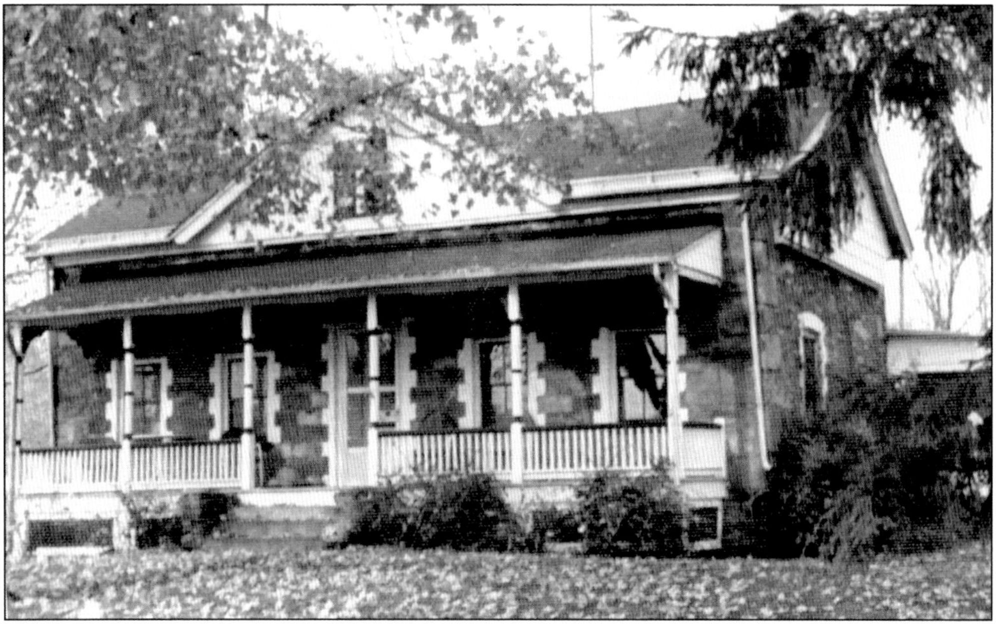

In April 1925, the Elmer Lemon property on Mud Mills Road, formerly known as Sands Station Road, was auctioned off in the city of Middletown. The *c.* 1860 stone house and 76 acres of farmland went begging when no purchaser could be found. The executors of the Lemon estate would not accept the highest bid of $4,800. The next day, Clarence Anson Dart boosted the price to $5,000, which was accepted. (Dart family photographs courtesy of Willard Dart.)

Shown is Clarence Anson Dart in 1890 at seven years old.

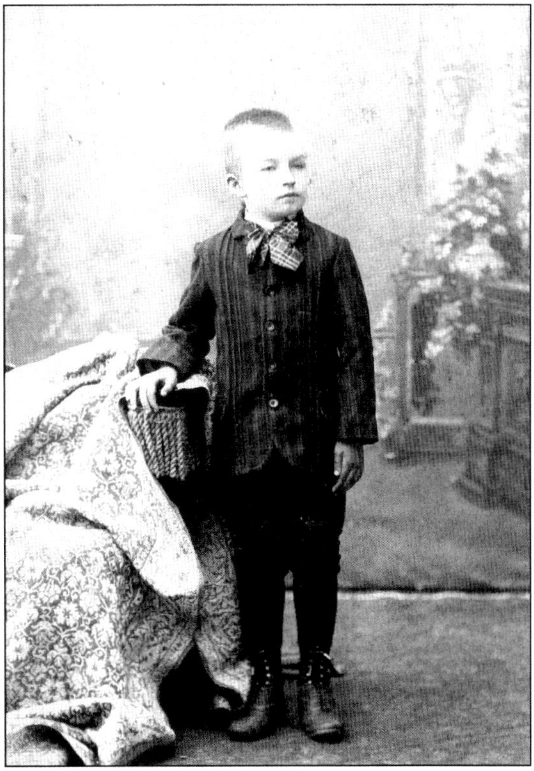

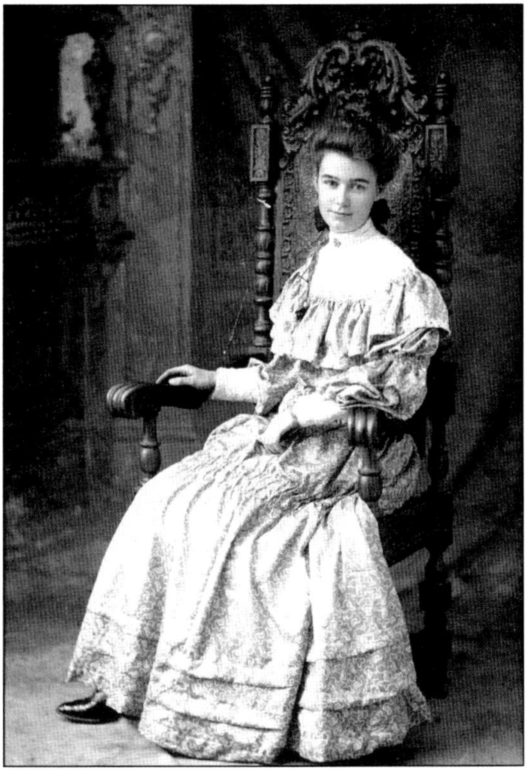

Pictured here is Blanche Henderson at 16 years old.

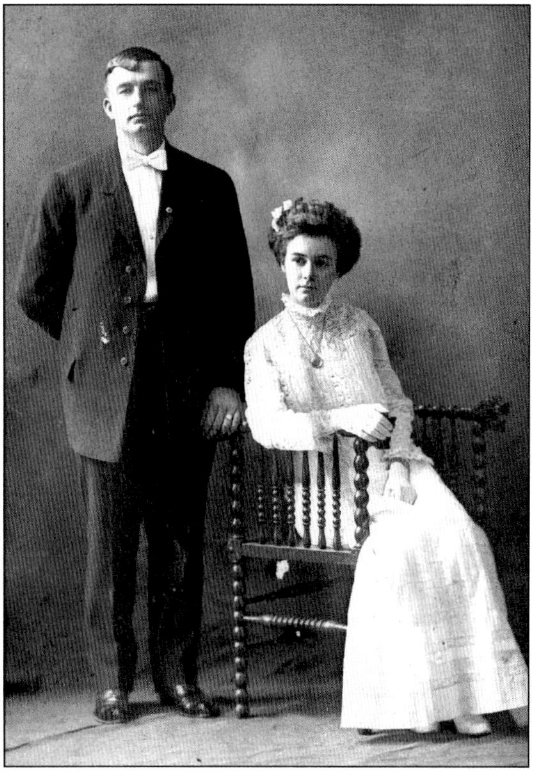

Clarence Anson Dart and Blanche Henderson pose for their wedding photograph on June 21, 1910.

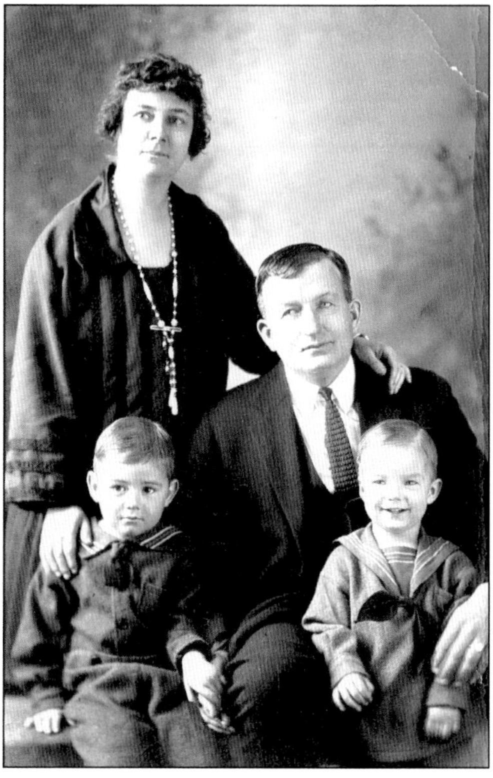

In this Dart family photograph are, from left to right (first row) Clarence Avery Dart, (born October 10, 1921) and Willard Henderson Dart (born December 31, 1922); (second row) Blanche Dart and Clarence Anson Dart.

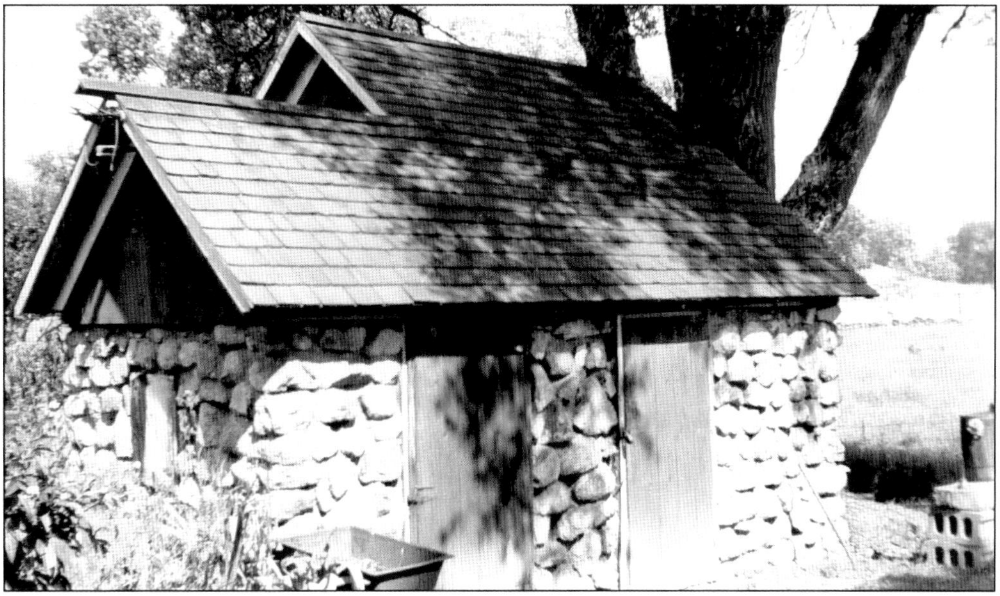

This stone springhouse stood next to the Dart home.

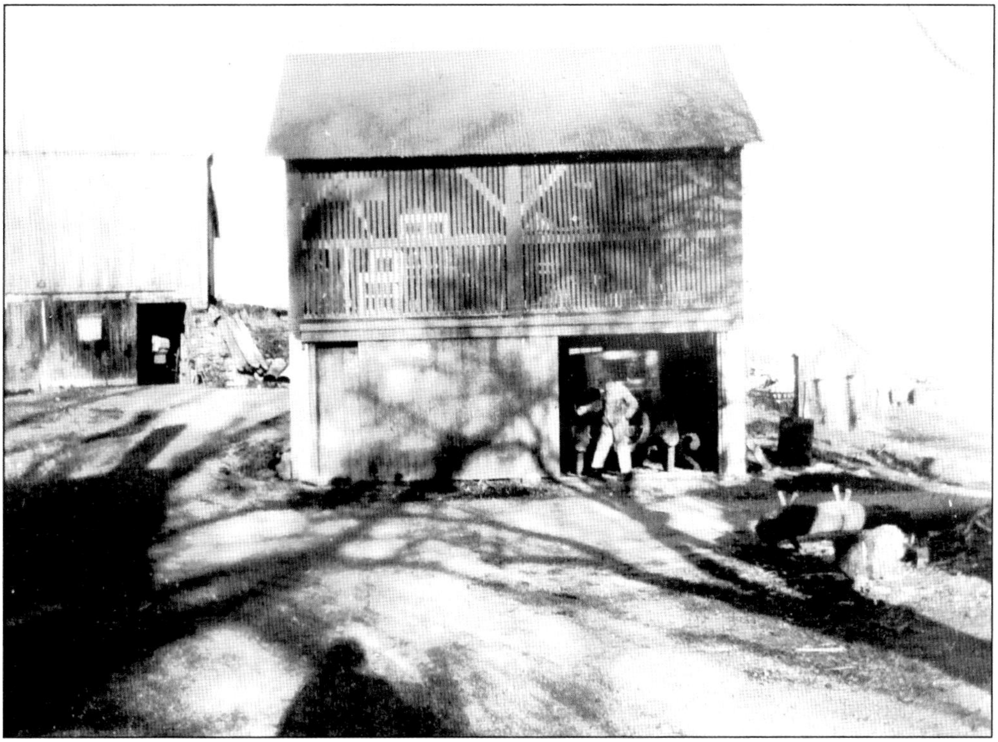

Seen in this view are the granary, the garage (below), and the back of a 1927 car.

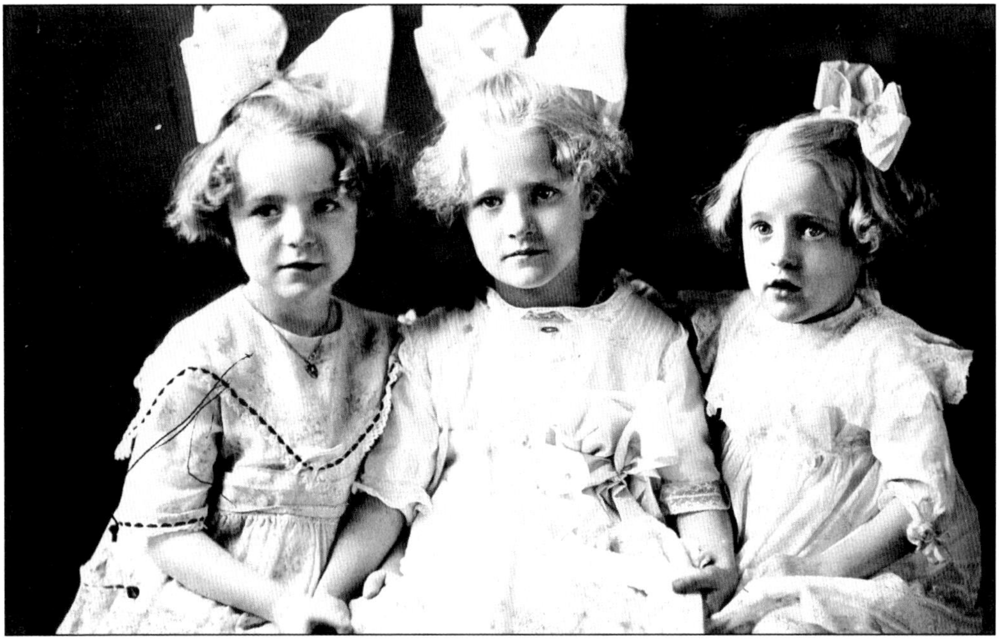

The Taylor girls are, from left to right, Marjorie, Julie, and Marie—cousins of Clarence and Willard Dart.

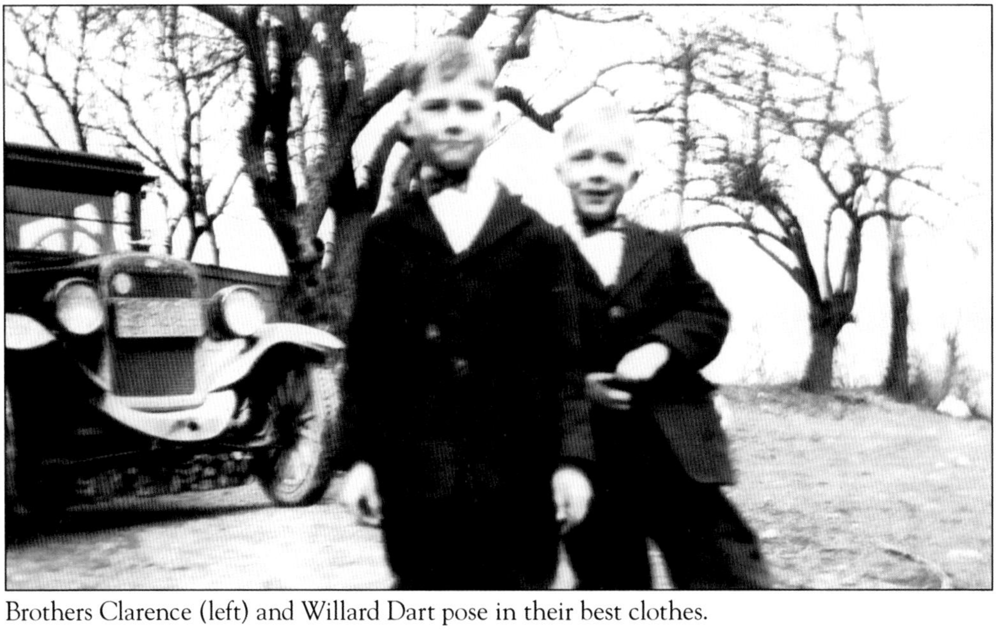

Brothers Clarence (left) and Willard Dart pose in their best clothes.

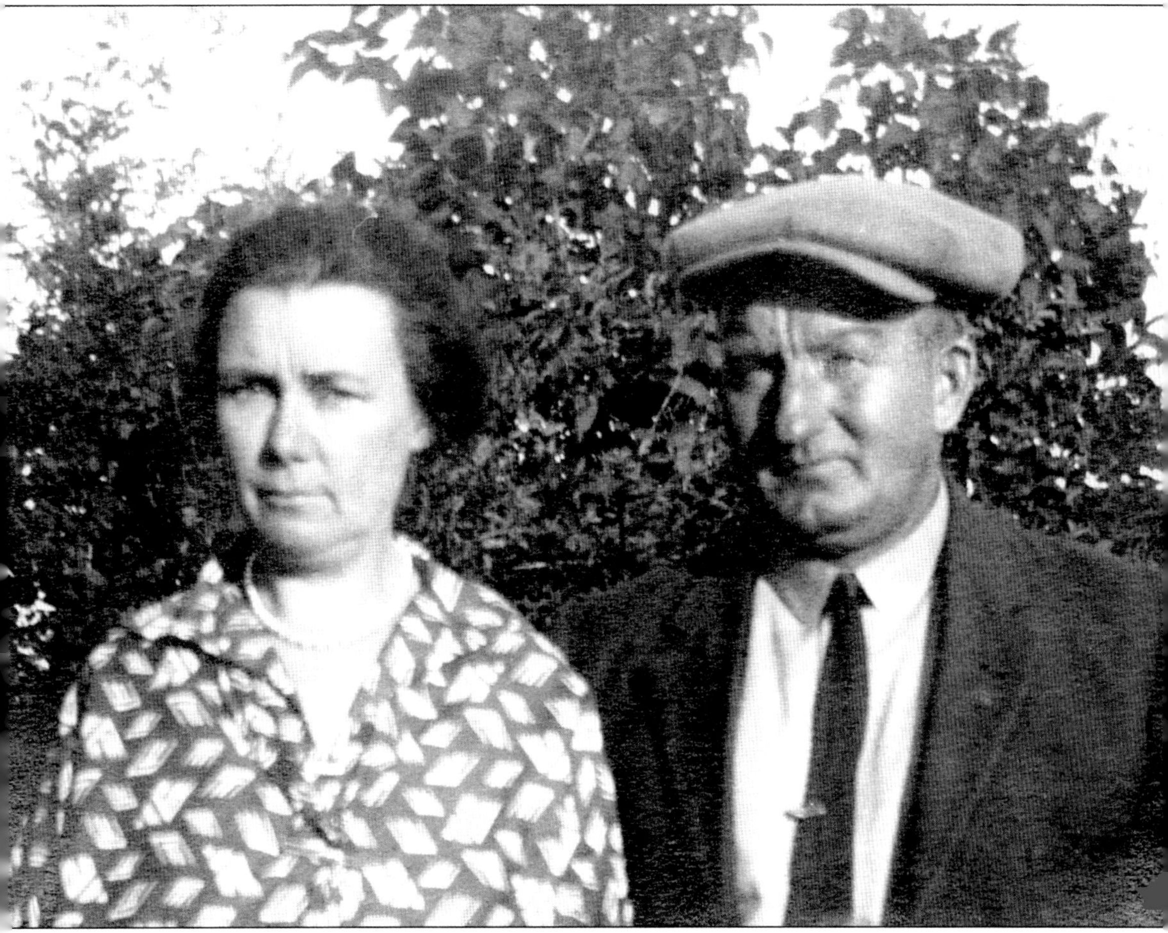

Pictured are Blanche and Clarence Anson Dart in 1930. On December 31, 1930, Clarence Dart was making his first run on a new train schedule, the Ontario and Western Milk Train No. 11, when he was hurled from the snow-covered roof of a boxcar at Walton and was killed. He was 47 years old.

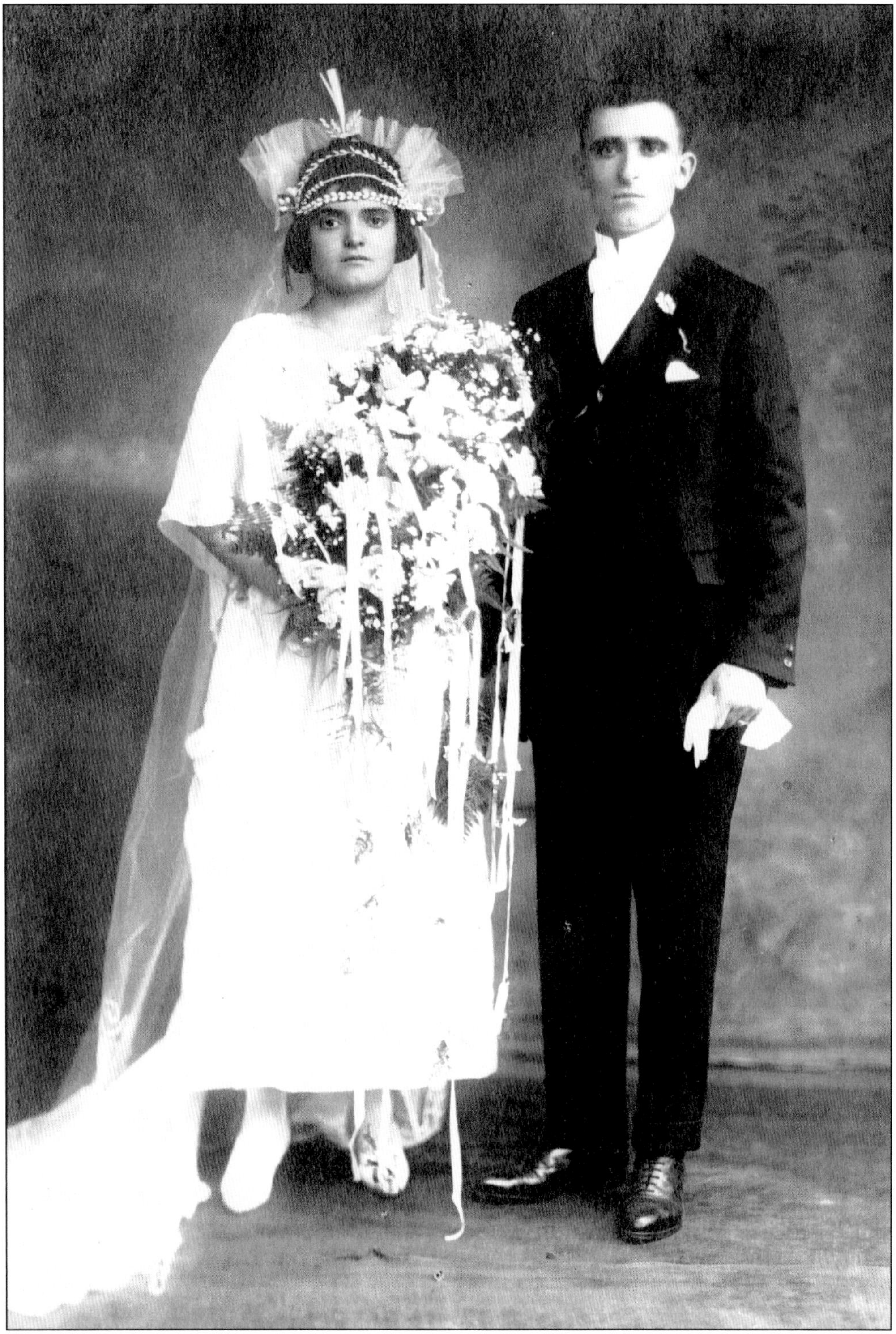

Maria Dina looked elegant on the day of her wedding to Guiseppe (Joseph) Ingrassia, June 27, 1920. Both arrived in the United States in 1913 from Sicily. (Courtesy of the Ingrassia family.)

Five

Recreation and Entertainment

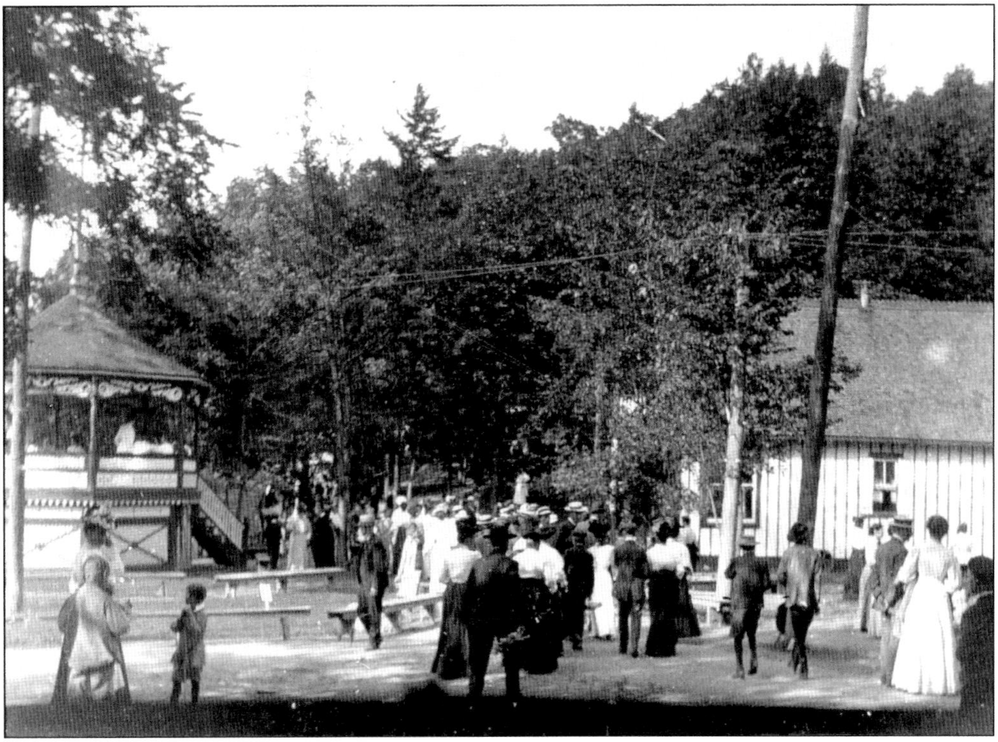

Midway Park was owned and operated by the Middletown-Goshen Traction Company, which built a trolley line in 1894 that ran from Middletown to Goshen. On opening day, August 25, 1894, Midway Park's attendance reached 9,600 people. (Photographs not otherwise identified, courtesy of the Historical Society of Middletown and the Wallkill Precinct.)

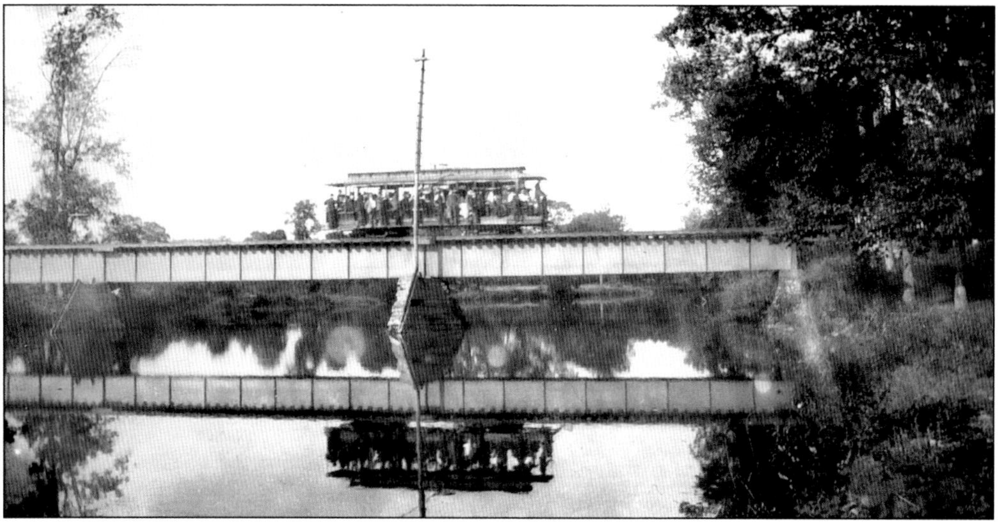

A well-filled open car crosses the bridge over the Wallkill River en route to a day's outing at Midway Park.

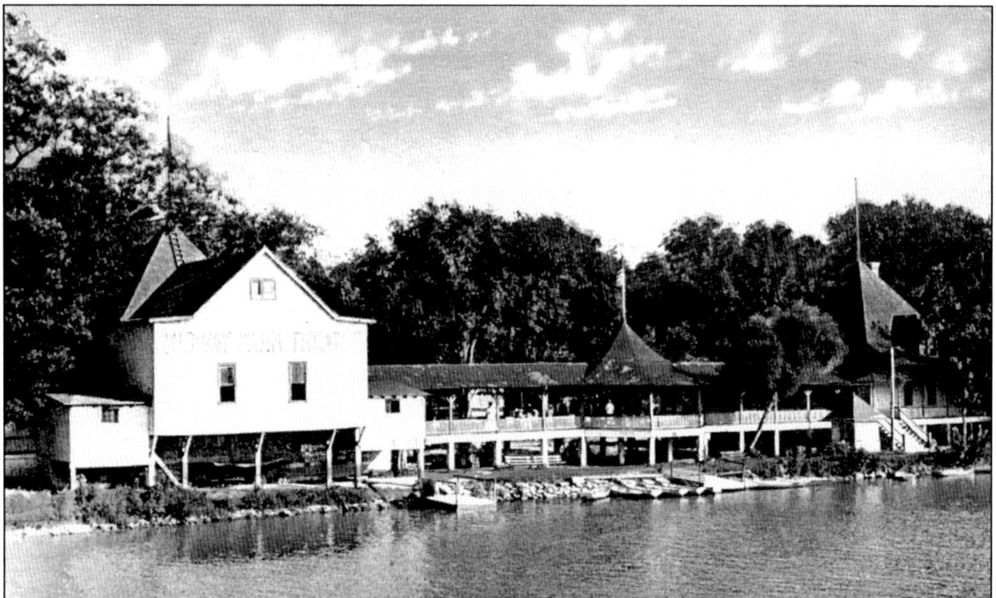

A covered pavilion, 232 feet long, was built for roller-skating, dancing, or audience seating when vaudeville shows or plays were given.

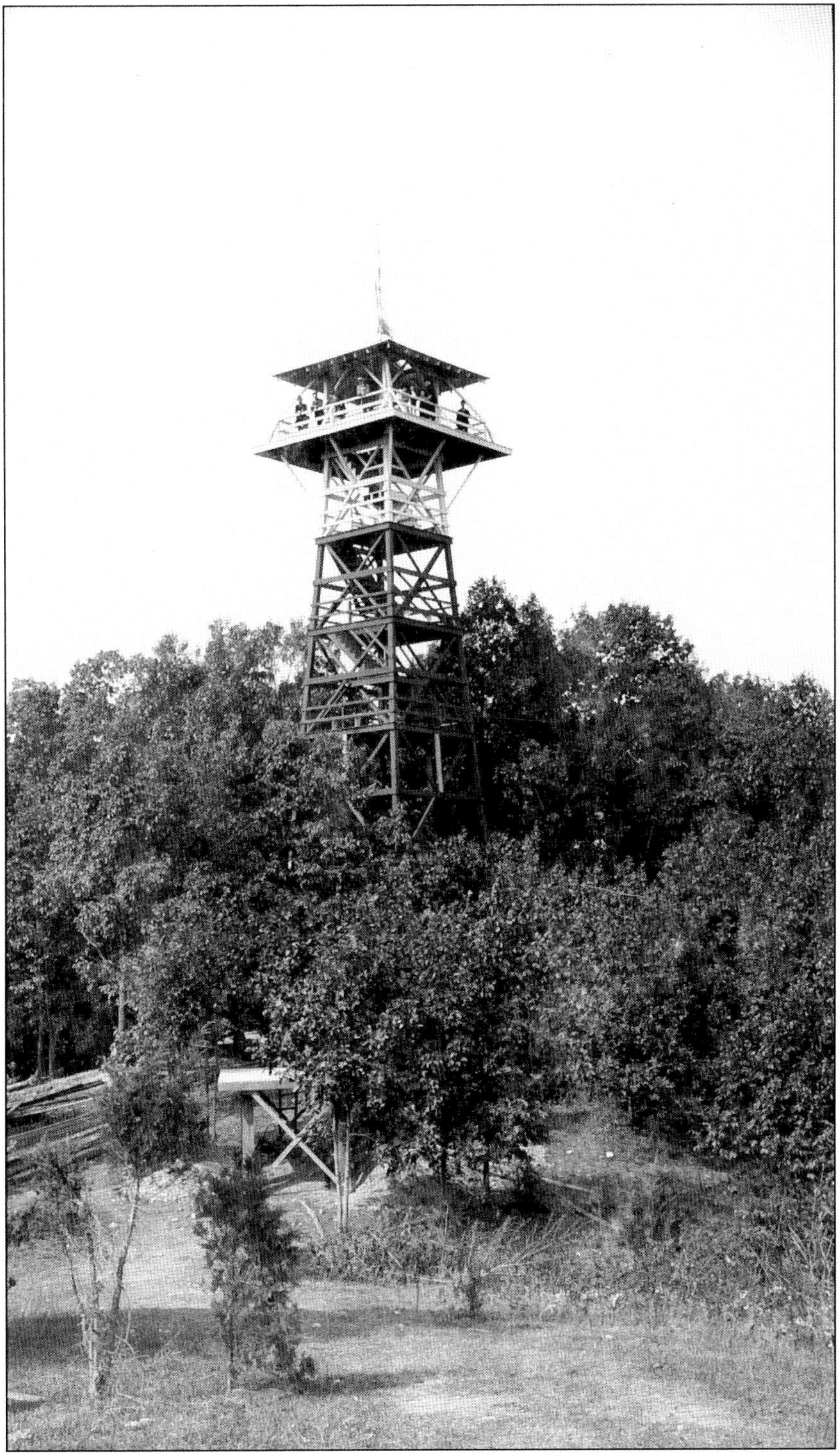

An observation tower, 75 feet high, was constructed on top of Hopper Hill, from which superb views could be seen in all directions. The hill was so named because its shape resembled the hopper of a gristmill.

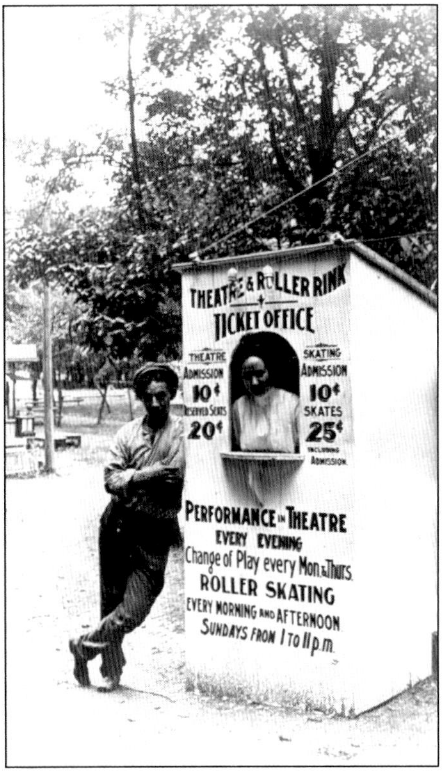

This is the ticket office at Midway Park.

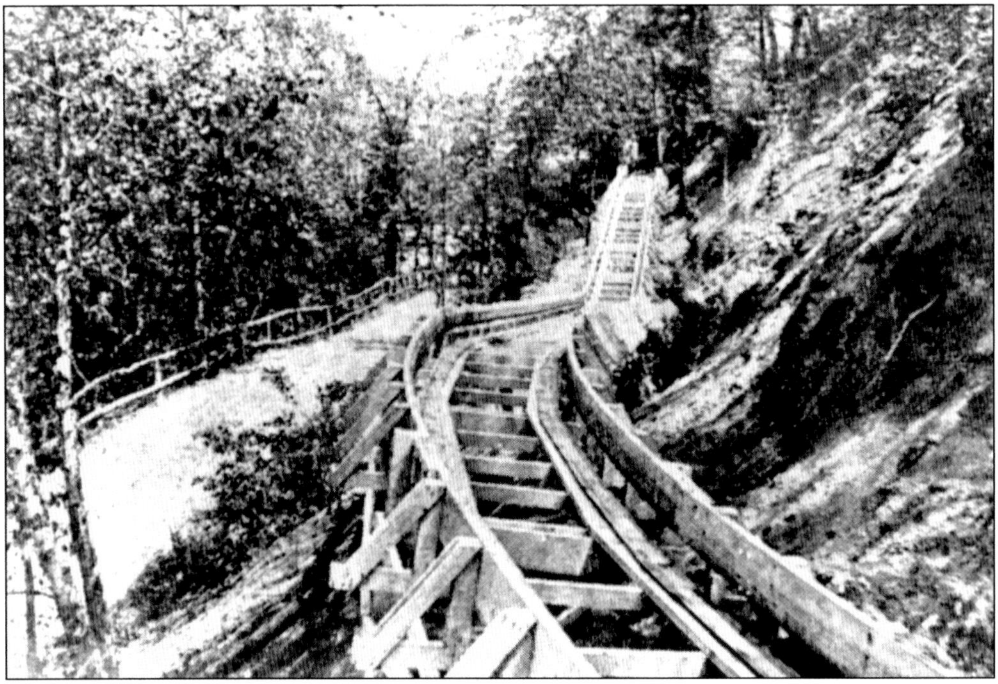

Patrons had to climb a 250-foot incline to board the roller coaster to ride as it "wound its way through meadow and woods, across ravines and along precipitous hillsides for three fourths of a mile."

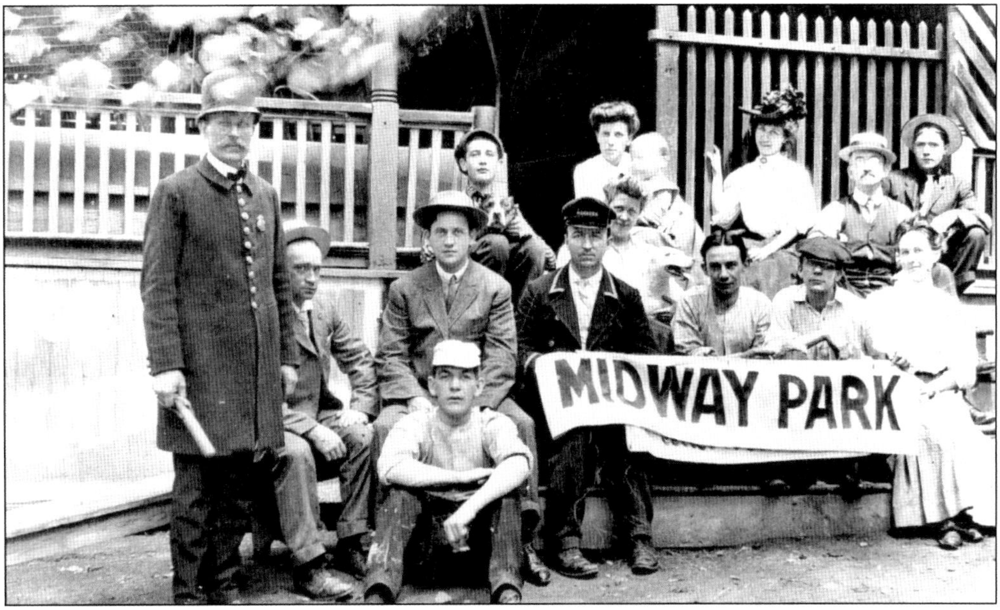

The uniformed policeman is John Durham.

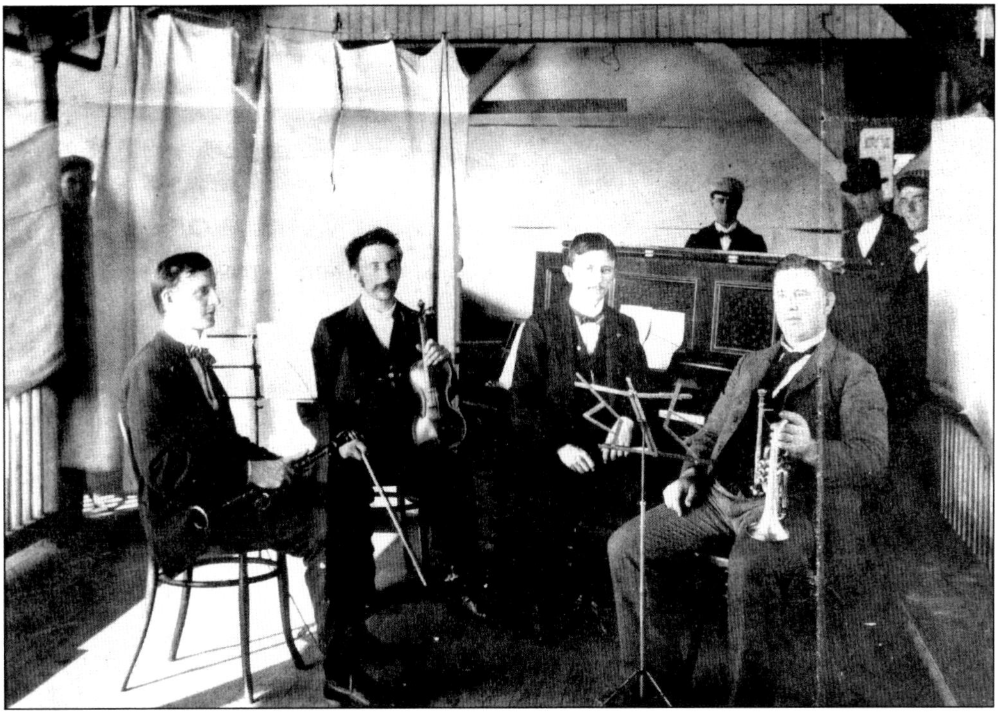

Ready to perform in 1898 are, from left to right, musicians Frank Brady, Prof. William Roescher, Edward C. Vollmer, and Art Parkins.

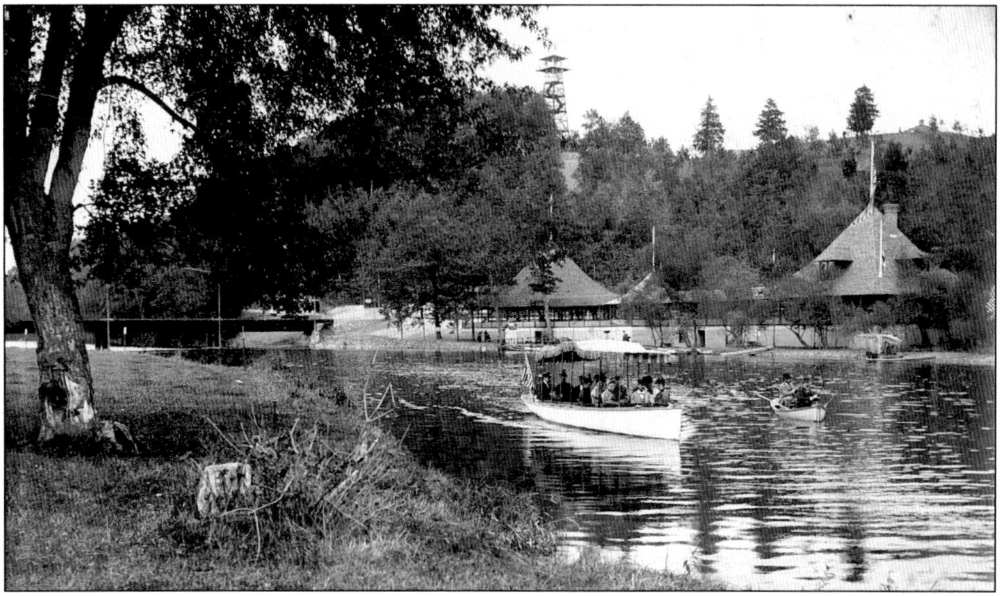

A powered launch was available for those who did not want to row a boat, and the boaters were able "to glide over a smooth stretch of water for a distance of half a mile on the north and one and a half miles on the south affording the voyager beautiful views." The restaurant is on the right, and the trolley car bridge is at the far left.

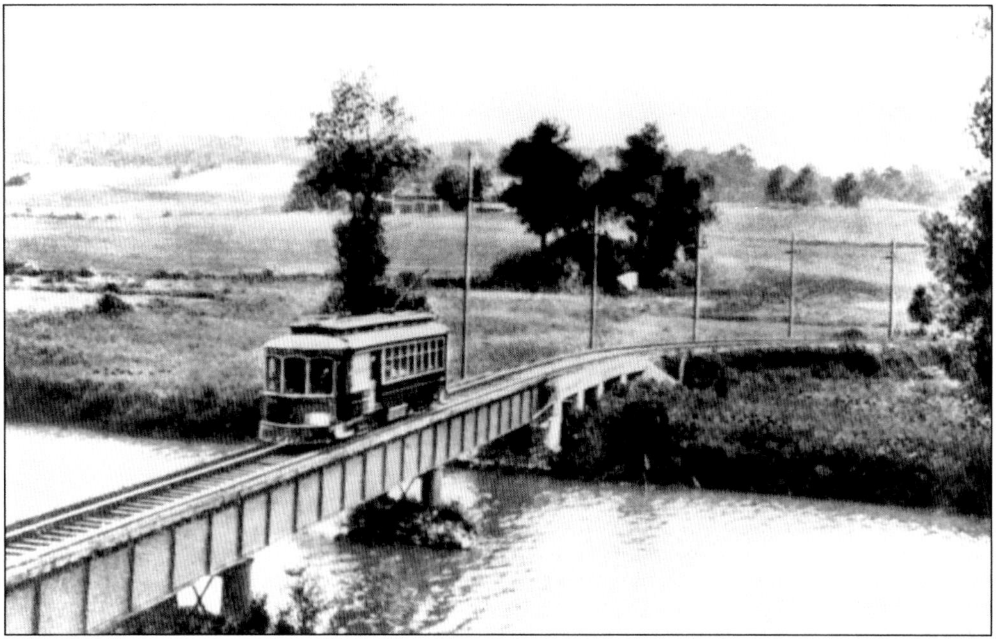

Shown is a trolley crossing the Wallkill River at Midway Park.

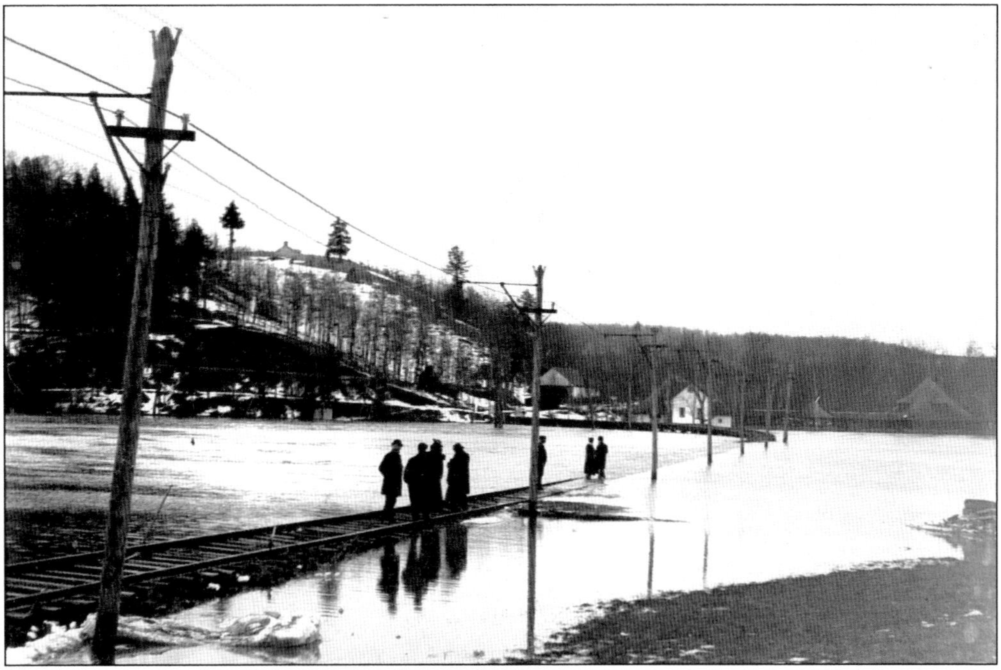

The Wallkill River overflowed the trolley tracks between Orange County Golf Club and Midway Park on March 3, 1902.

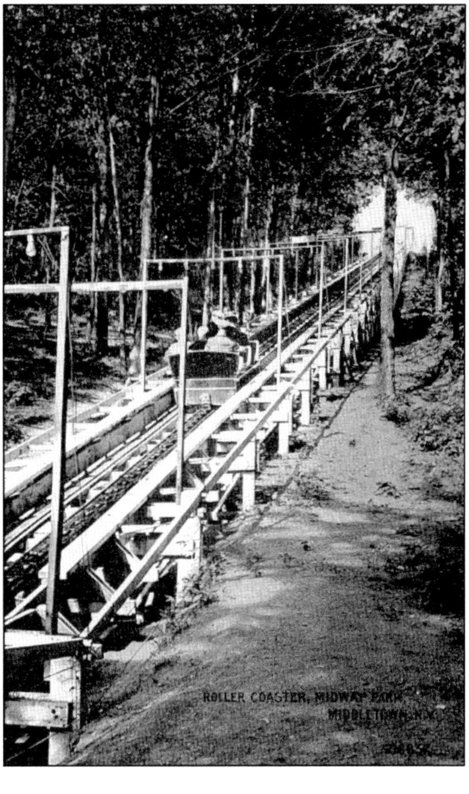

In 1904, the season opened with a disaster. The roller coaster burned as it ran through the woods. The dry leaves and dead branches under and along this wooden structure caught fire from a spark. In 1911, a new trolley was installed, financed by a group of Middletown businessmen. Passengers did not have to climb the hill since the cars were pulled up by cables operated by electric motors. The ride was 3,500 feet long and followed the natural contour of the ground.

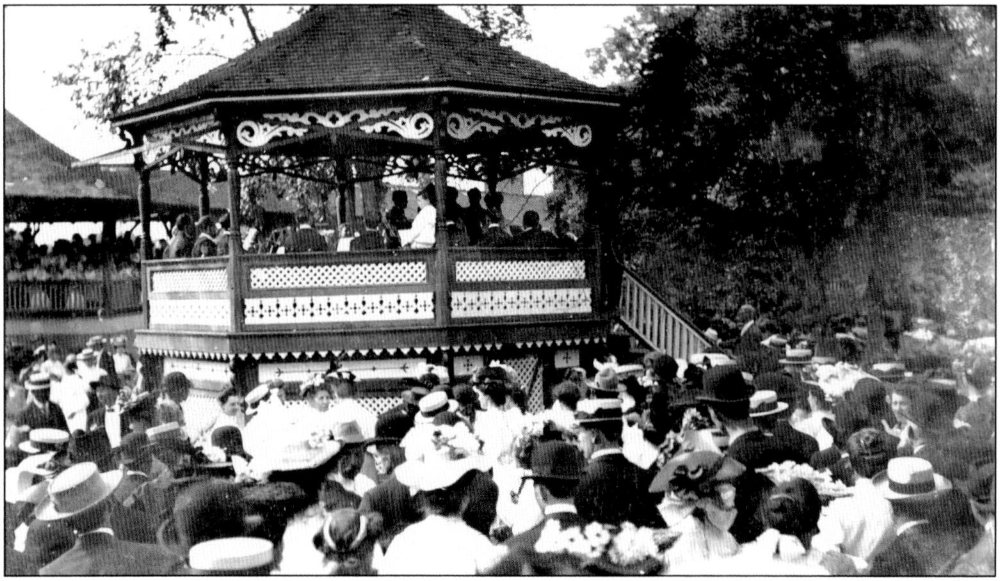

Margaret "Maggie" Dailey became a sensation at Midway Park on June 4, 1906, when on a dare, she persuaded Professor Kelly, the regular aerialist, to allow her to go up in the balloon instead of him. She was examined by local attending physician Dr. J. B. Hulett, who found her to be "sound." "With a life preserver around her waist—in case she came down in the Wallkill River—and with a parachute for her descent, she took off." Her instructions were to cut loose from the balloon when the altimeter showed about 1,000 feet, but she kept on going. It was estimated she was up 2,500 feet when she cut loose and parachuted safely to earth. In 1907, she returned to Midway Park to make some ascensions and to be married there. The event on the Fourth of July brought thousands to Midway Park and it was reported 18,000 people rode the trolleys that day. She made a successful flight in the early afternoon but landed in the Wallkill River. She was married to C. Arthur Brockett at 4:00 p.m.

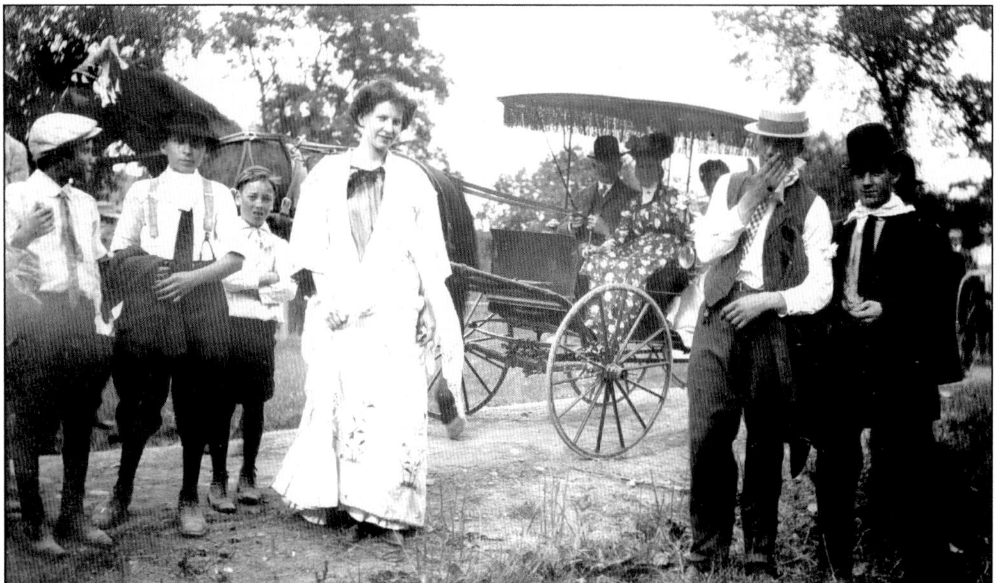

Maggie Dailey Brockett returns from a balloon ascension. (Courtesy of William Maxwell.)

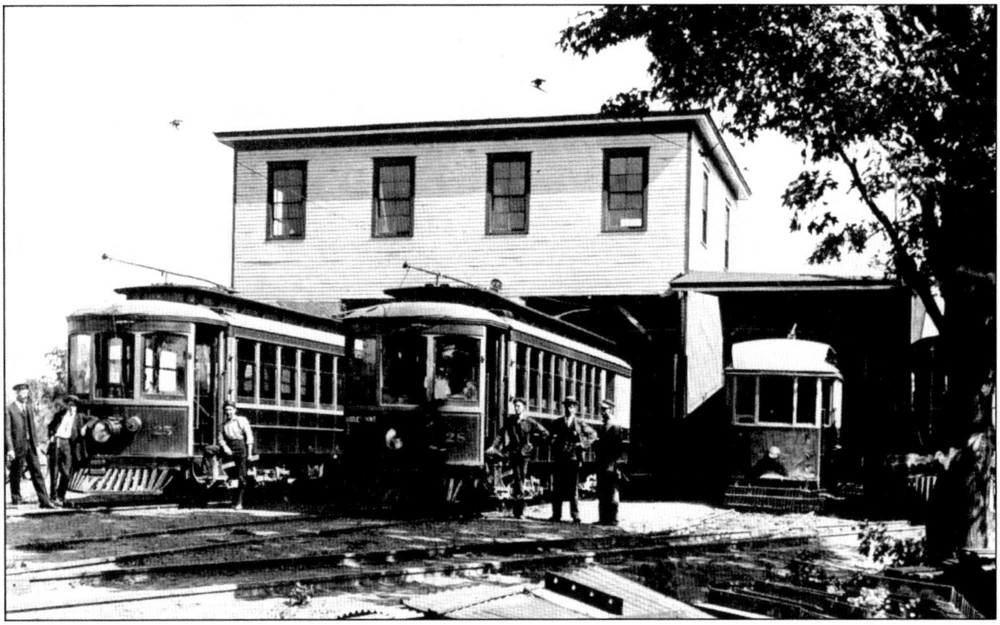

Shown are the trolley barns on East Main Street in Mechanicstown. The barns were there from 1894 to 1924. (Courtesy of William Maxwell.)

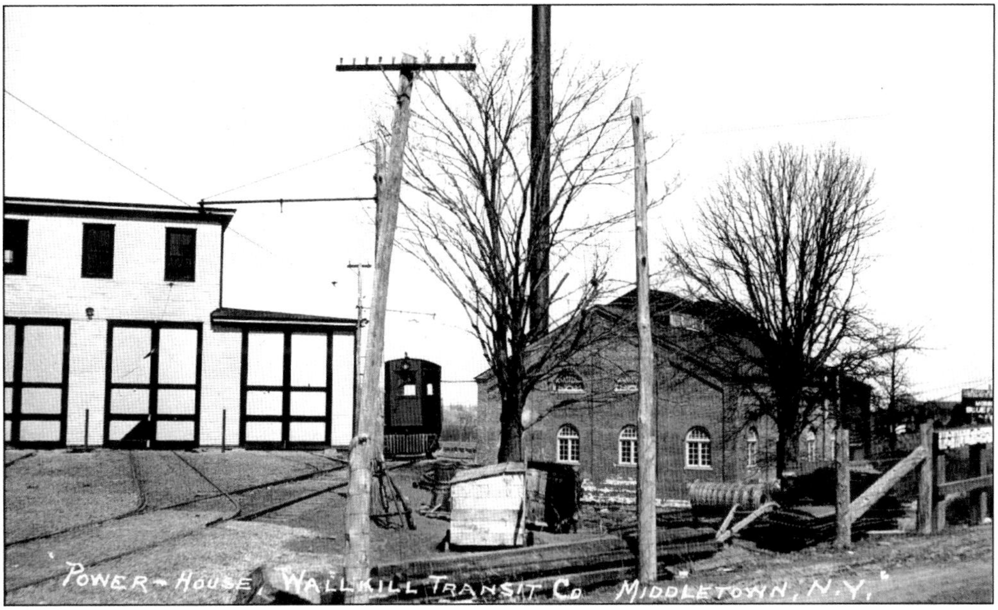

The electric powerhouse (now the C. R. Wolfe Heating Company) was located next to the trolley barns in Mechanicstown. Notice the very tall smokestack on the back of the powerhouse. (Courtesy of Jim Wolfe.)

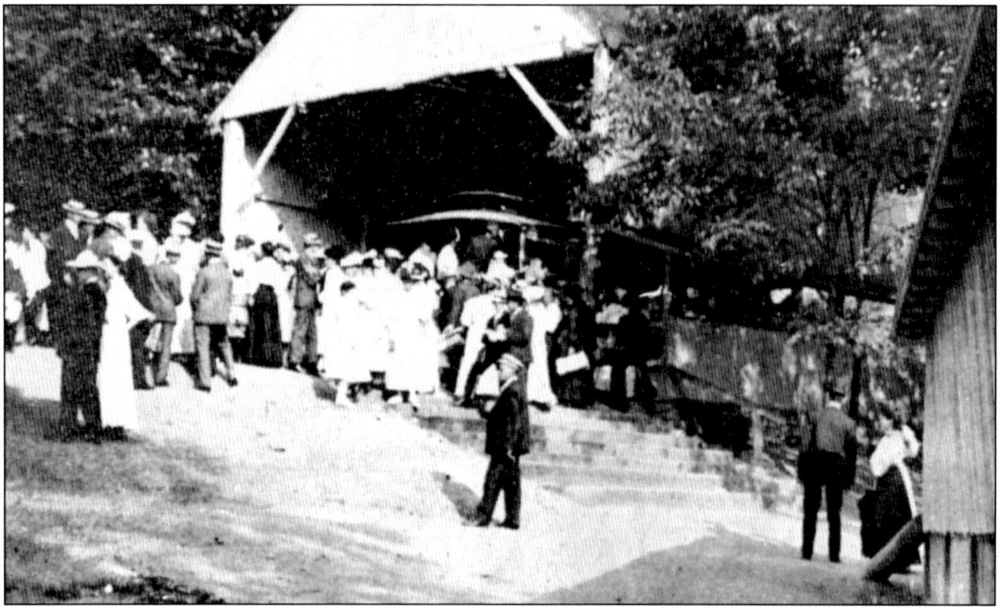

Visitors board trolleys that will take them home to Goshen or Middletown.

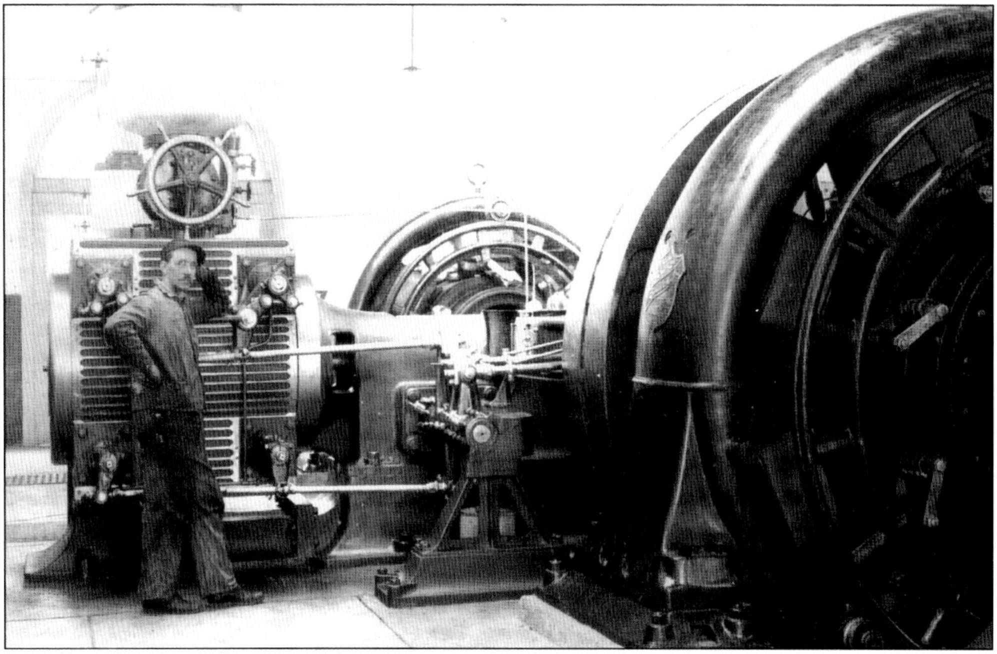

The steam engines and massive generators supplied power for the Wallkill Transit Company's trolley cars. On October 21, 1924, due to the lack of money to make repairs, the power plant broke down. Without electricity the cars could not move, and on that date the trolleys stopped running between Middletown and Goshen forever. (Courtesy of Jim Wolfe.)

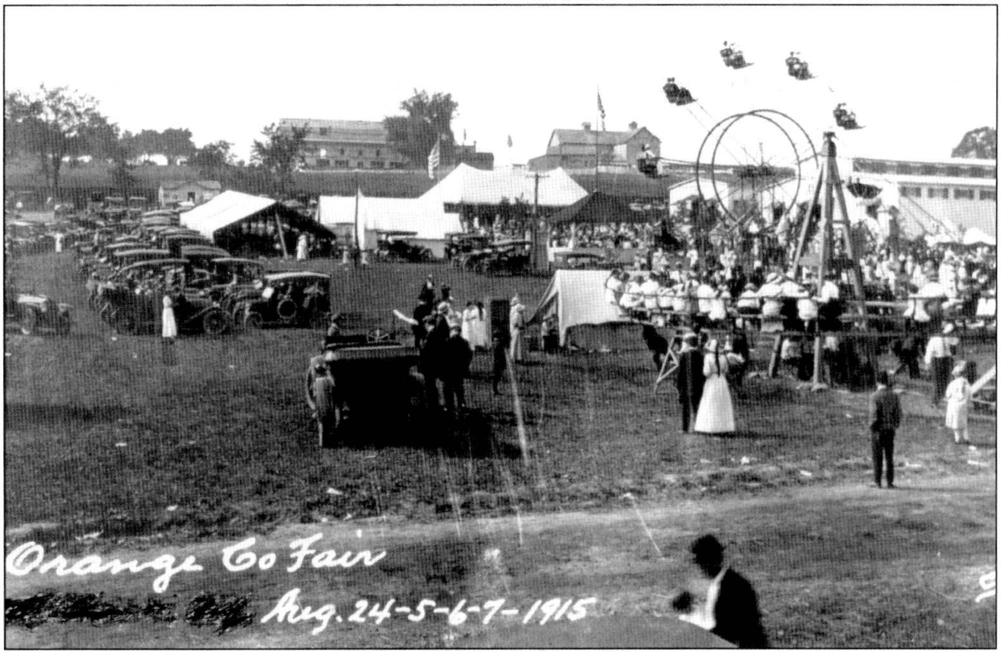

The Orange County Agricultural Society Fair was established in 1841. In 1897, the Willis Stock Farm in the Town of Wallkill became the permanent home of the Orange County Fair. Only two rides can be seen in this 1915 photograph. Fairmont Farm is on the hill in the background. (Photographs courtesy of the Historical Society of Middletown and the Wallkill Precinct.)

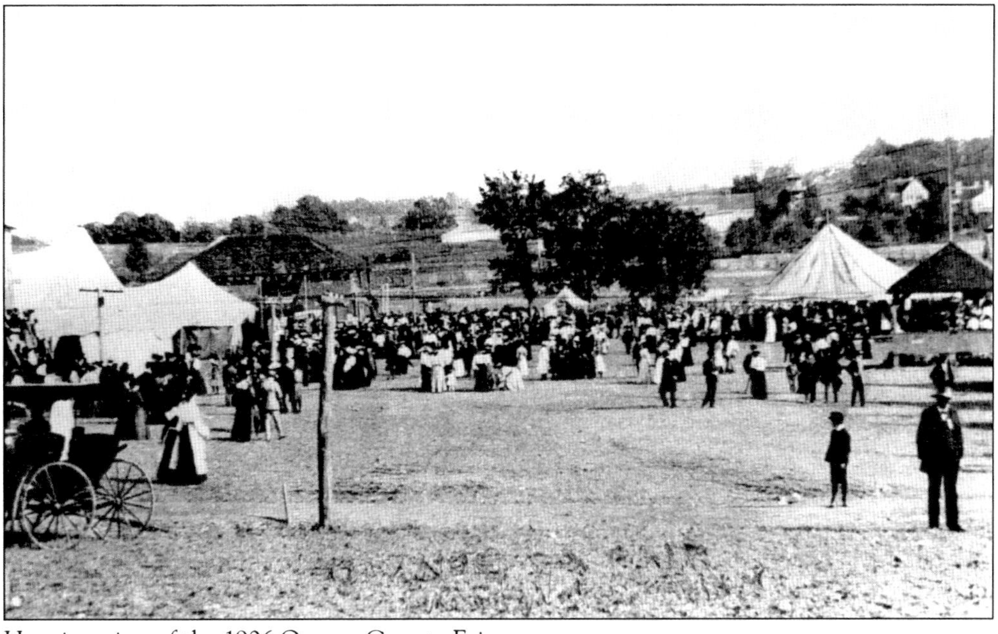
Here is a view of the 1906 Orange County Fair.

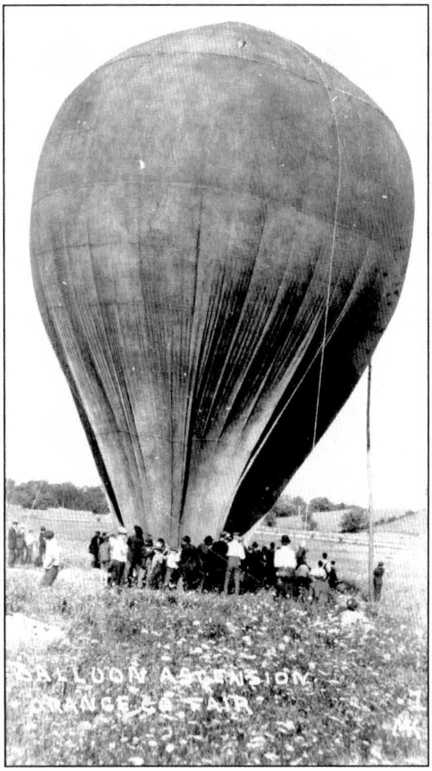

A balloon ascends at the Orange County Fairgrounds in the early 1900s.

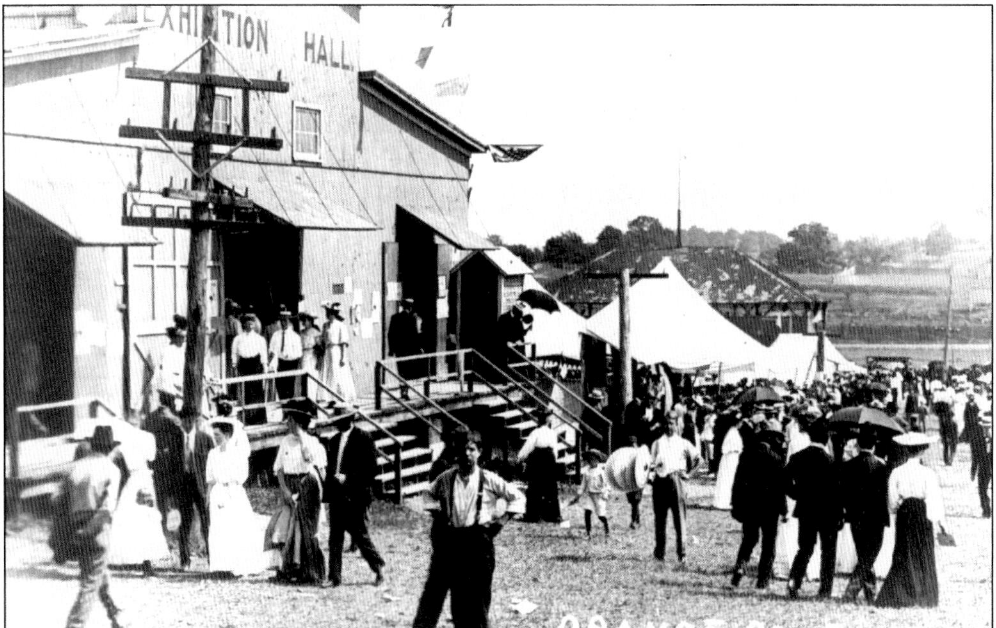

Shown is the Exhibition Hall in 1906.

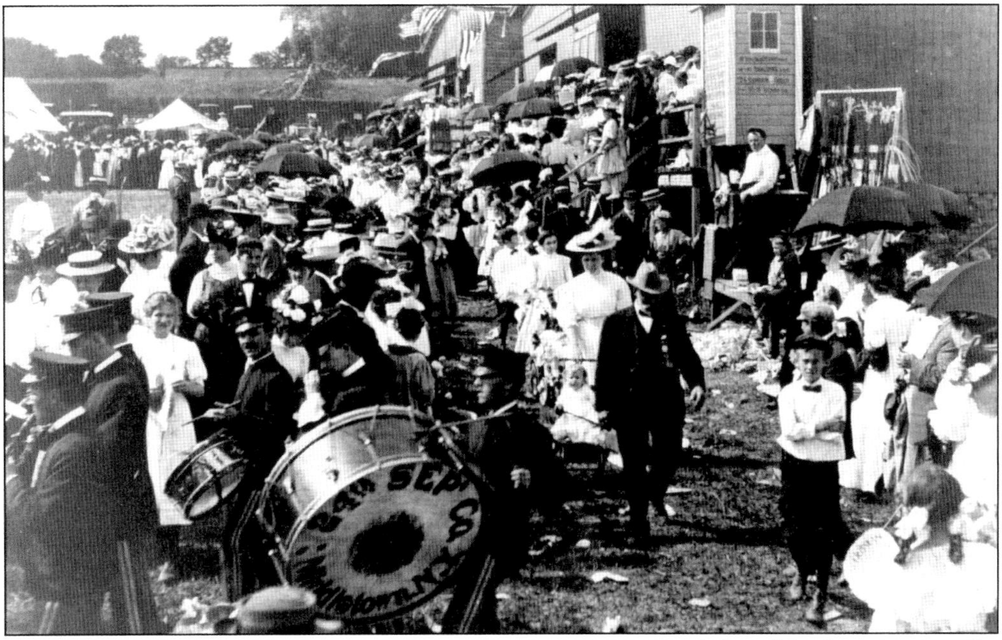

With the band of the 24th Separate Company New York National Guard leading the way, the Baby Parade begins at the Orange County Fairgrounds on September 22, 1908.

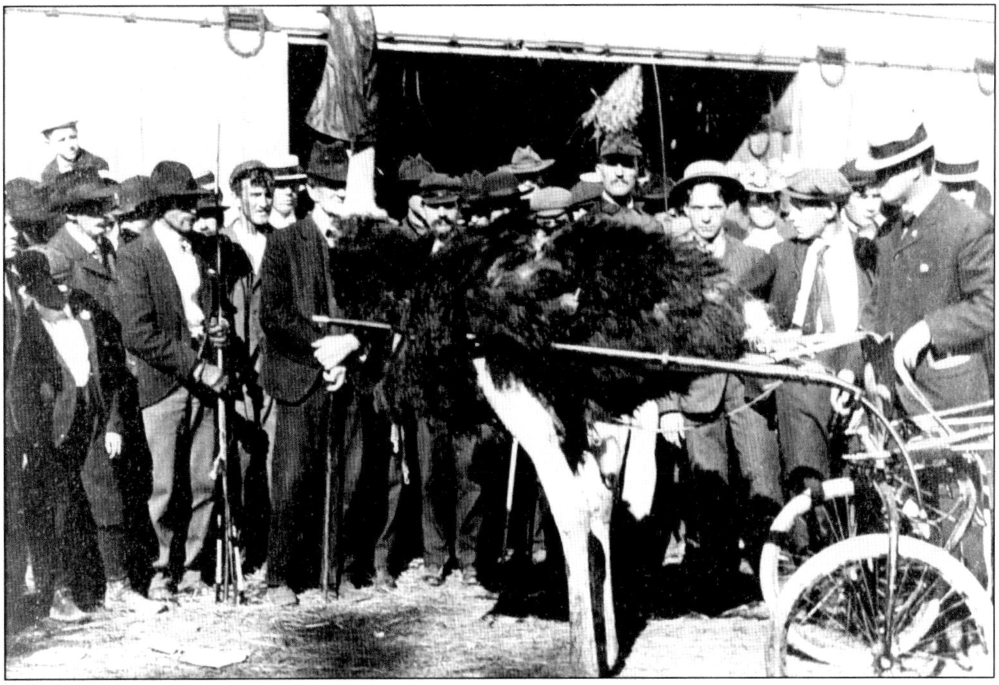

A hooded ostrich gets ready for his race in the early 1900s.

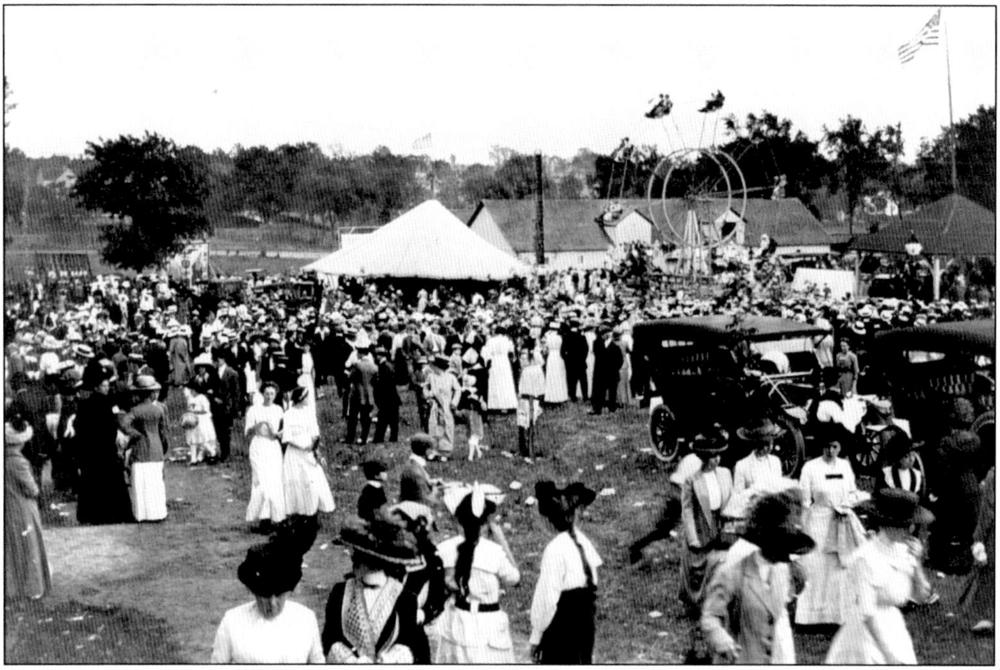

The ferris wheel is full of riders in this 1913 photograph. Notice the women with their beautiful hats in the foreground.

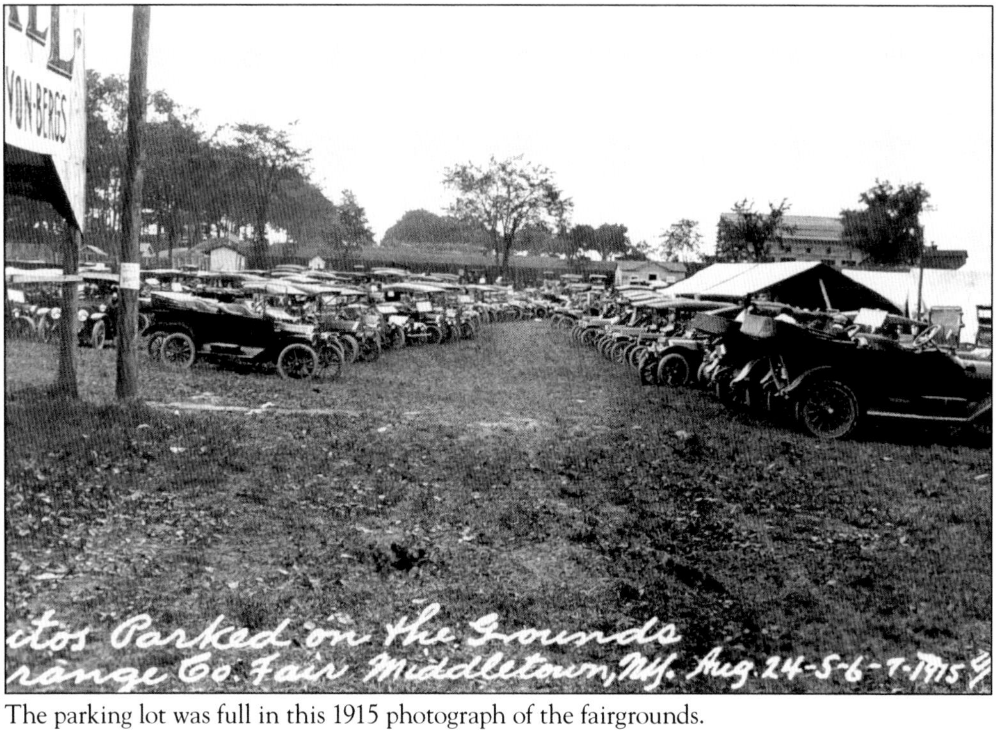

The parking lot was full in this 1915 photograph of the fairgrounds.

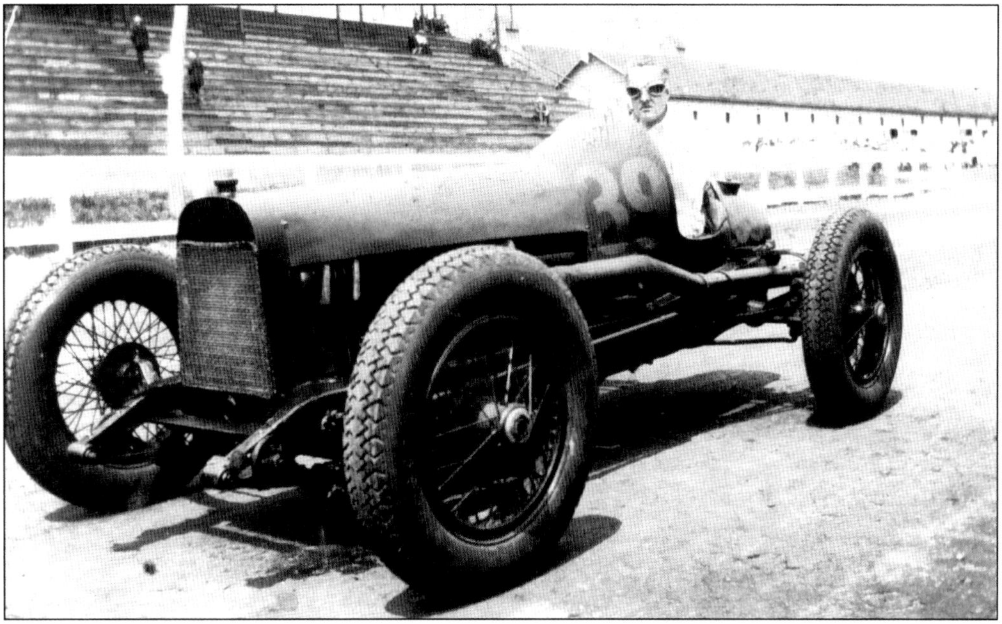

The original Orange County Speedway track at the fairgrounds was built in 1857 for horse racing. The track was rebuilt in 1924 by Joseph Coates of Goshen with clay dug from Finan's Pond in Goshen. In 1909, George Martin was appointed the director of the Orange County Fair Society. Being a race car enthusiast, he had an idea to add auto racing to the show, and it became a reality. This racing car photograph was in 1918.

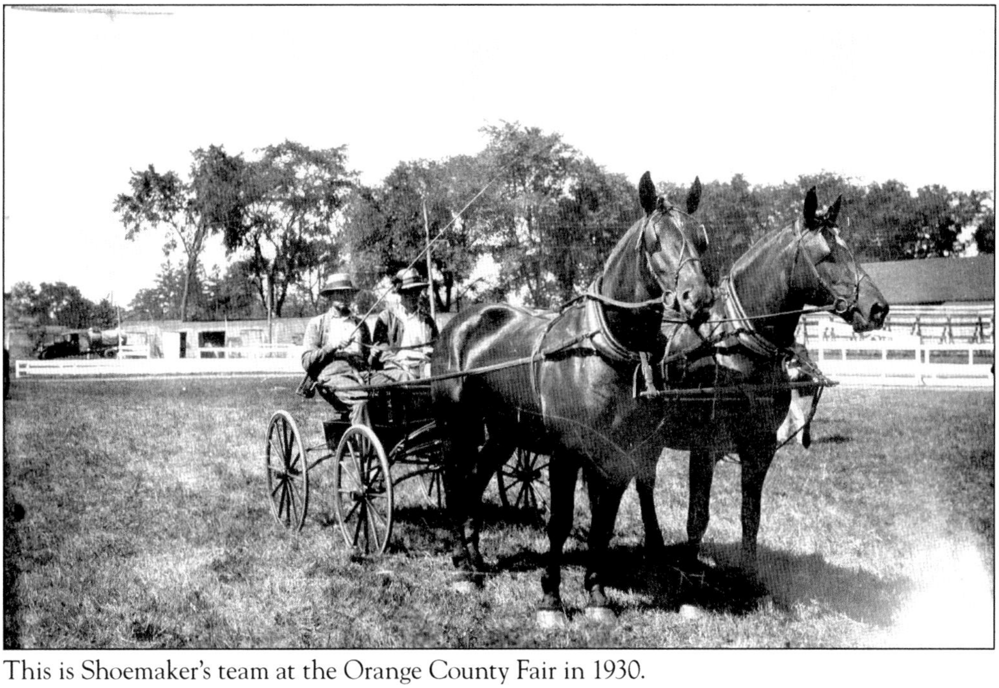

This is Shoemaker's team at the Orange County Fair in 1930.

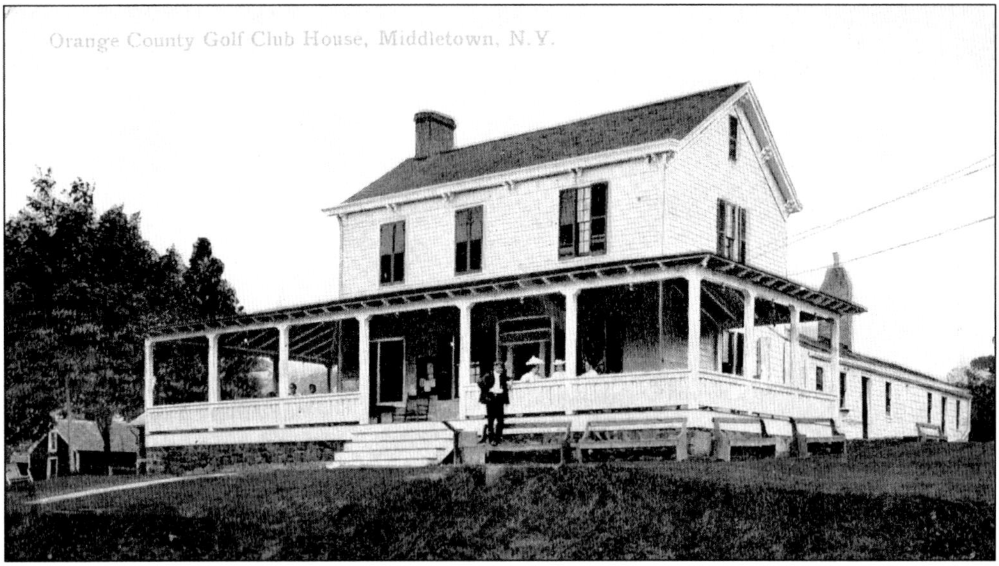

On April 26, 1899, a group of prominent area residents met at Midway Park, directly across the Wallkill River from the Rhinehart lands, to organize the Orange County Golf Club. The group incorporated in May 1899, and Henry Bacon was chosen as the first president. Arrangements were made to lease the clubhouse—a farmhouse—and land for $450 a year, and an expert was hired to help lay out the course. On Memorial Day 1899, the club members gathered for the opening of the links for play. The former Theodore Rhinehart farmhouse served as the club's headquarters for nearly 80 years. (Courtesy of William Maxwell.)

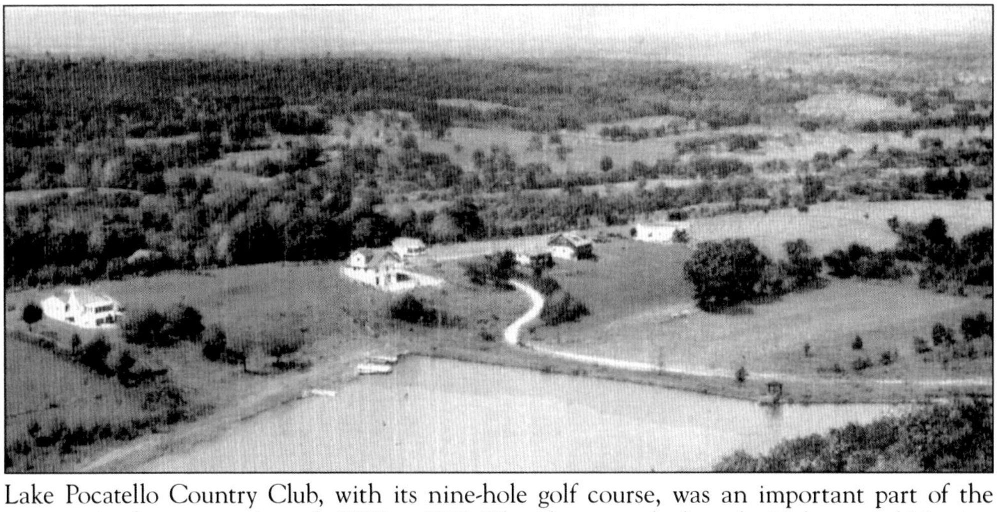

Lake Pocatello Country Club, with its nine-hole golf course, was an important part of the community from approximately 1929 to 1941. The idea started when the Nelsons and Merritts built a small miniature course on a flat piece of land near their properties. It proved so popular that A. C. N. Thompson, Frank Simpson, and Mr. Merritt decided to build a regular course. A man by the name of Bellows was the pro, and a Mr. Stacy was the groundskeeper. Mr. and Mrs. Ebner ran the bar and dining room. The course had seven holes on the southeast side of the road and two on the northwest. The first hole went from the clubhouse down to the dam at the lake. The second tee was on the dam. Being a public golf course, many Middletown people played there and enjoyed the activities and meals at the clubhouse. (Photograph courtesy of William Maxwell and information courtesy of Helen S. Van Wie.)

Six

Reservoirs

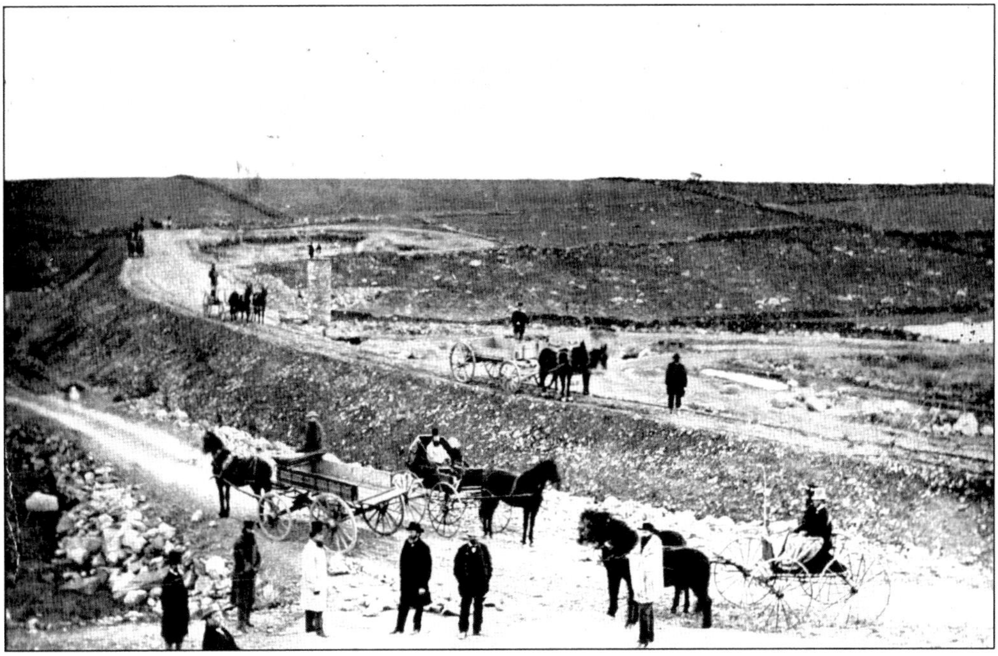

Under way is the building of the first reservoir at Monhagen Lake in 1913. (Courtesy of the Historical Society of Middletown and the Wallkill Precinct.)

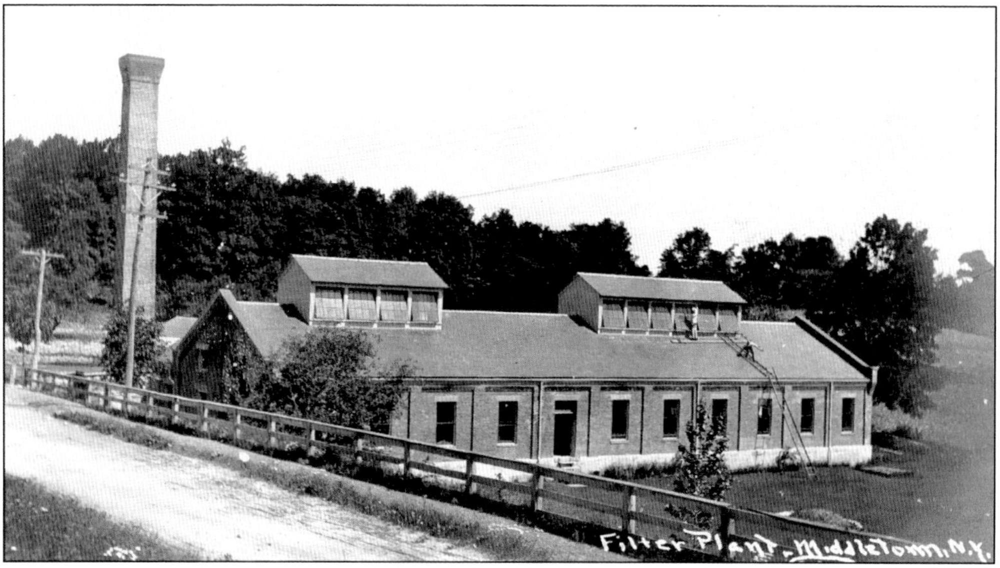

Shown is the filter plant at Monhagen Lake.

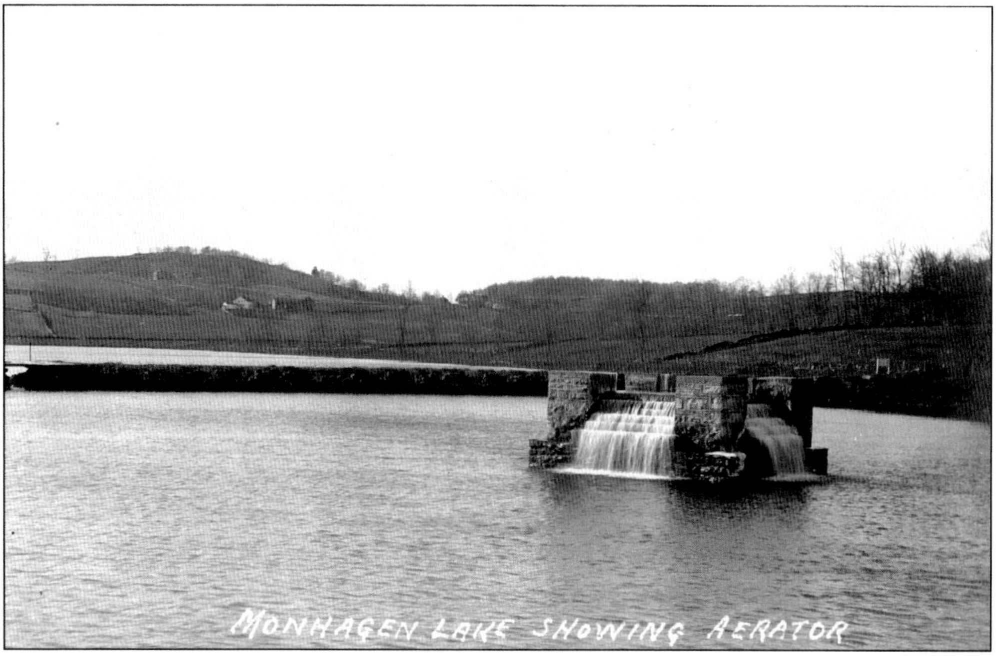

This view of Monhagen Lake includes the aerator.

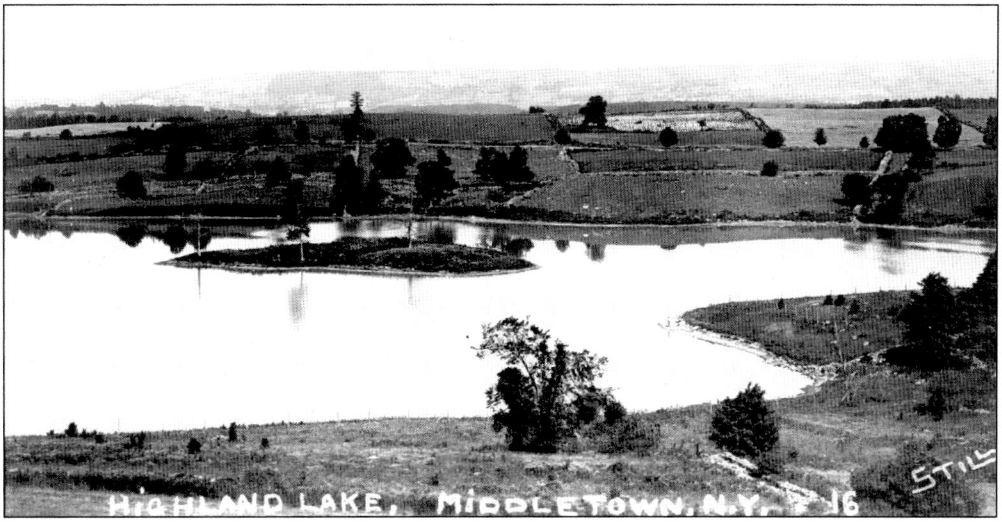

Highland Lake was another reservoir site.

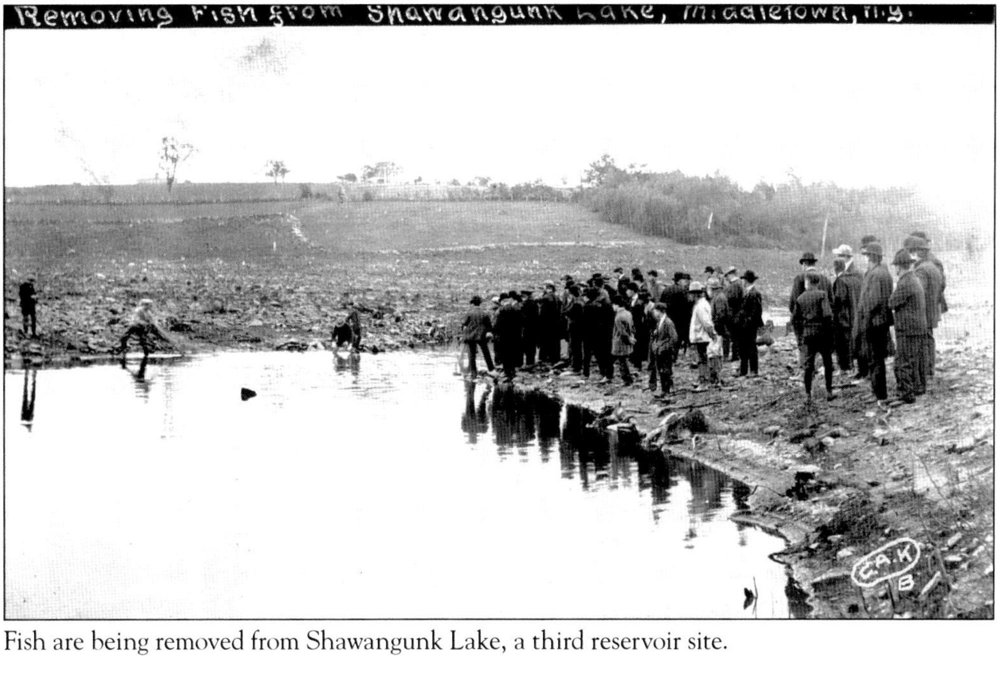

Fish are being removed from Shawangunk Lake, a third reservoir site.

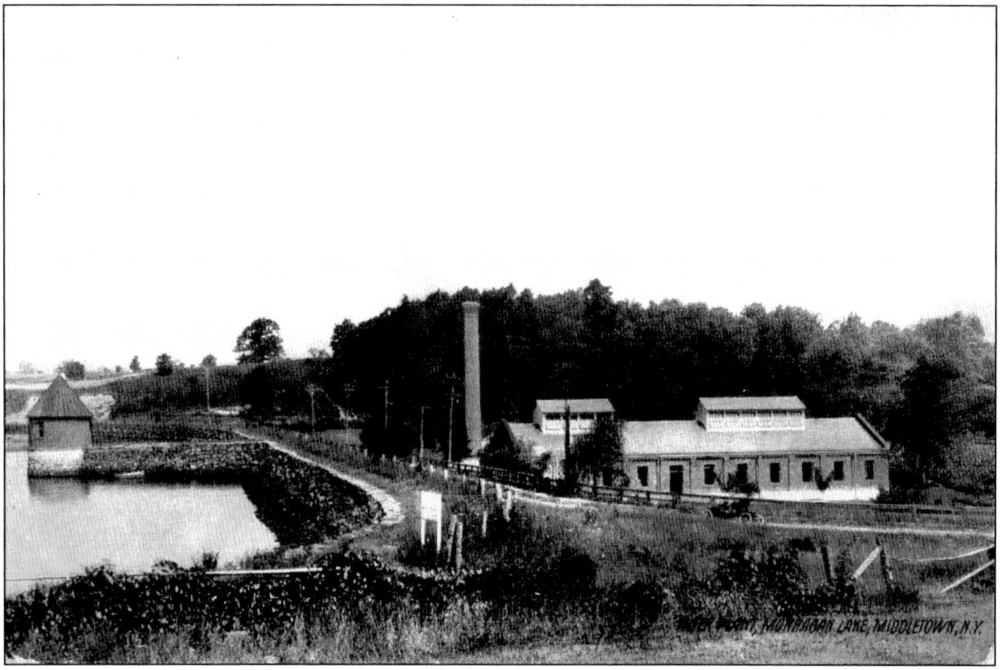

Pictured is the Monhagen Reservoir.

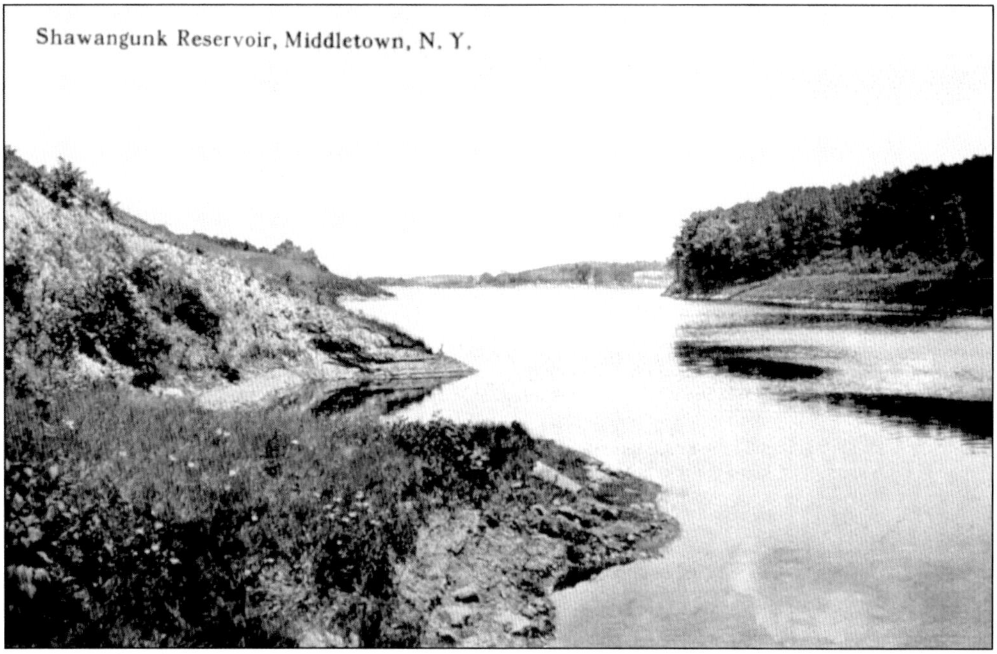

Shown is the Shawangunk Reservoir.

Seven

EARLY CHURCHES AND CEMETERIES

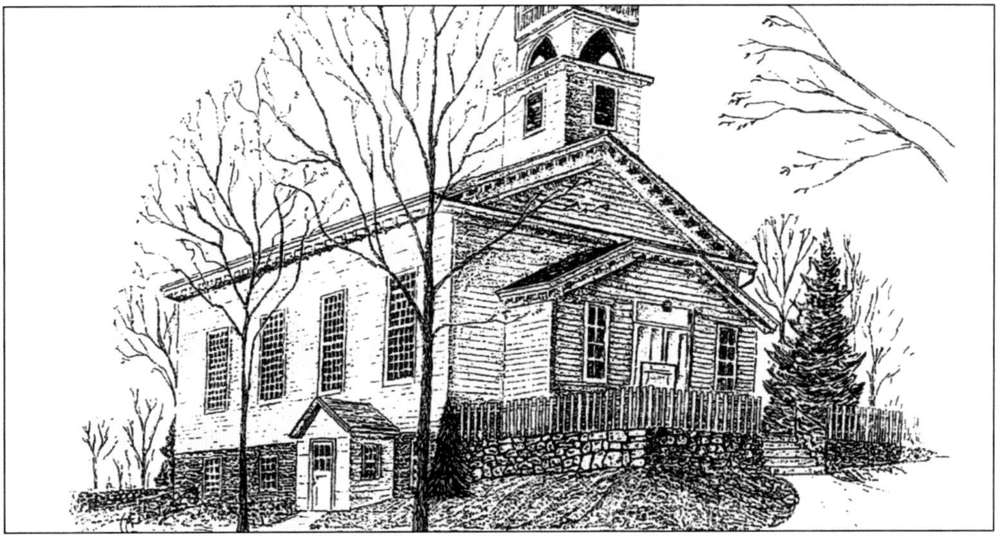

This congregation was organized on July 3, 1782, and is said to be the second Congregational Church established in the state of New York. The first place of worship was an old log schoolhouse, unheated and candlelit. The church was incorporated in 1810 under the name of the Congregational Church and Society in Wallkill and Deerpark Patent in the County of Orange, State of New York. At this time a church was built at "the place known as Mapestown" on what is now Tally Ho Road. Named the Galilee Church, it was fondly referred to as "the Little Yellow Church" because of its color. On July 6, 1847, the name was changed to the Congregational Church and Society of Mount Hope. By 1849, when the Erie Railroad was in operation and the hamlet of Howells began to flourish, the society decided to build a new church building on the hilltop of that place. The present building was erected in 1850. In 1937, the name was changed to the Congregational Church of Howells. (Courtesy of the Historical Society of Middletown and the Wallkill Precinct.)

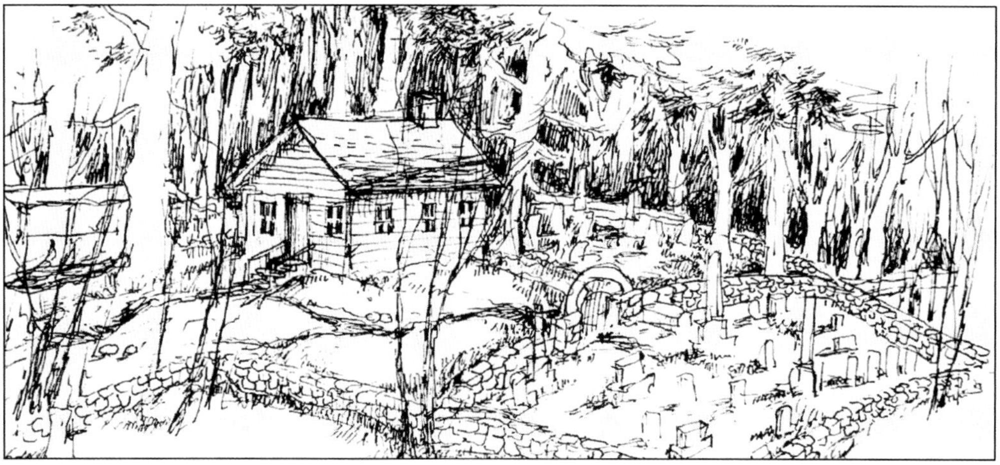

The Old School and Primitive Baptist Church of Middletown and Wallkill was constituted at Middletown on October 4, 1792. There were 30 constituent members in all. The first deacons were Silas Hulse and John Green. Church members continued to hold meetings in the free meetinghouse in Middletown, in which they all had joint interest with the Congregationalists until about 1820. Then, to accommodate members living north of the village of Middletown, they built a frame meetinghouse less than three miles north in the hamlet of Rockville, north of Maples on Van Burenville Road. At the time of the erection of the Primitive Baptist Church at Rockville, a certificate of incorporation was filed dated on December 10, 1821. The proceedings were signed by Thomas P. Tarry and Silas Horton as inspectors of election. The meeting was held at the Van Burenville Schoolhouse, District No. 16. Although the church is no longer there, the Pine Hill burial grounds surround its location. (Artist's rendition of the church by Harold Card and information courtesy of Irving J. Gibbs, former Historian of the Town of Wallkill.)

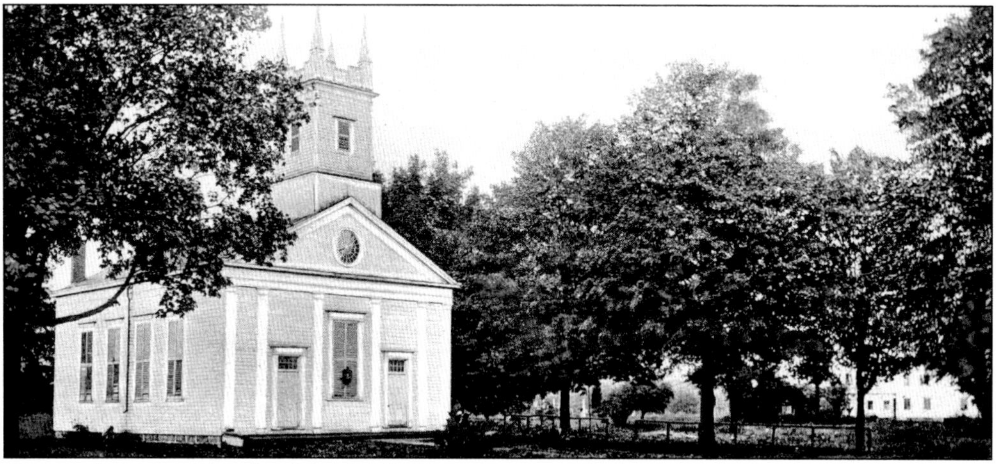

The Presbyterian Church of Circleville was incorporated on January 4, 1842. The proceedings were signed by Josiah Crane and Samuel Bull. Samuel Bull, who had built a stone house nearby, donated five acres of land for building a house of worship and a parsonage. A committee was appointed to draft a plan for building the house of worship, which was to be 40 feet by 54 feet. The contractor was Daniel Bush, who was paid $425, and the residents of the area donated the timber. Lumber was drawn from Sullivan County free, and the mason work, under the direction of Samuel Bull, was donated. The parsonage was not built until 1845 adjacent to the church. Previous to the building of the parsonage, Bull had given the ministers the use of a dwelling house owned by him. (Photograph courtesy of Leona Trimmer and information courtesy of Irving J. Gibbs.)

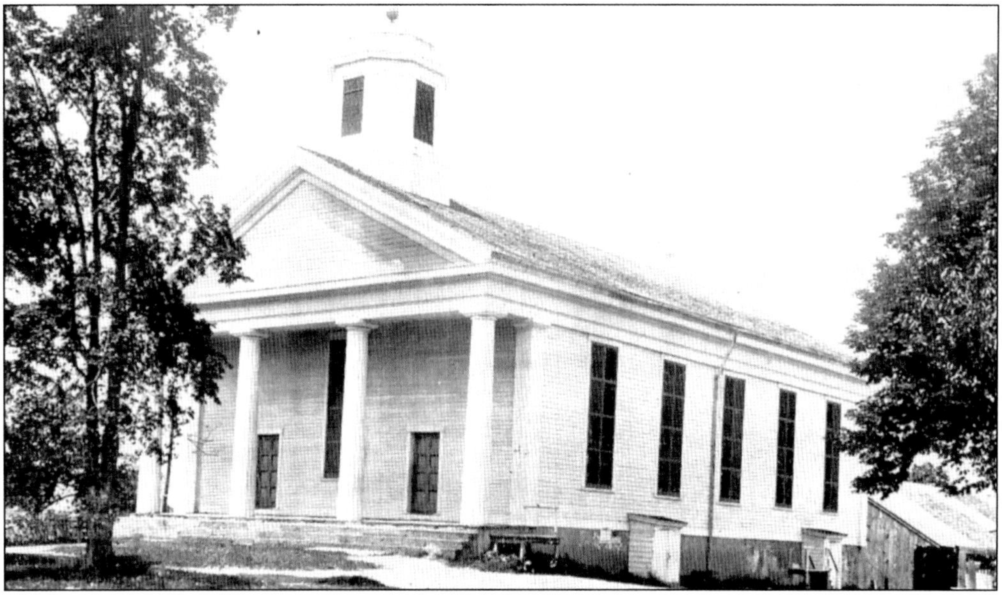

In December 1795, a small group of settlers resolved to build a meetinghouse at "the corner of the road above the house of George Houston." With a church came the need for a name for the small community, and it was named Scotchtown in tribute to the ancestral home of most of its inhabitants. "The Meetinghouse was raised the first day of July 1797 and enclosed and painted the 17th day of September following." The building remained a simple enclosure, without plaster, pews or pulpit, and without stoves for nine years, although it was occupied regularly for worship. After standing for 57 years, the building as torn down, and in 1854, the present Scotchtown Presbyterian Church was erected. (Information courtesy of Scotchtown Presbyterian Church's booklet *Yesterday, Today and Forever.*)

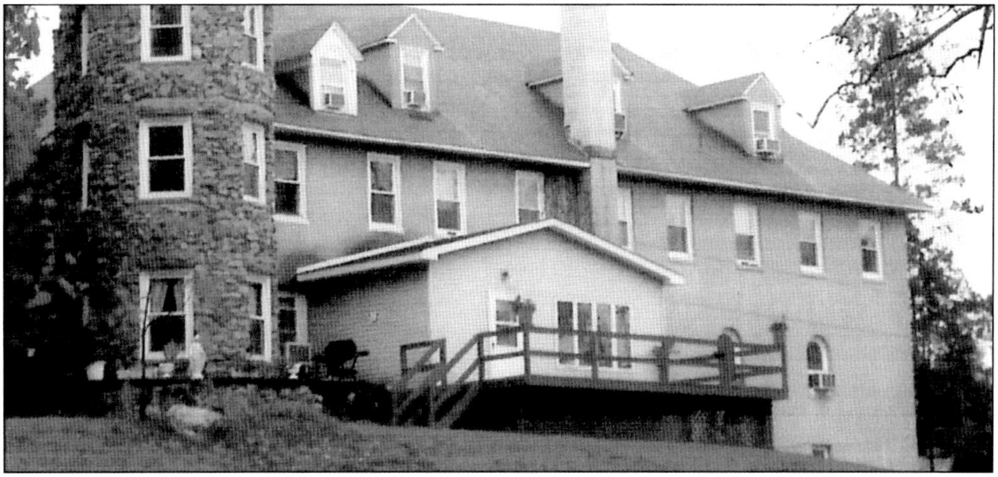

In 1887, Horace Corey, along with two partners, purchased the Casino Rink in Middletown and converted it into the Casino Theater. He married Sadie Mapes, and they lived in his home, Locksley Hall, on an expanse of 15 acres in the Town of Wallkill off Wawayanda Avenue. A fire struck in February 1889, causing extensive damage. Restoration of Locksley Hall was made, but Corey died soon afterward and the property was sold to James Wallick, a theatrical producer. James Wallick added the stone tower portion to the existing building and a cornerstone, renaming it the Thistle's dates this as 1902.

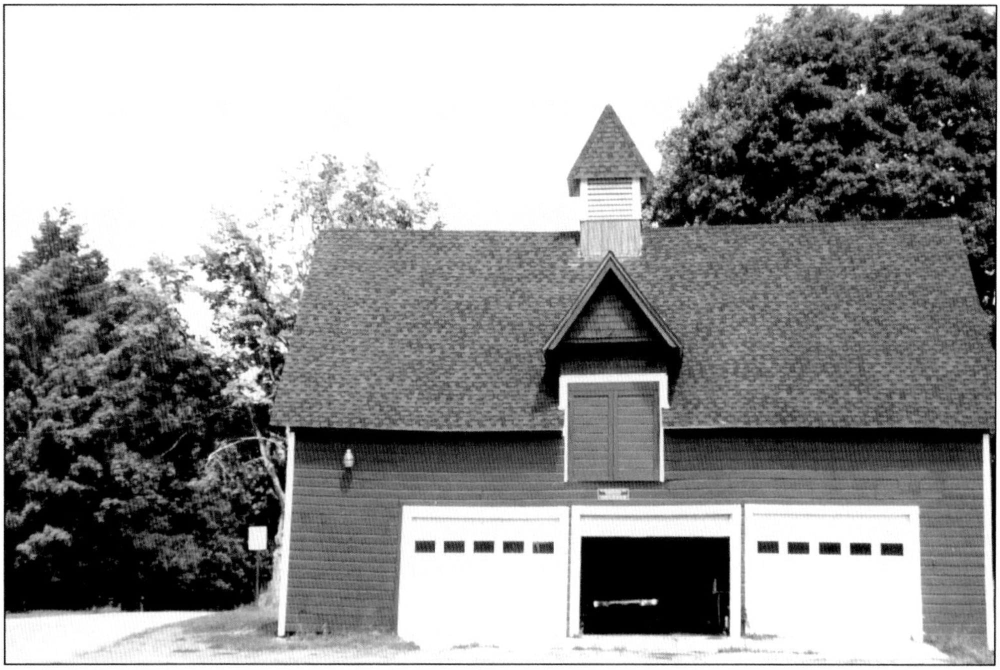

Wallick held play rehearsals in the loft of the present barn and garage. The play was then performed at the Middletown Casino Theater, owned by Horace Corey. If the play was successful in Middletown, Wallick took it to Broadway in New York City.

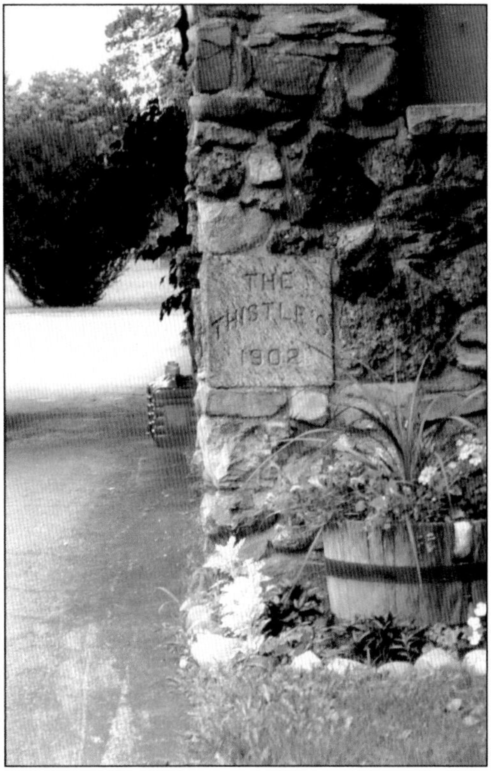

The Carmelites, under Archbishop John Cardinal Farley, purchased the Thistle's and surrounding land for a preparatory novitiate. The St. Albert's Seminary, Carmelite Order, was the owner in 1917. (Information from *A History of St. Albert's Jr. Seminary*, by Alfred Isacsson, O. Carm.)

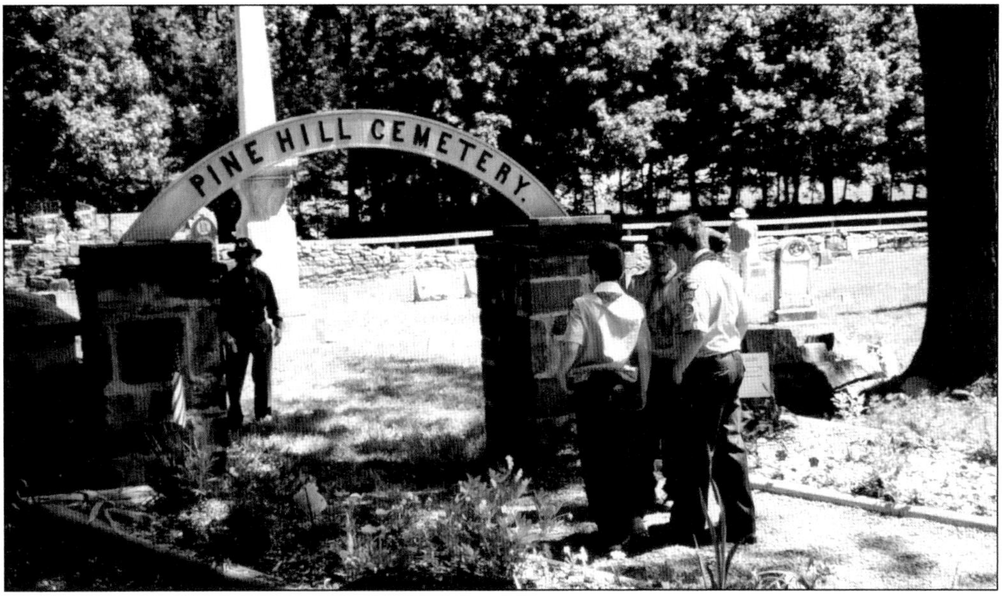

These two cemeteries are combined and located on Van Burenville Road, off Route 17M, in the Town of Wallkill. The hamlet of Rockville was settled in 1700. The Old School Baptist Church was established in 1792, in the center of the combined cemeteries. The Pine Hill Cemetery, 1820, was memorialized in 1990 as the Rockville Pine Hill Cemetery. Carpenter, Clark, Denning, Godfrey, Gregory, Horton, Remson, Uptegrove, and Wilkinson are but a few of the names found in this well kept burial ground.

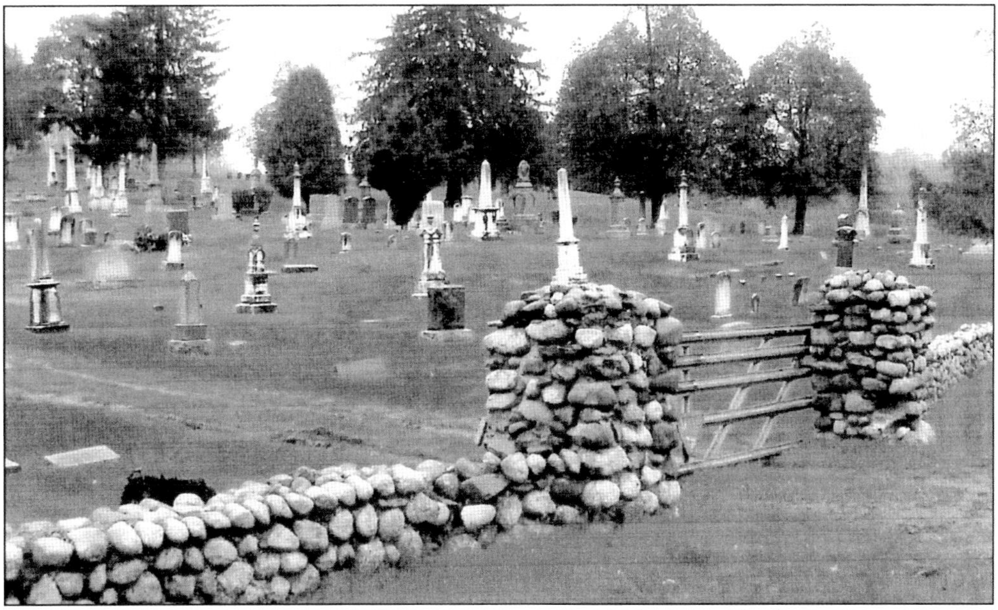

The Wallkill Cemetery is located off East Main Street on Midway Road. This cemetery is one of the oldest in the Town of Wallkill, with burials dating from the 1790s to the present day. This is a nondenominational cemetery with family monuments of Carpenter, Wisner, Butterfield, Phillips, Forthoffer, Crawford, Mapes, and Forster.

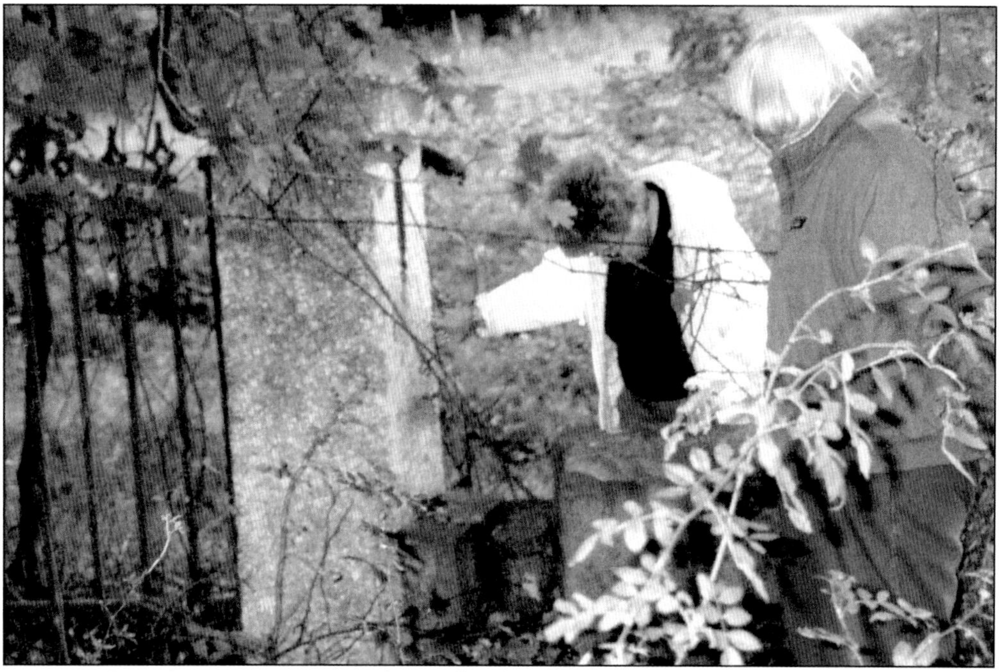

Historian Dorothy Hunt-Ingrassia and Priscilla Thompson negotiate the once beautiful entrance, with iron fencing and pillar gate, of the Hollyrood Cemetery.

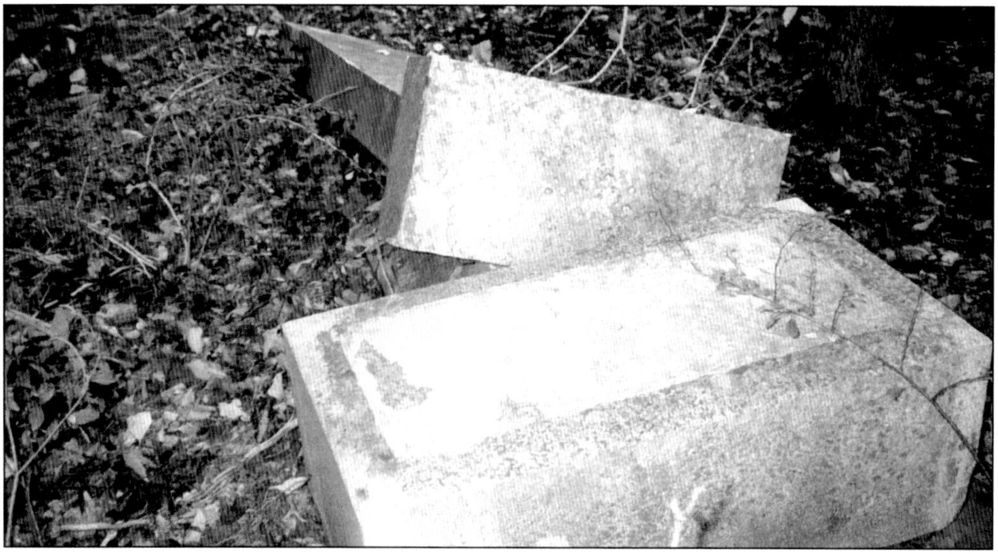

Hollyrood Cemetery is located on Hufcut Road, just east of Circleville. The adjacent farm was owned by R. S. Hume. The cemetery lies northwest of the elegant white farmhouse, with several barns and other buildings on the property. The burial ground is surrounded by stone walls. It has flowering shrubs and cedar and deciduous trees that have overgrown the cemetery. Many of the stones are very large and are lying on the ground. Some are readable, but others have fallen face down. The Hollyrood Cemetery dates back to the burial of Thomas Brunson, who died on January 29, 1813, at the age of 52. Other stones reveal the burial of Winter, Hill, Moore, Gowdey, Weller, and Shorter. The latest date of interment is that of Mary Shorter, who died January 17, 1872, at the age of 65.

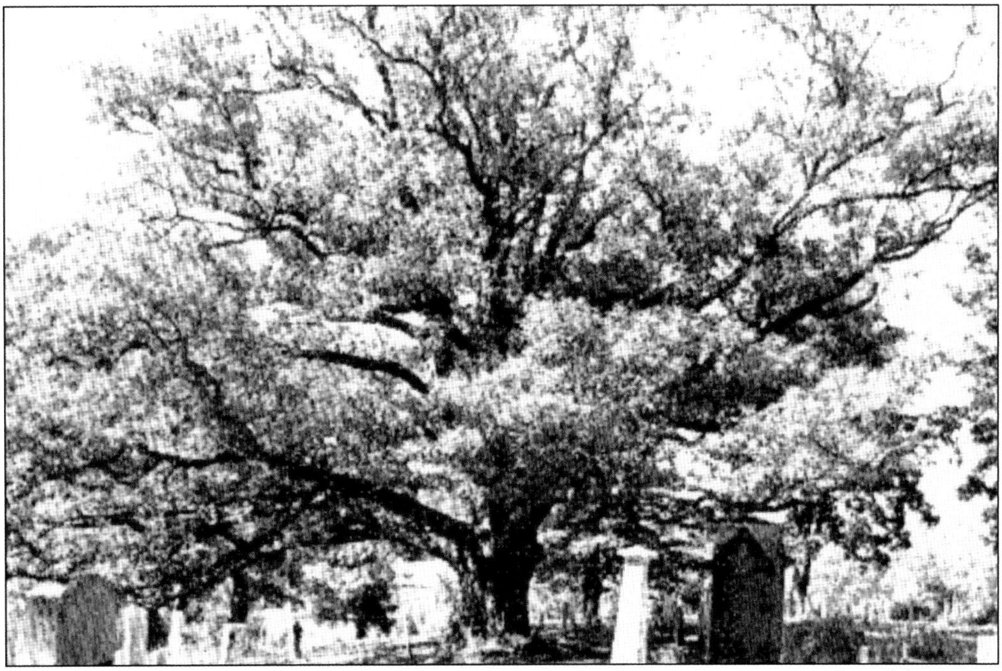

The Bloomingburg Rural Cemetery is located on Route 17M on the western edge of the Town of Wallkill just before the Sullivan County line. The Minisink Chapter of the Daughters of the American Revolution (DAR) has installed a plaque on the historic iron fence that once stood in front of the New York City Hall. The cemetery was the home of one of Orange County's largest trees that unfortunately fell some years ago. This tree was near the location of the Union Baptist Church. The cemetery was formed in late 1809 in conjunction with the Union Church. The old section is in poor condition with many stones toppled by nature and vandalism. The newer sections are well kept and contain many familiar names such as Stitt, Crane, Weld, Gillen, Stringham, Miller, Jordan, Johnson, Carpenter, Hultslander, Niven, Jessup, and Beakes.

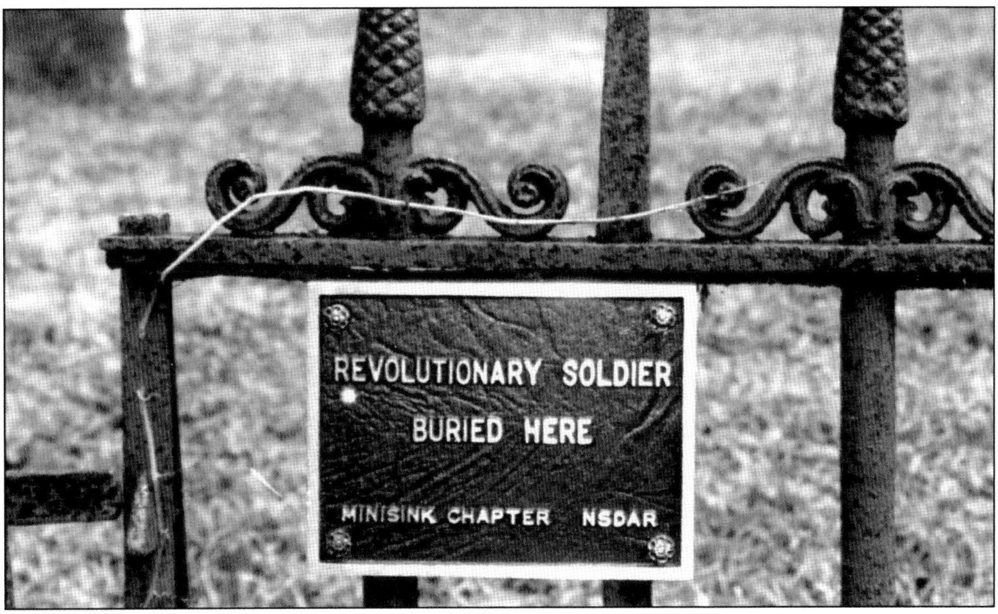

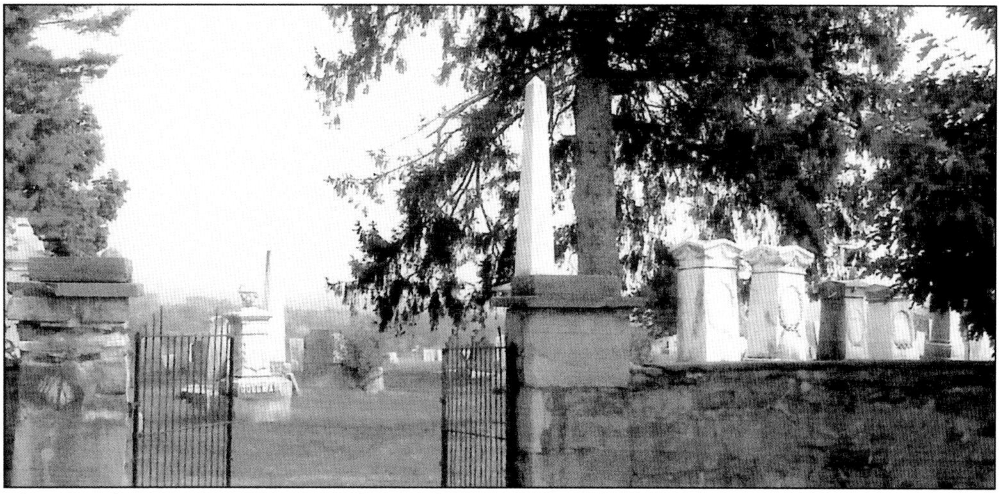

The Scotchtown Cemetery is in the southwest corner of the intersection of Blumel Road and Silver Lake Scotchtown Road in the hamlet of Scotchtown. The cemetery is directly across the road from the Scotchtown Presbyterian Church. Some Revolutionary War soldiers, as well as many Civil War soldiers, are buried there. Some family names that are memorialized with fine monuments are Bookstaver, Puff, Stitt, and Comfort.

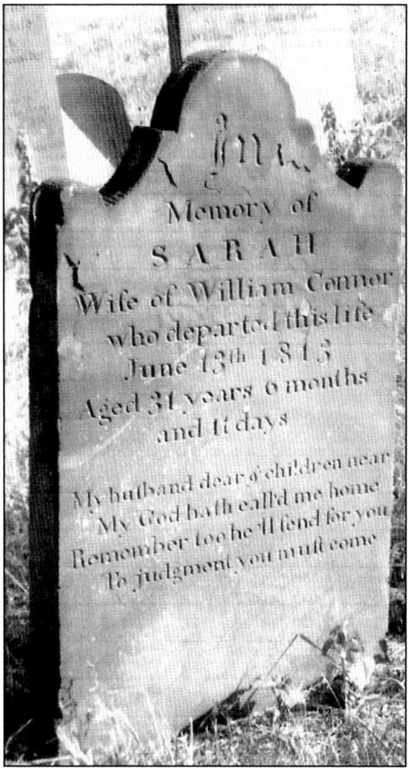

Shown is the monument of Sarah Conner, who died on June 13, 1813, at 34 years, 6 months, and 11 days.

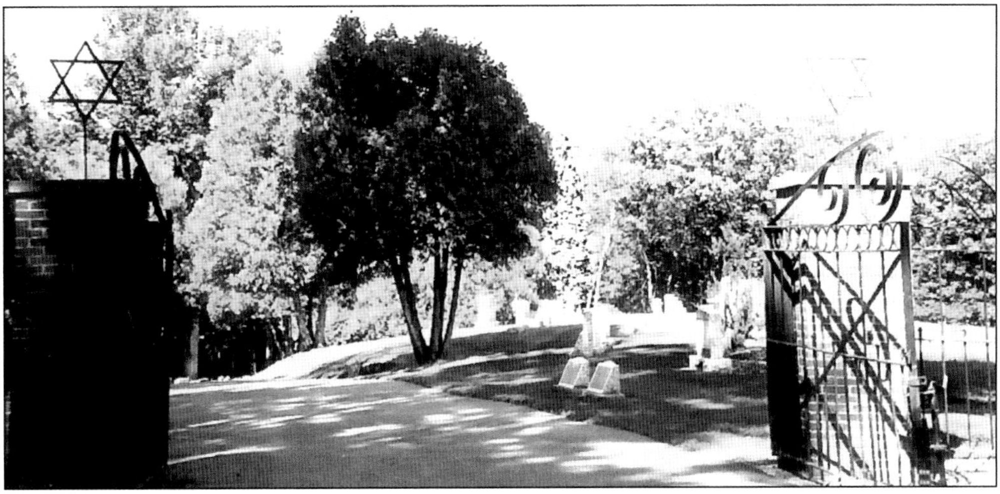

The Middletown Hebrew Association purchased a tract of land near Circleville for a Jewish cemetery in the year 1917, although the cemetery did not open until October 15, 1921. Since that time a great majority of the local Jewish residents have been interred in the impressive Temple Sinai Cemetery, located on Route 302 south of the hamlet of Circleville.

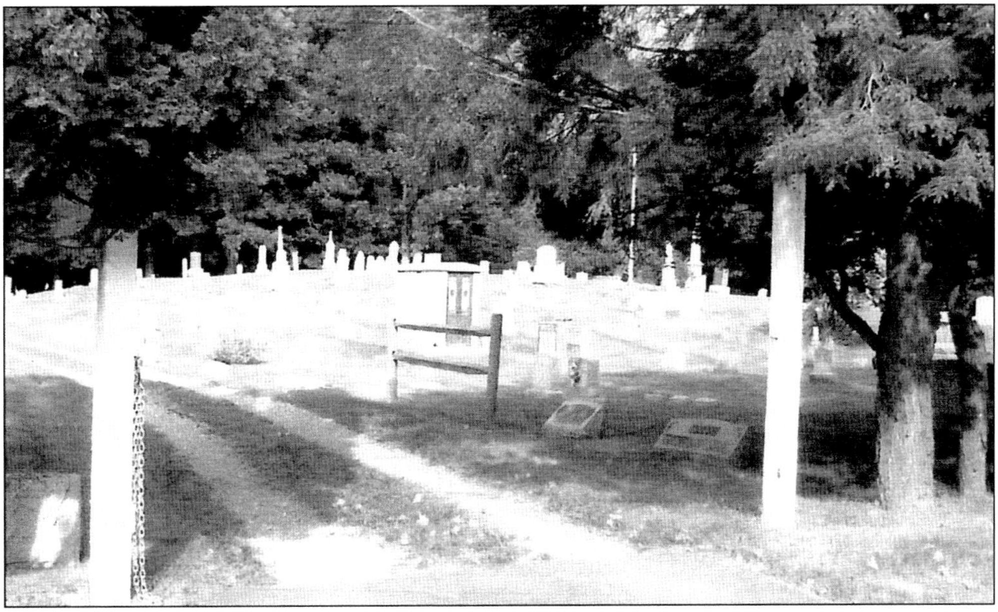

The Circleville Cemetery is located off Goshen Turnpike in Circleville. It is directly behind the Circleville Presbyterian Church and manse. This is a burying ground of the early 1840s, with the church being constructed in 1843. It has had several expansions, with the oldest graves starting on the hill and spreading outward. A few of the names memorialized are Cox, Herman, Howell, Finch, Rupello, and Brown. The cemetery is well kept but has had some stones fallen and broken by nature, tree roots, and human misbehavior. The entrance is off the church parking lot.

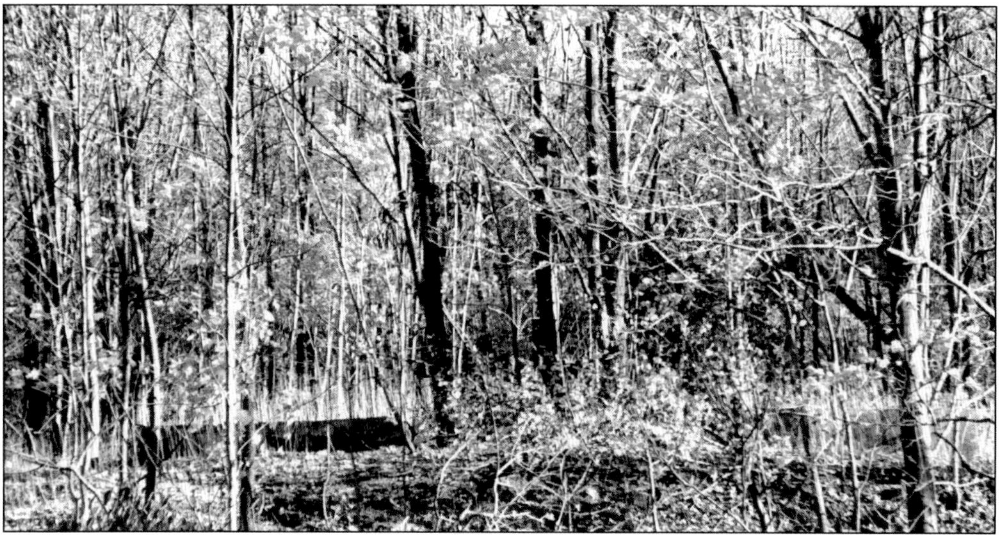

The old Guinea Cemetery is located high on a hill off Midland Lake Road. It is proclaimed to be a burying ground of manumitted black slaves and slave children connected to Colonel McLaughry of New Windsor. The little settlement of Guinea was inhabited by an industrious group of people who attended local schools and churches. A recent trip to the cemetery found it in poor condition. Most of the monuments have been toppled, either by nature or vandals. Some of the inscriptions include: Cloe, wife of John McLaughry, died June 10, 1845; John McLaughry, died November 9, 1855, age 86 years; William McLaughry, died April 12, 1842, age 83 years. The name is believed to derive from the country of Guinea in West Africa.

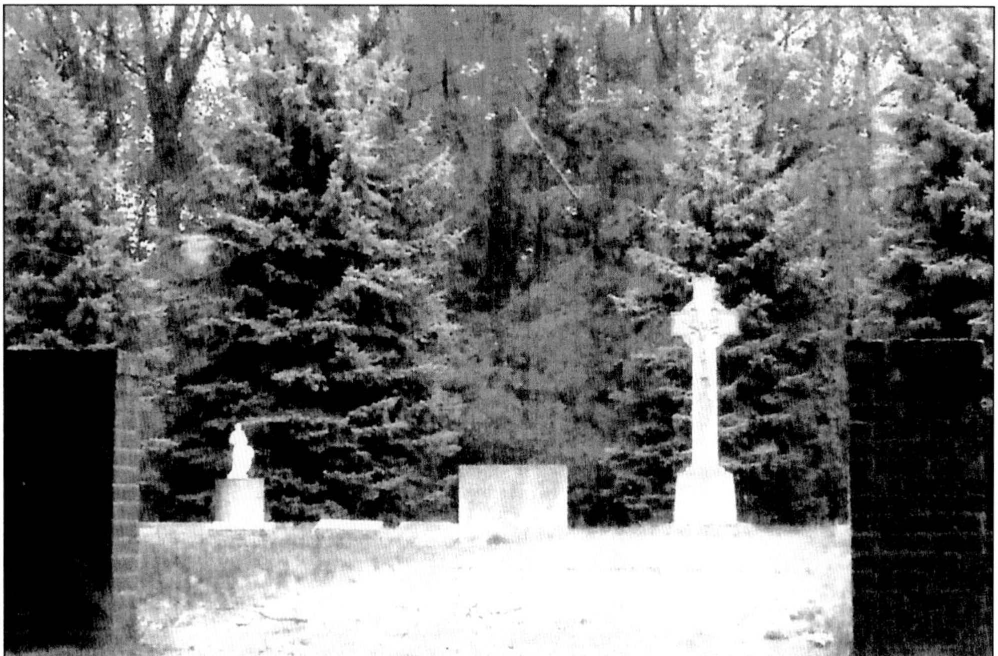

St. Albert's Cemetery is located on the grounds of St. Albert's Seminary off Wawayanda Avenue in the Town of Wallkill. The cemetery is in memory of the Carmelite reverends. The Rev. John Bartley is the first recorded, November 28, 1895, on the monument of record.

Eight

SCHOOLS

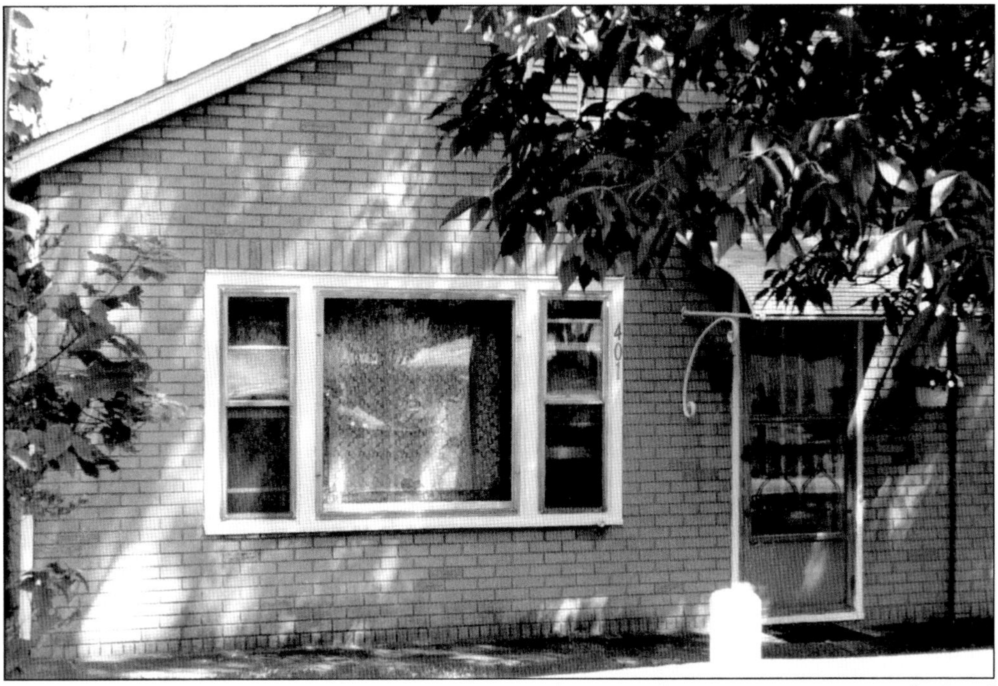

Pine Knot School, District No. 2, is located next to the Pocatello Fire House on Pocatello Road (formerly Sayers Hill Road). According to the three Dutcher sisters who attended, one teacher was Clara Eidel, 18 years old, who walked to school every day. One day she was harassed by a man, and from that day forward she always carried a gun.

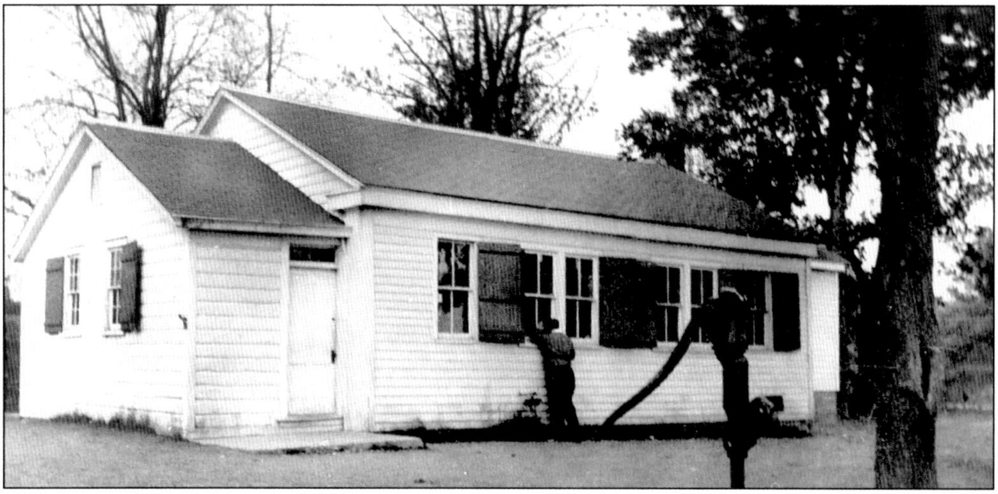

Mud Mills School, District No. 4, located on Mud Mills Road, served the district for over 100 years. The original section of the school was built around 1840, and later additions were built to the front and the back. An early teacher was Mrs. Harold Holland.

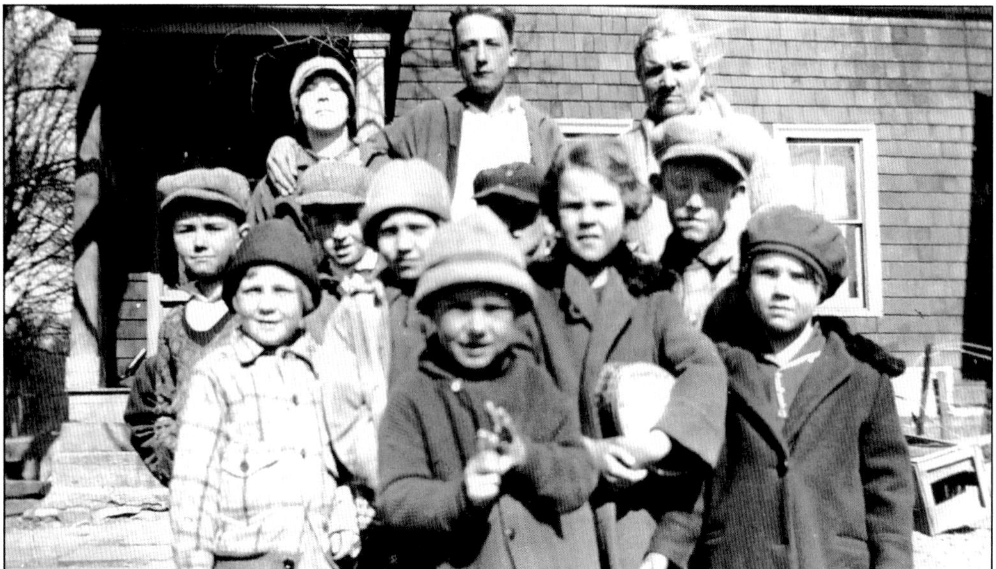

Pictured are Mud Mills School students in 1932. Clarence Avery Dart is the first student in the second row on the left. (Courtesy of Willard Dart.)

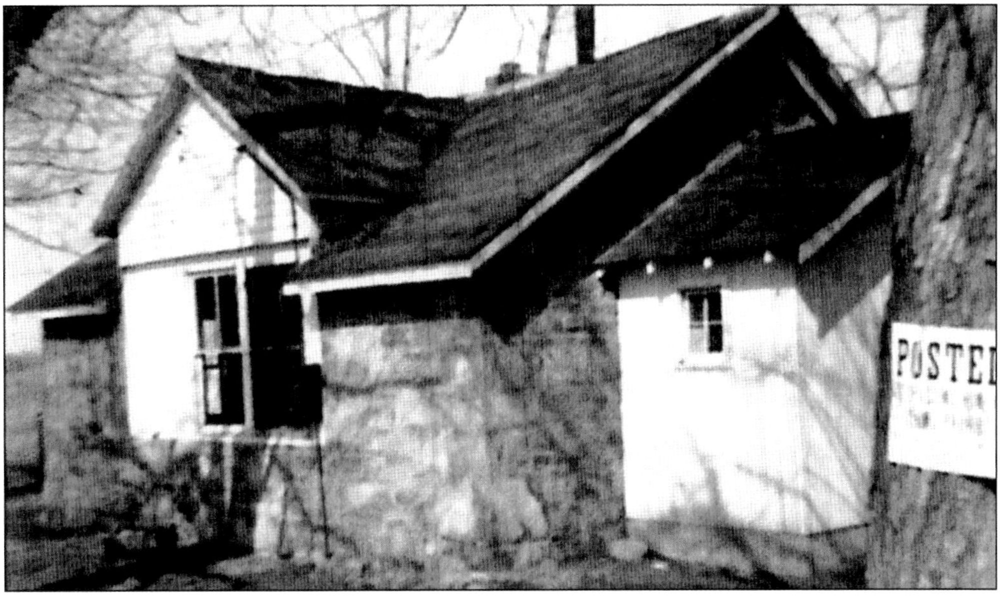

Brimstone School, District No. 5, a small stone building, is located near the intersection of Brimstone Hill and Lybolt Road. It was built around 1840 and was named as a result of a story told of a drinking spree in a nearby log tavern. Short of glasses, one was brought in that was used to mix up brimstone, and a quantity had been left in the glass. A patron who drank from that glass ran into the road shouting, "Brimstone, Brimstone" and the area was so named.

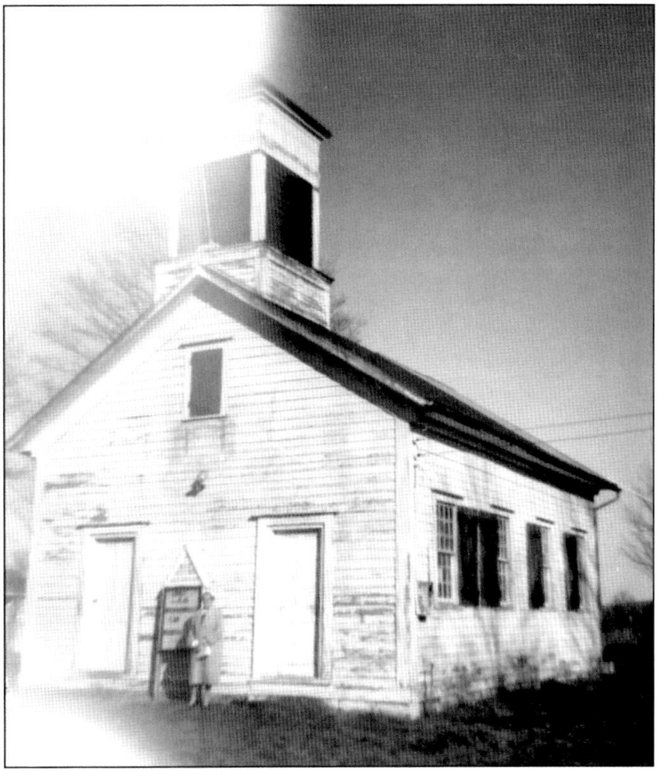

Franklin Square School, District No. 6, was built around 1855. Teams of farmers brought lumber from Sullivan County in one day for the construction of the new school. A former teacher, Doris Halsey, said in an interview that "one day the stove got too hot for a family of skunks living under the school so they left . . . but left the odor behind. In spite of the cold and snow, school was held outdoors for the rest of the day, fortunately it was a Friday."

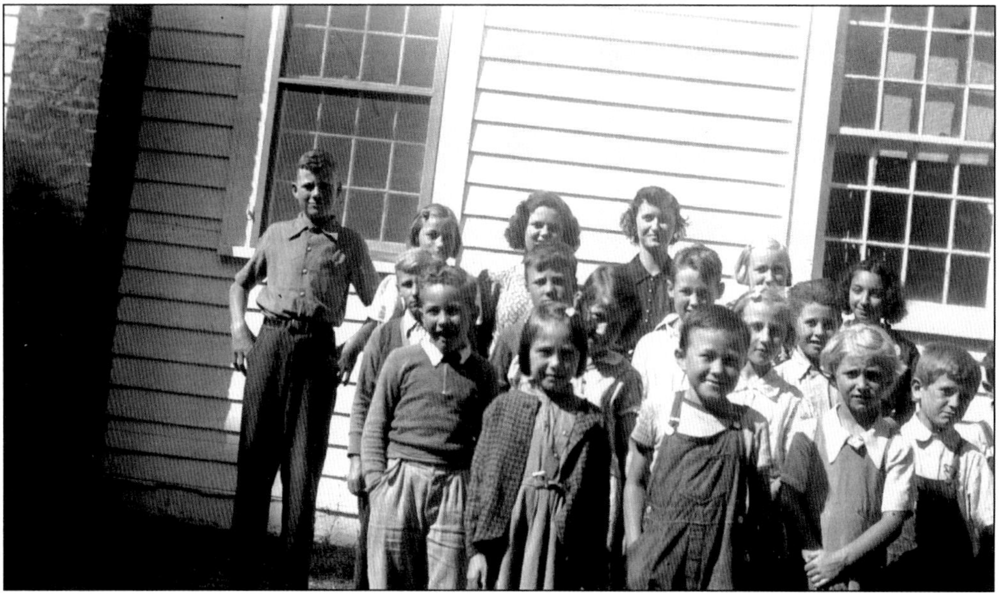

Franklin Square School students pose for the photographer around 1930. (Courtesy of former teacher Susan Zickler Vanderburgh.)

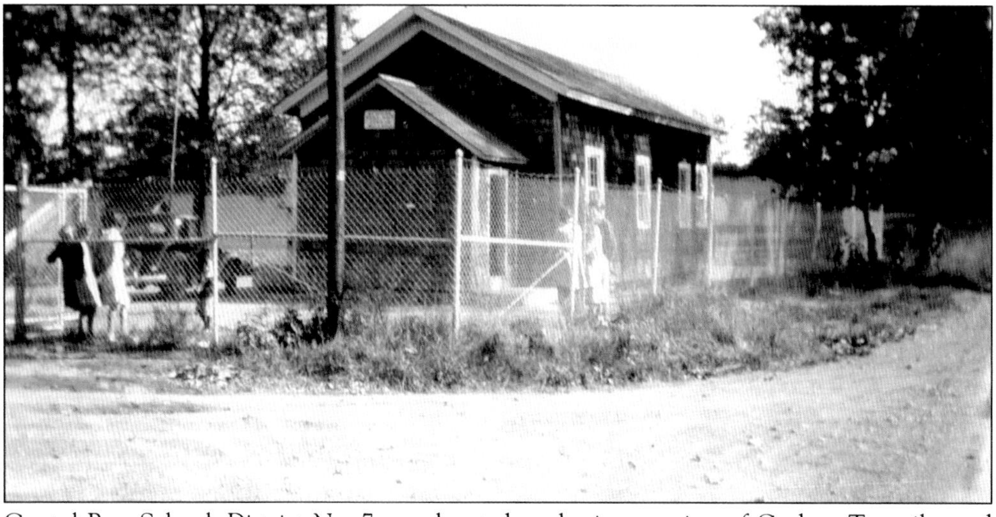

Crystal Run School, District No. 7, was located at the intersection of Goshen Turnpike and Stony Ford Road. Susan Zickler taught here from 1933 to 1937, beginning at age 18. The active 4-H Club members earned money for trips. Card parties were held at the school to raise money for playground equipment and school necessities.

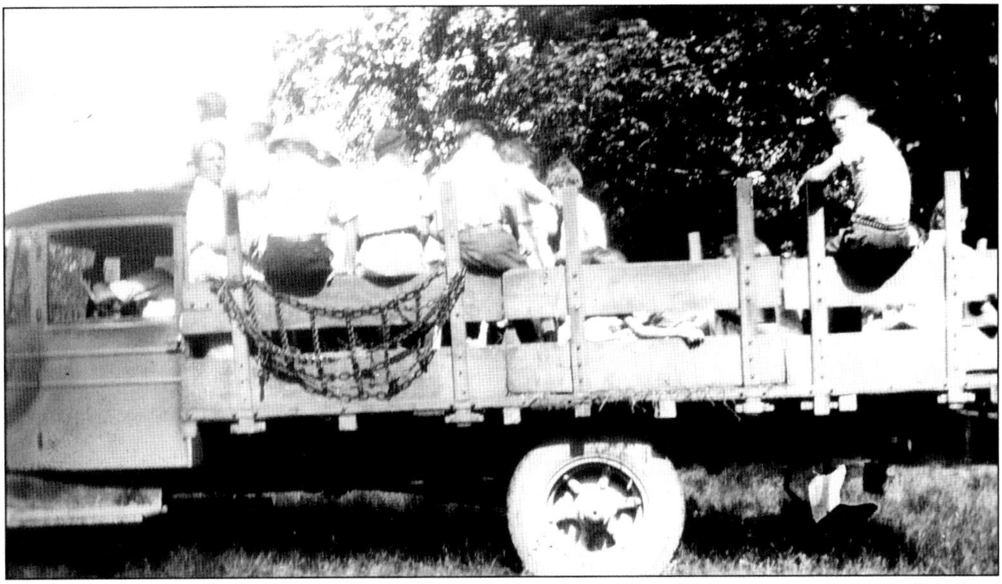

At the end of the school year, students would climb aboard Clarence Crist's truck for their annual trip to Pine Bush Recreation Park.

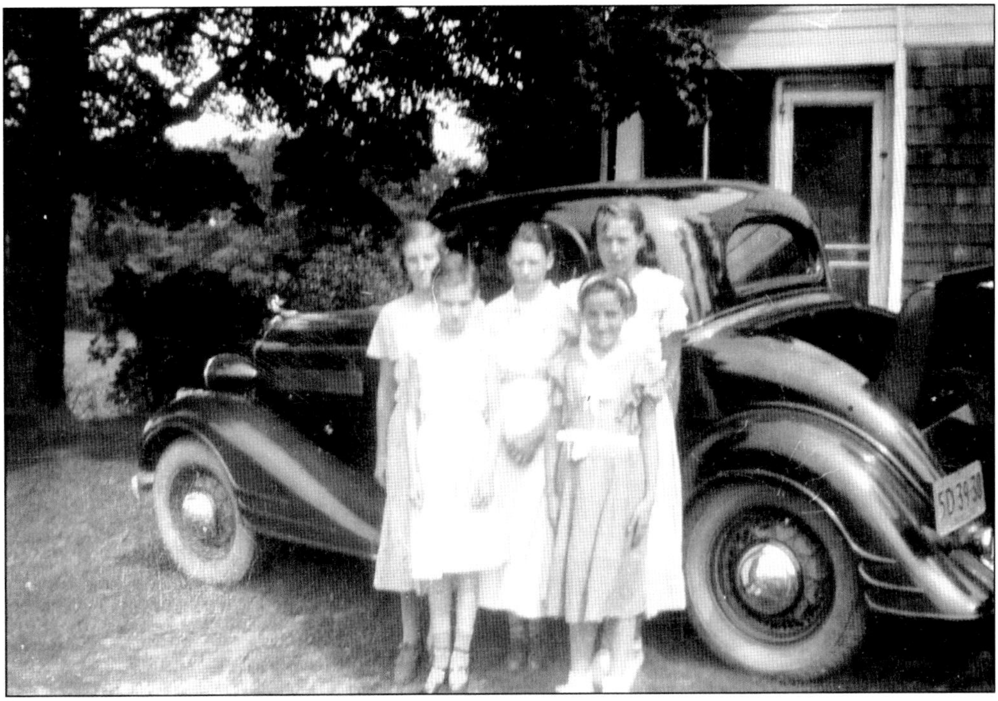

Some 4-H girls are seen at Zickler Farm in the 1930s. From left to right are May Stage, Betty Elston, Mary Elston, Sara Wicks, and a Kelley girl. (Courtesy of Susan Zickler Vanderburgh.)

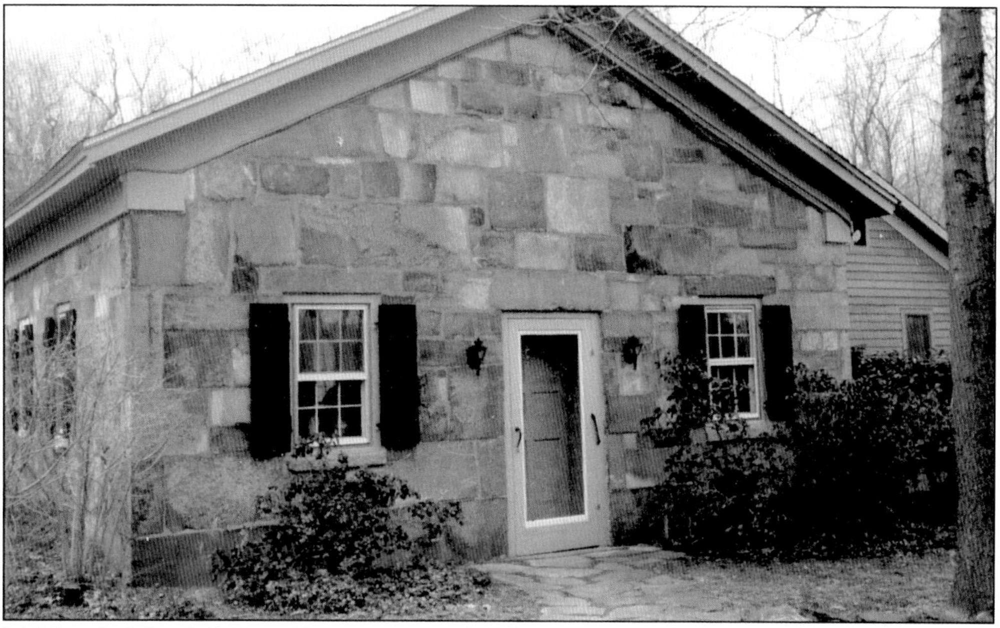

Millsburgh School, District No. 8, a stone schoolhouse, is located on the Scotchtown Collabar Road. There is a date on a stone near the entrance of the building reading 1853, but also a date of 1813 on a patch of plaster on the back wall. The interior of the building is 22 feet by 30 feet, and the walls are two feet thick. The stones were believed to have been quarried from the Millsburgh farm.

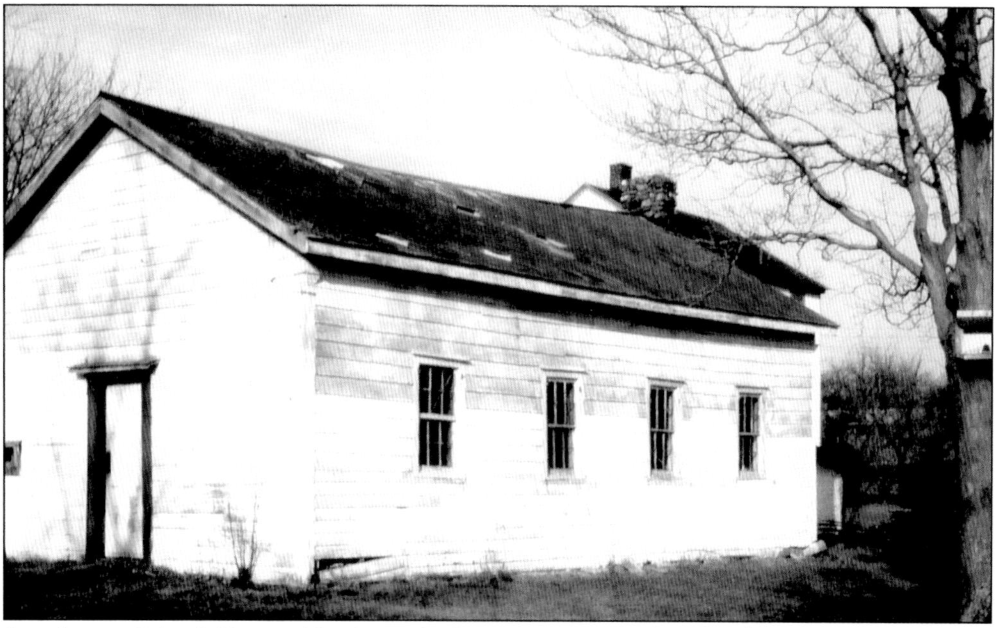

Scotchtown School, District No. 9, was built in 1842 at a total cost of $400. Charles Comfort, a former student, told the story of an incident in which the floor weakened near the stove and the students liked to jump on the loose and springy boards. Finally a board was broken, and the students found a new exit out of school—through the floor and the stones in the foundation. The school closed in 1942 after 100 years of service.

This April 1932 photograph is of Scotchtown school student Gordon Hasbrouck. (Courtesy of Gordon Hasbrouck.)

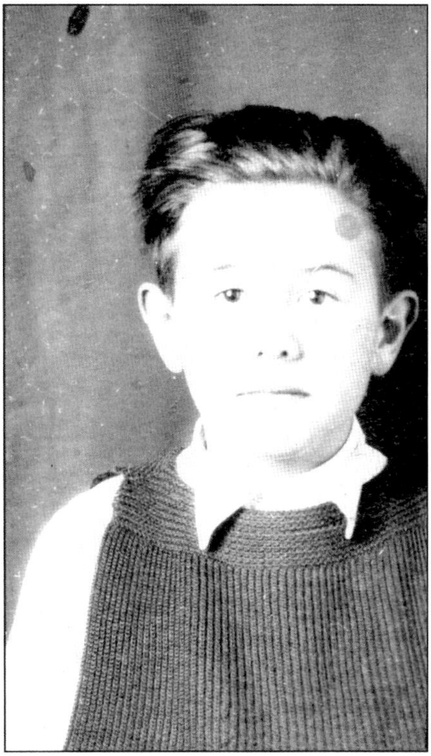

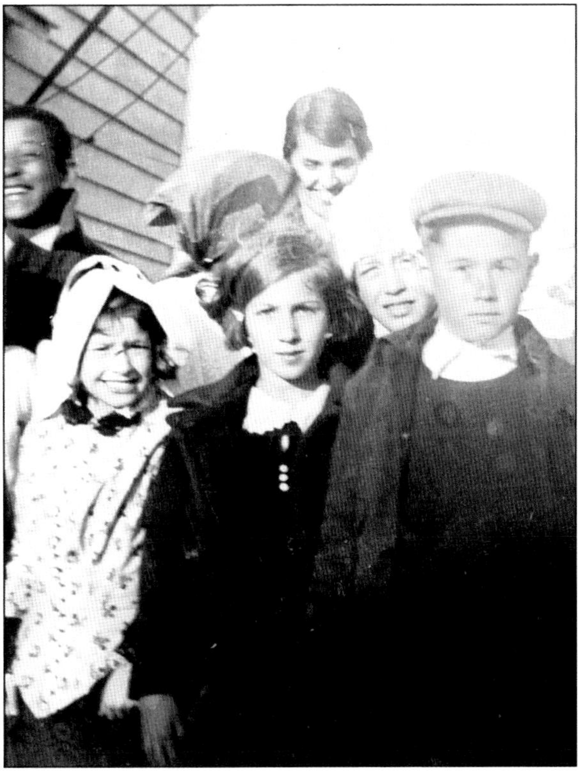

This Scotchtown School photograph was taken on February 22, 1932. From left to right are (first row) Elaine Wilkin, Mildred Lauer, and Gordon Hasbrouck; (second row) Walter Whiting, Neva Whiting (head turned), Mrs. Hubbard, and William Comfort.

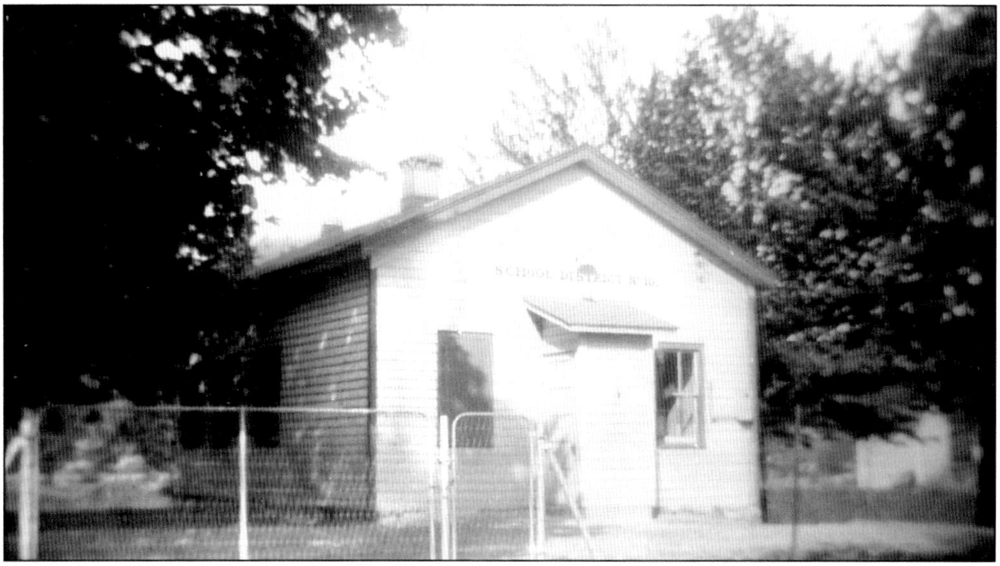

Rockville School, District No. 10, was located on Maples Road near the intersection of Route 17M. From 1930 to 1950, Julia Robinson was the teacher. One snowy day as she was leaving school, she noticed that some students had piled snow in front of her car. She got in, started her Ford Model A, "gunned" the engine and went through the snow, laughing, because she knew the students were hiding nearby, watching. (Information from Town Historian Dorothy Hunt-Ingrassia's personal interview with Julia Robinson.)

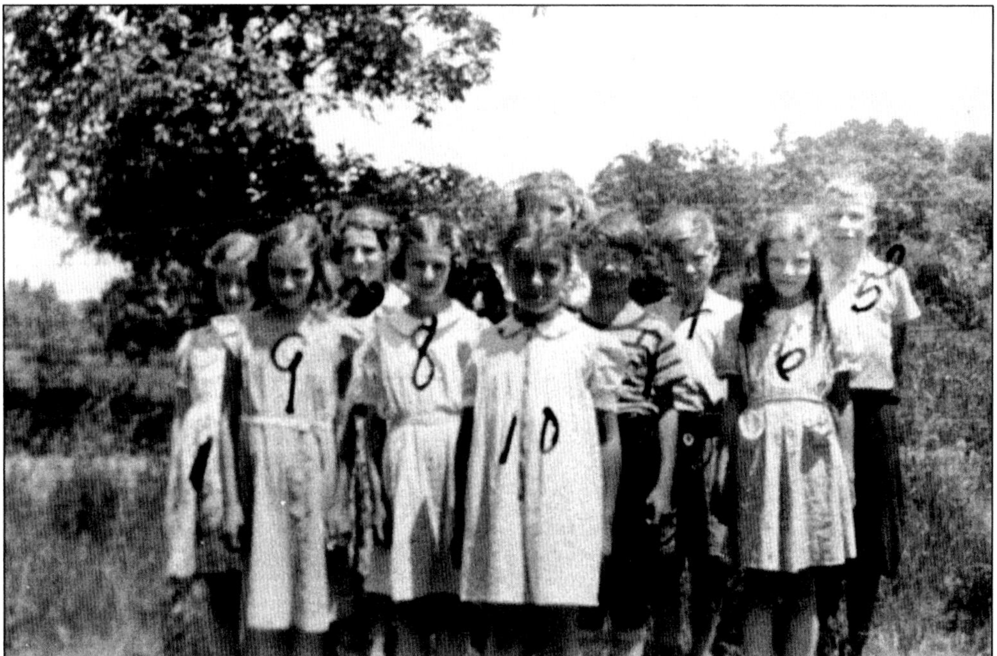

Pictured are Rockville students 1 Catherine LaScala, 2 Annie Deserto, 3 Shirley Nehls, 4 Albert Krull, 5 Frank Grasberger, 6 Eleanor Austin, 7 Joseph Ingrassia Jr., 8 Annie Van Kleeck, 9 Dorothy Salvagin, and 10 Phyllis Ingrassia.

Mechanicstown School, District No. 11, built in the 1800s, was at the intersection of East Main Street and Golf Links Road and was the first Mechanicstown school. At times, 50 students were taught there, although it was designed to accommodate 35 pupils. Miss Niering was the teacher when the school closed in 1926, after the little red schoolhouse, the second Mechanicstown school, was built.

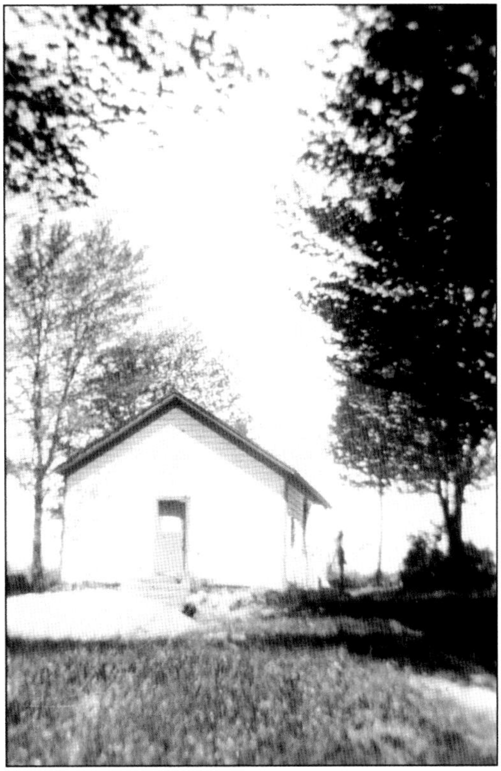

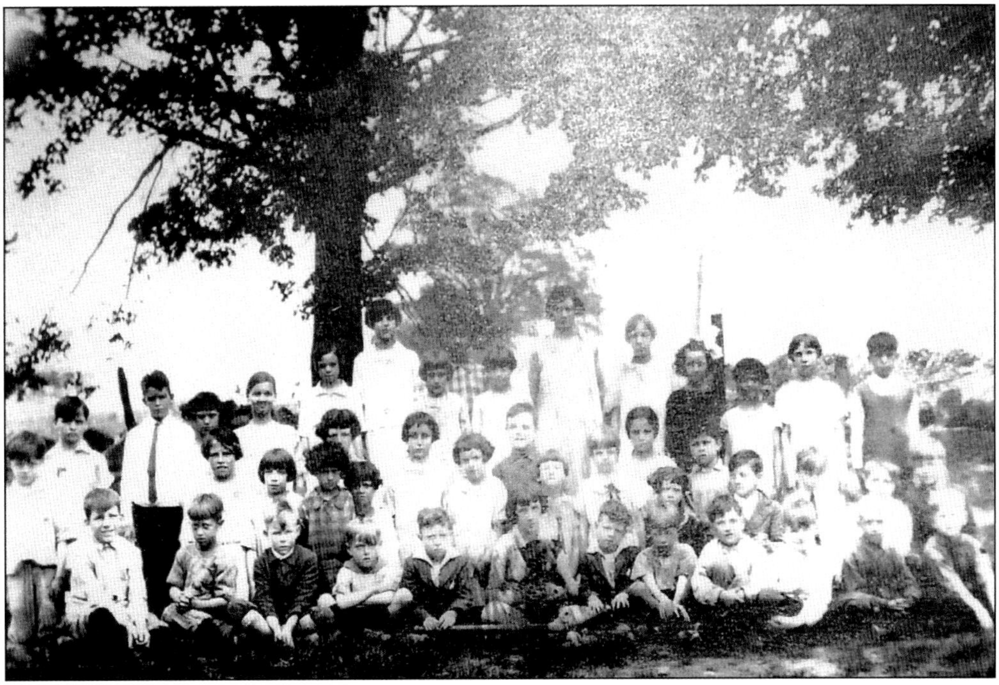

This was the last class to attend the first Mechanicstown School, in 1926, under the oak tree next to the school, which was located at the intersection of East Main Street and Golf Links Road.

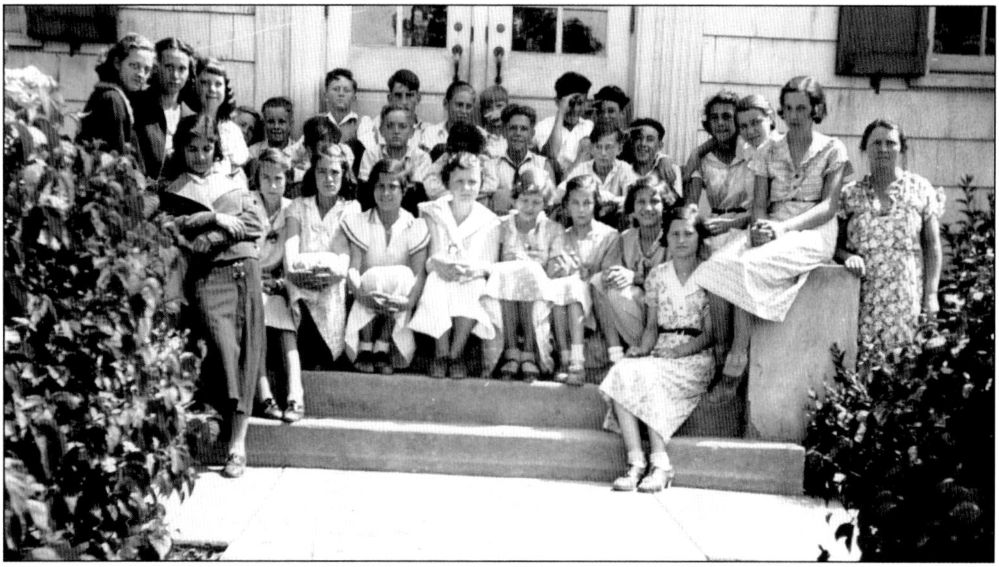

Students at the little red schoolhouse in 1934 are identified as Conjet Guzzetti, Esther Purdy, Ada Davis, Arlene Green, Gladys VanBenscopen, Frances VanBenscopen, Easter Zoffanero, Elizabeth Caffery, Louise Freer, Helen Keener, Evelyn Black, Minnie Zoffanero, Ralph Smith, Vincent Budd, Richard Perry, George Simpson, Salvatore Gulle, Floyd Truex, Henry Frank, Teresa Muer, Marion Gardner, Effie Terwilliger, teacher Blanche Taylor, Robert Maxwell, George Booth, Everett Menshen, George Brown, Dominick Muer, Douglas Miller, and Robert Van Pelt. Absent were Frances Brewster, Emily Perry, and Catherine Miller. (Courtesy of Helen Keener.)

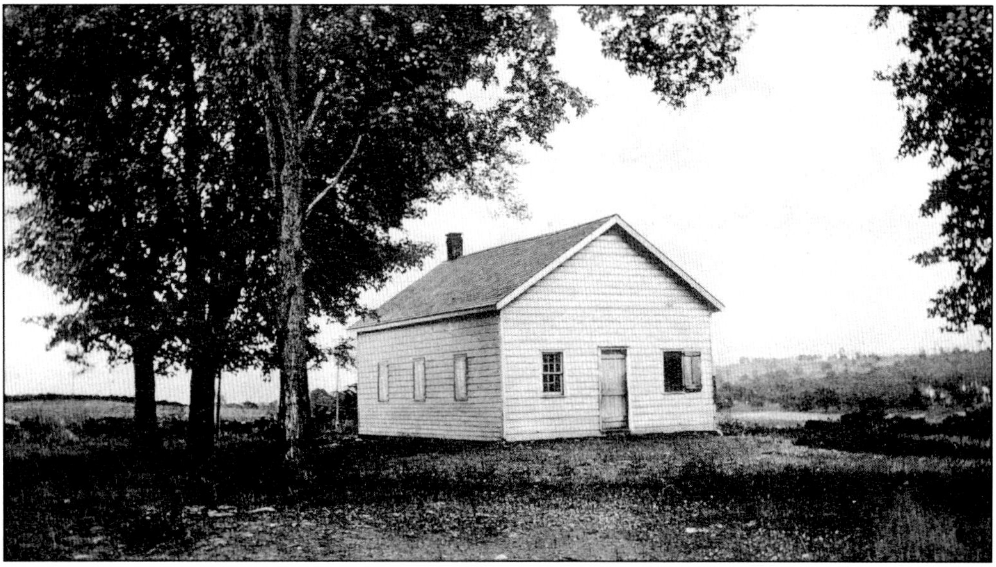

White Schoolhouse, District No. 12, was formed around 1828 when two small districts were united. The school was built on the southwest corner of James Morrison's farm, about one mile from Circleville. James Morrison donated the land. Bradner Little had the contract for building it for $300. Samuel Bull did the mason work. Most of the timber was donated by the McLaughrys, a family of manumitted slaves who lived on Guinea Road (now Midland Lake Road). Guinea is an African name for community. This District No. 12 ceased operation when Circleville School was built in 1907.

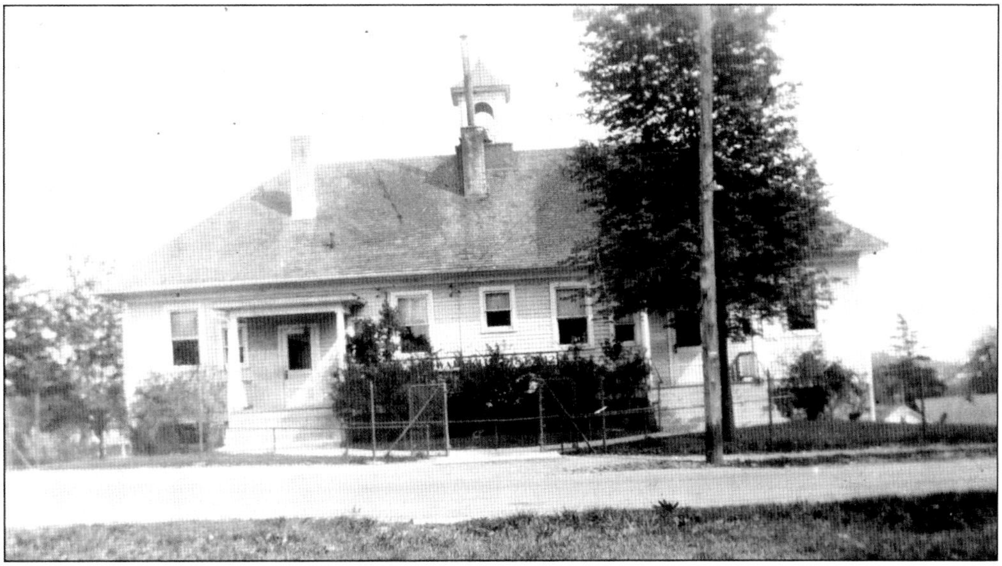

Washington Heights School, District No. 12, was built in 1925. A very active neighborhood school, it was acquired by the Middletown School District in the 1950s. Formerly District No. 12 was the White School on Shaw Road in Circleville, but was discontinued as a school when the new school, No. 19, was built in Circleville in 1907. When the Washington Heights School was built in 1925, the Commissioner of Education designated it District No. 12.

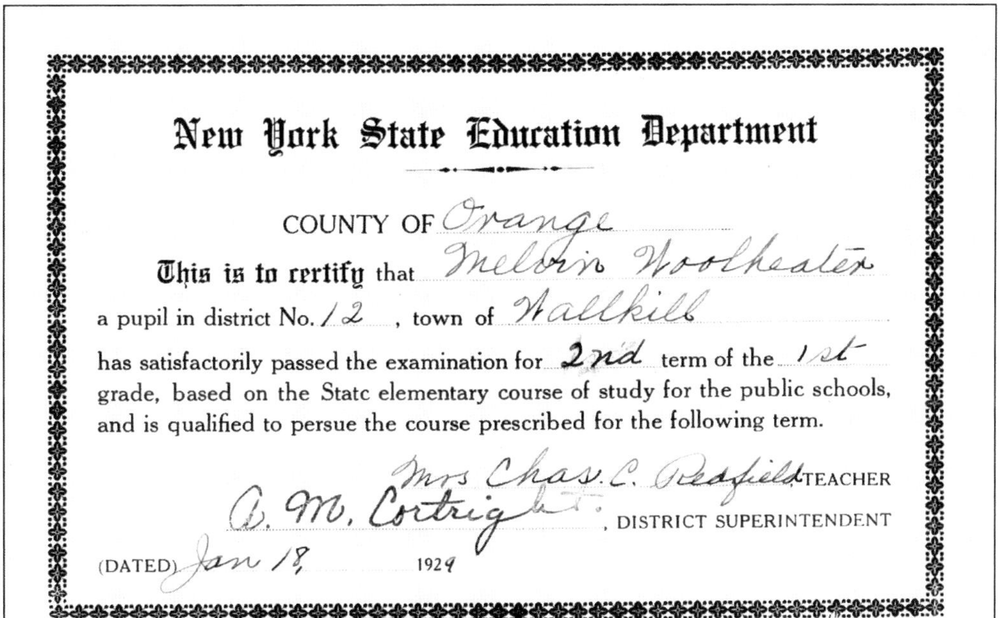

New York State Education Department

COUNTY OF Orange

This is to certify that Melvin Woolheater

a pupil in district No. 12, town of Wallkill

has satisfactorily passed the examination for 2nd term of the 1st grade, based on the Statc elementary course of study for the public schools, and is qualified to persue the course prescribed for the following term.

Mrs Chas. C. Redfield TEACHER

A. M. Cortright, DISTRICT SUPERINTENDENT

(DATED) Jan 18, 1929

Melvin Woolheater graduates to the second term of first grade at District No. 12 in 1929. He is awarded a certificate by teacher Mrs. Charles C. Redfield. The district superintendent was A. M. Cortright. (Courtesy of Melvin Woolheater.)

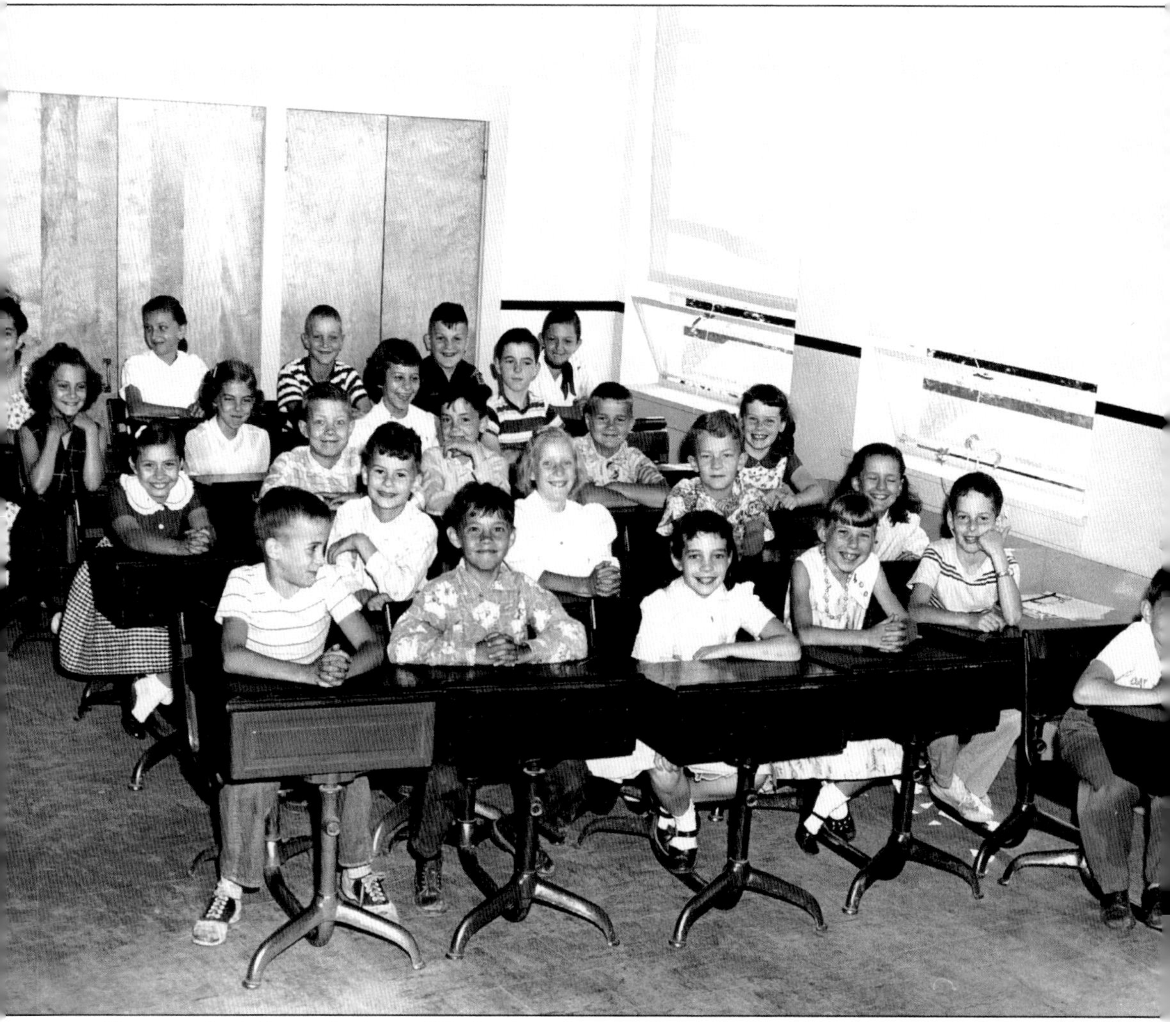

Shown is the fifth-grade class of Washington Heights School in 1956. From left to right are (first row) Philip Morse; (second row) Fred Myers, Wesley LaBagh, Betsey Tuthill, Linda Vanalstyne, and Elihue Sussman; (third row) Joseph Kehm, Linda Barnes, Allan Brinckerhoff, and Coretta Needham; (fourth row) Sandra Pizza, Dennis Eckerson, Gene Sigler, Edward Brown, and Nancy Clauson; (fifth row) Linda Fuller, Susan Meyers, Cathy Brown, and Lynn Bliven; (sixth row) Linda Berry, Donna Ruppert, Samuel Barnes, Robert Carey, and Bonnie VanInwegen. (Courtesy of Joseph and Alida Brinckerhoff.)

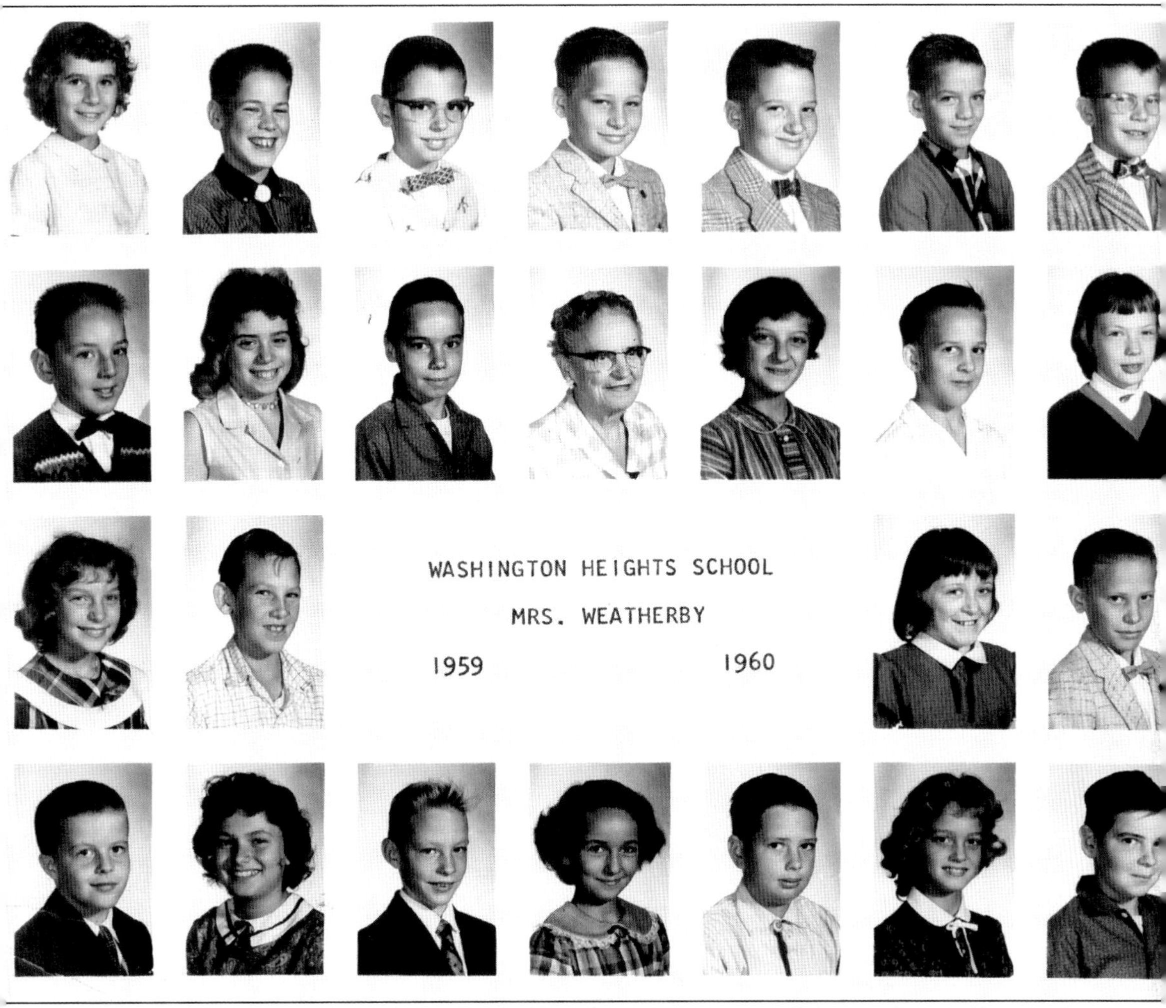

This is the Washington Heights School class of 1959–1960. From left to right are (first row) Danny Furlin, Connie Turi, Samuel Mitchell, Delores Barnes, unidentified, Jane Dunn, and Dickie Thorpe; (second row) Cathy Doty, David Dumond, Leah Penny, and William Ott; (third row) unidentified, Lorlie Foster, unidentified, teacher Ina Wetherby, Janice Martine, unidentified, and Carol Davis; (fourth row) unidentified, David Malmad, Joe Dziengeil, Walter Ott, Jerry Sayer, Ernie Wagner, and Carl Brinckerhoff. (Courtesy of Joseph and Alida Brinckerhoff.)

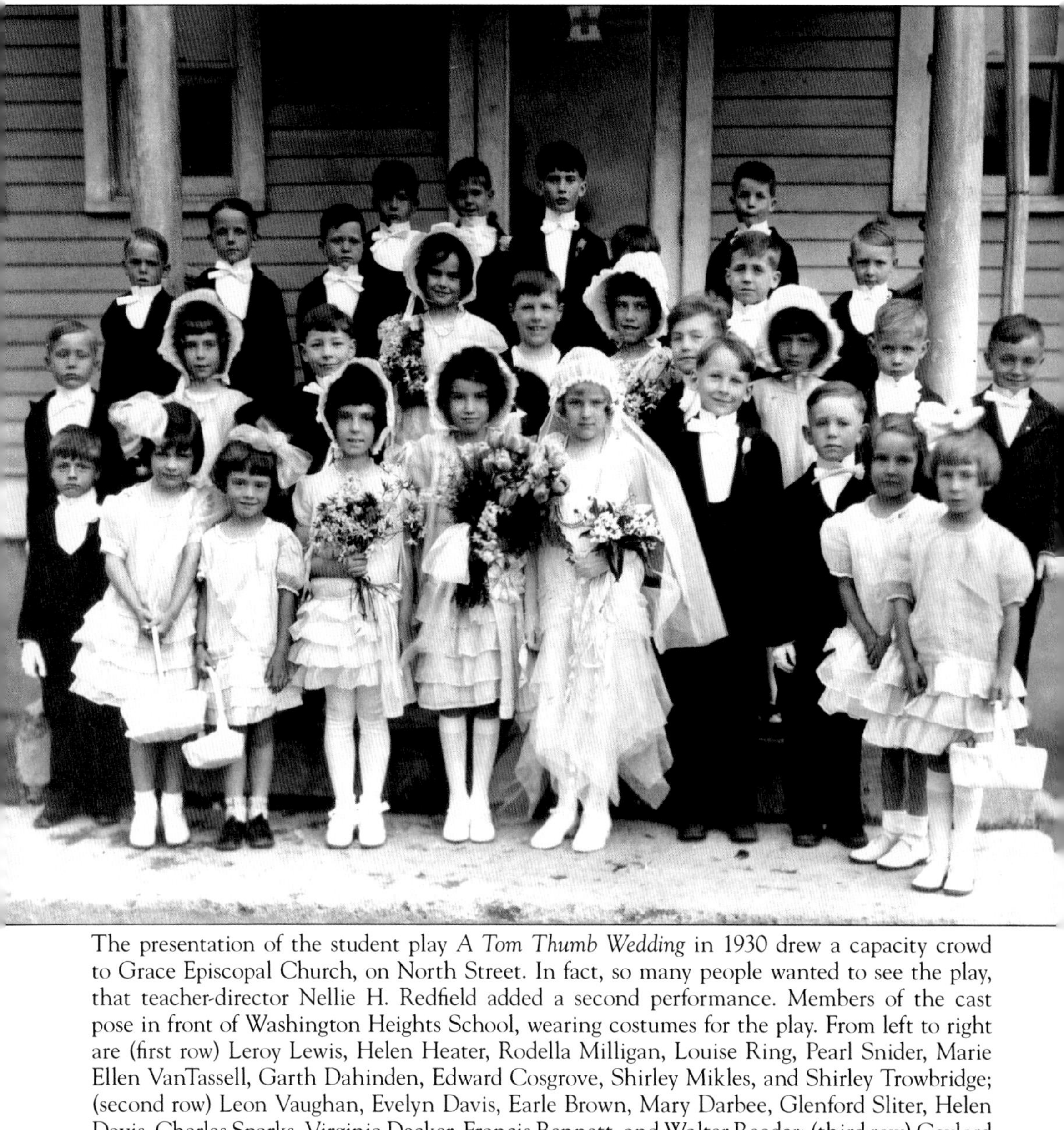

The presentation of the student play *A Tom Thumb Wedding* in 1930 drew a capacity crowd to Grace Episcopal Church, on North Street. In fact, so many people wanted to see the play, that teacher-director Nellie H. Redfield added a second performance. Members of the cast pose in front of Washington Heights School, wearing costumes for the play. From left to right are (first row) Leroy Lewis, Helen Heater, Rodella Milligan, Louise Ring, Pearl Snider, Marie Ellen VanTassell, Garth Dahinden, Edward Cosgrove, Shirley Mikles, and Shirley Trowbridge; (second row) Leon Vaughan, Evelyn Davis, Earle Brown, Mary Darbee, Glenford Sliter, Helen Davis, Charles Sparks, Virginia Decker, Francis Bennett, and Walter Reeder; (third row) Gaylord Winner, Thomas Stack, Donald Sliter, Albert Brown (face hidden), Dwight Joslin, and Merritt Reynolds; (fourth row) Paul Sparks, Gurdin Fuller, Gilbert Arnold, and Harold Joslin. (Courtesy of Glenford Sliter, Lincoln, Nebraska.)

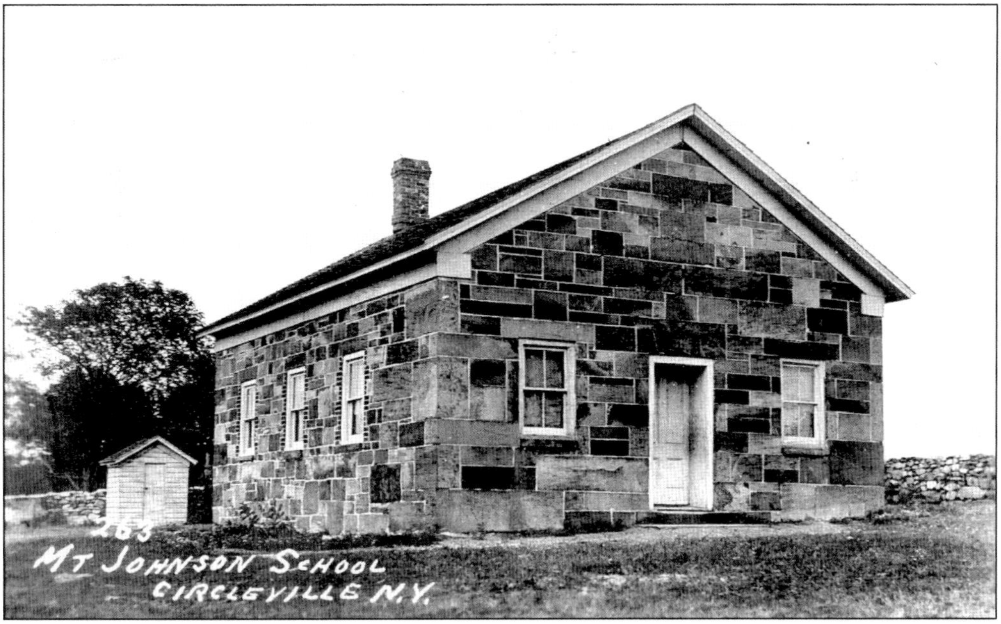

Mount Johnson School, District No. 13, is a stone building located on the Goshen Turnpike about a mile north of Circleville. Built around 1851 by Samuel Bull, who had built other stone houses in the vicinity, it was used as a schoolhouse until 1947. One of the early teachers was Belle Paterson, who taught between 1890 and 1912. The schoolhouse was sold at auction in 1953 for $3,050.

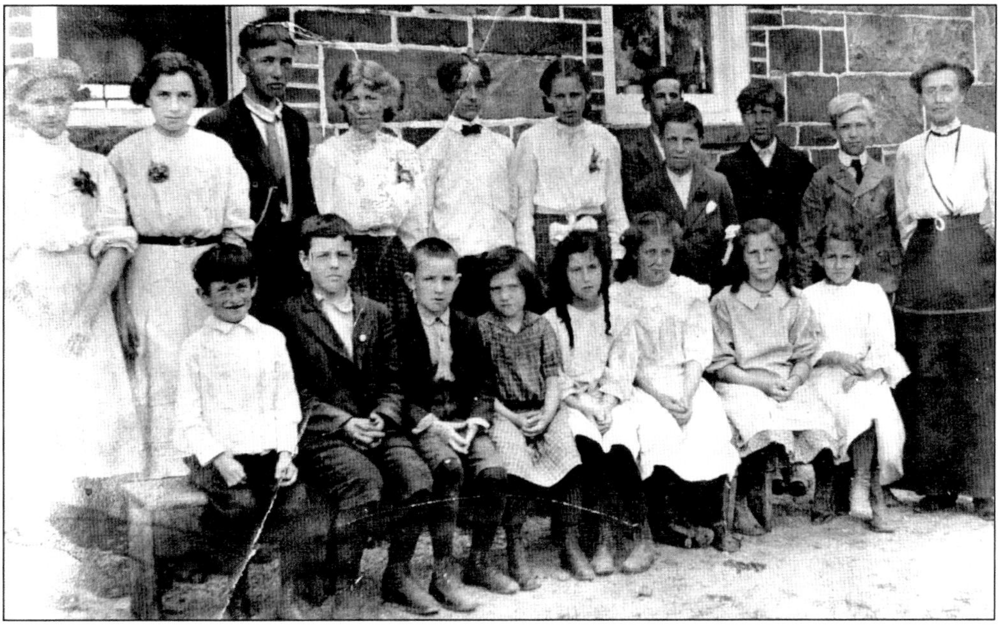

Pictured in this c. 1910 photograph of Mount Johnson School students are, from left to right (first row) Francis Carroll, Harry Dunham, Roy Finch, Clara Brown, Margaret Carroll, Hattie Brown, Marjorie Remsen, and Bessie Suffern; (second row) Edna Gillen, Flora Holley, Charles Gillen, Ethel Brown, Bernard Repelow, Anna Suffern, Walter Rhodes, partly hidden by Melvin Travis, William Kirk, Arthur Gillen, and teacher Belle Patterson. (Courtesy of Gregory Pryer.)

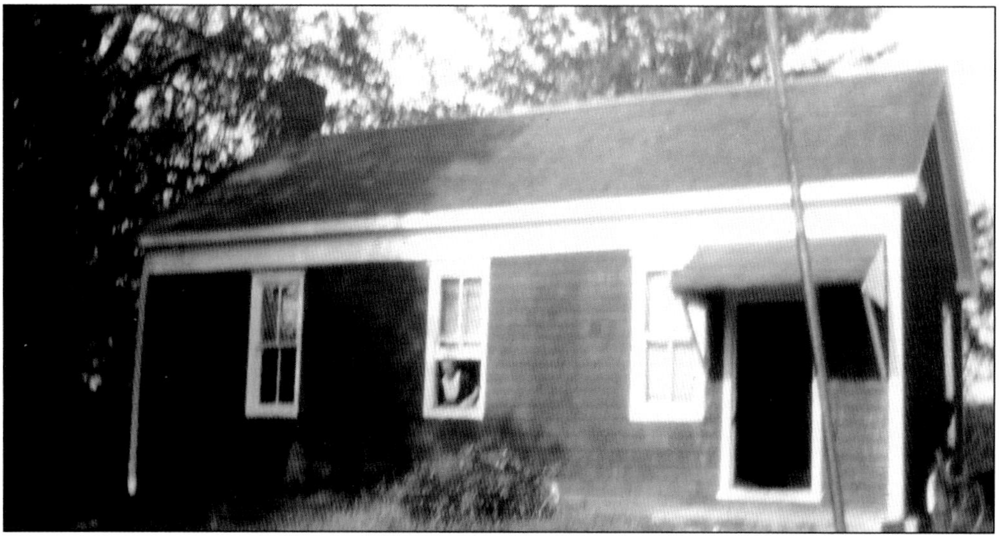

Cooper School, District No. 14, was located on what is now Route 17K, between Bullville and Bloomingburg. It was built next to the John Cooper farm, hence the name. In 1917, an old account book showed a balance of $1.44 and the teacher was given a note for $100 for the amount still due her. Ruth E. Fechner, a beloved teacher, taught there in the 1930s. Students attending in 1935 were Phyllis Behnke, Theresa Wild, Doris Dickinson, Shirley Goettman, Florence Wetzel, Marjorie Johnson, Marlin "Bud" Cooper, Kenneth Hayes, Andrew Wild, Donald Dickinson, Robert Dickinson, Henry Seaman, Leland Behnke, Edson Behnke, and Albert Wetzel. Prosperous Valley School, District No. 15, located on Prosperous Valley Road, was formed before 1844. Deborah Ann Everett was a teacher there in 1855, Mary Drake in 1856, and James E. Winter in 1857. No longer used as a school, it was sold at auction in 1963 for $2,100. (Courtesy of Shirley Ecker.)

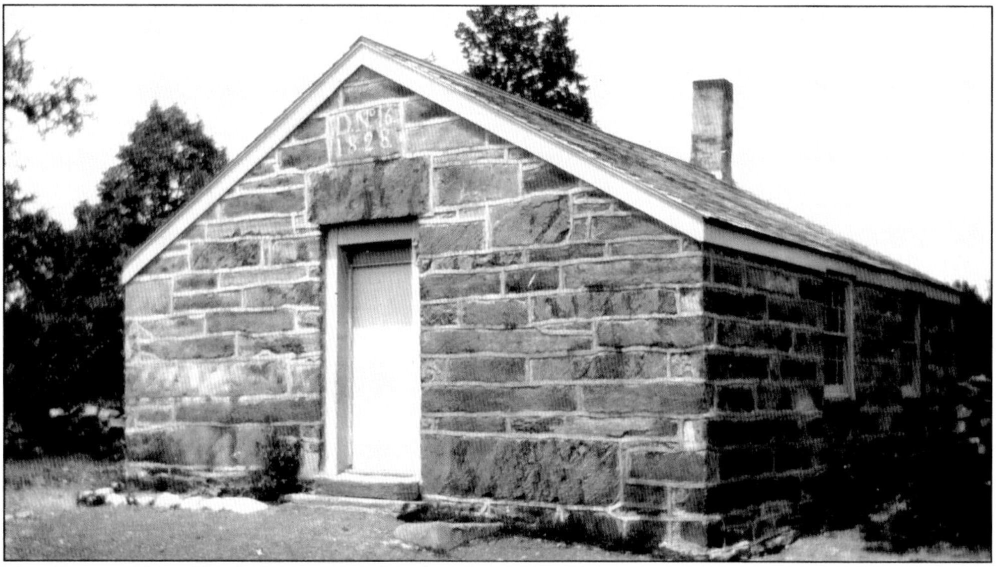

Van Burenville School, District No. 16, a stone schoolhouse with walls 18 inches thick, was erected in 1828, to replace a log cabin school. The 30-foot by 20-foot school is located on Van Burenville Road at the intersection of Derby Road. In 1815, there were 68 children in the district, and the district was entitled to $30.77 from the state. This historic building still stands.

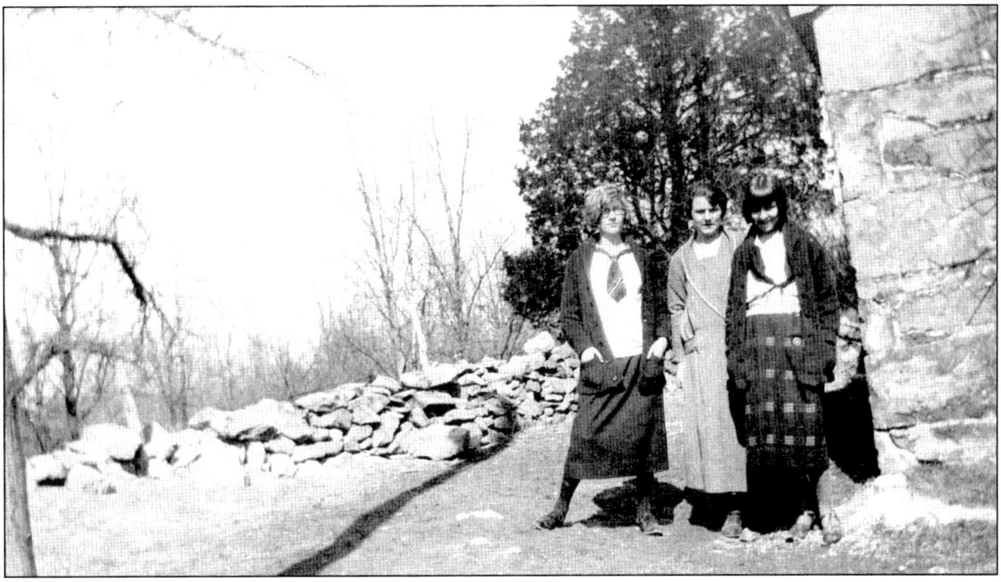

Pictured in the 1920s are, from left to right, Pearl Gillen, teacher Eleanor McCoach, and Isabelle Brown.

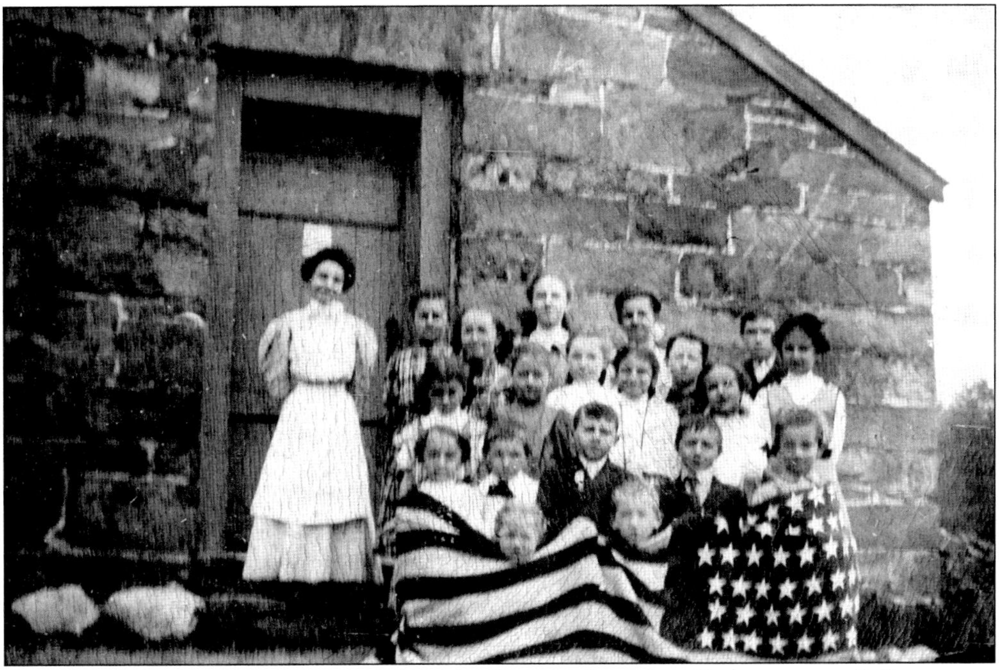

This Christmas card was given to students by their teacher, Marie Erchmann, in 1908.

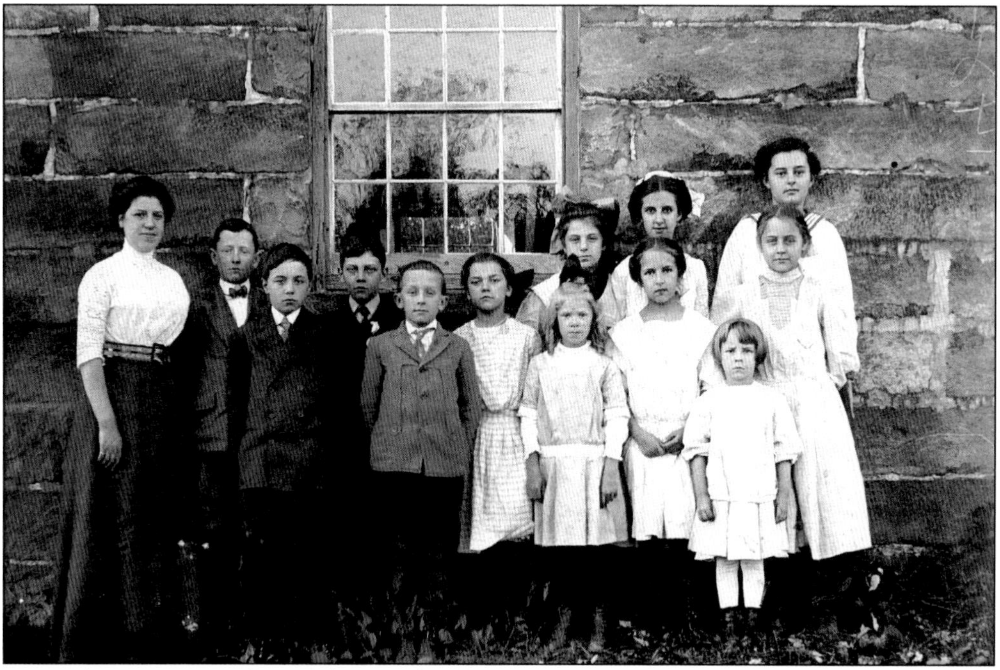

Pictured in 1911 are, from left to right (first row) Marion Crane; (second row) Clarence Dolaway, Kingsley Crane, Marion Weld, Maude Gillen, and Maude Anderson; (third row) Myrtle Hamilton, teacher Austin Anderson, John Decker, Marion Decker, Julia Carpenter, Laura Gillen, and Adeline Anderson. (Courtesy of the Historical Society of Middletown and the Wallkill Precinct.)

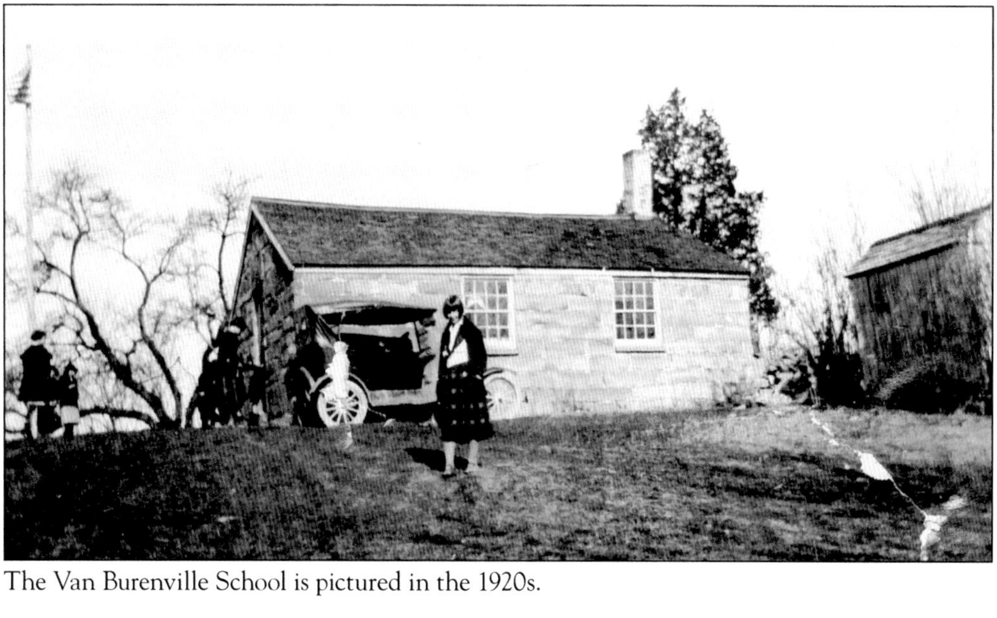

The Van Burenville School is pictured in the 1920s.

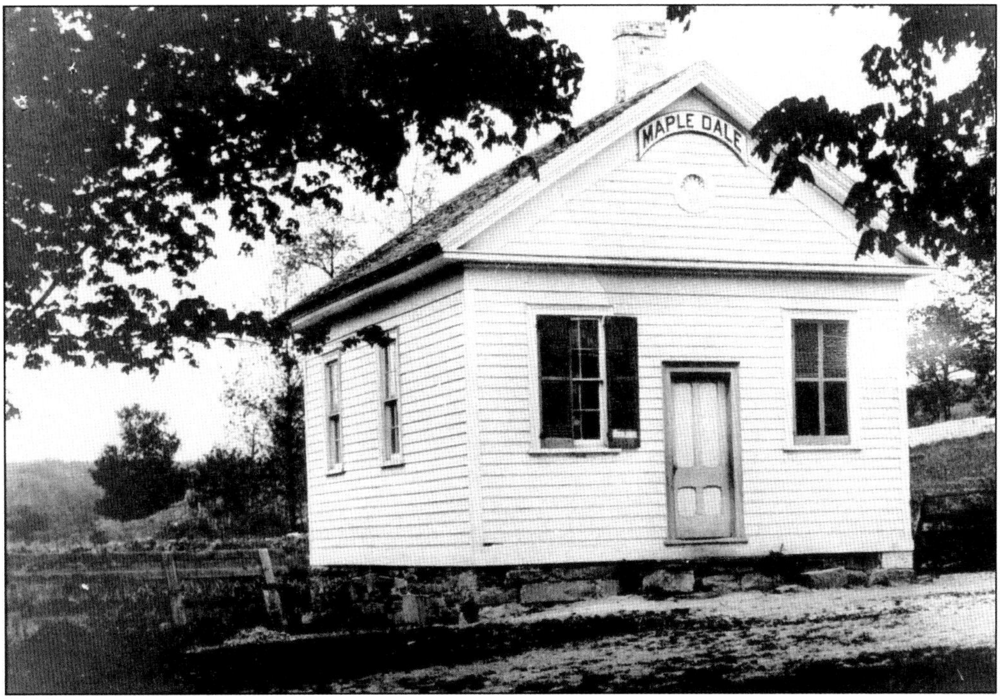

Maple Dale School, District No. 17 was built in 1867 on Mount Hope Road (formerly the Montgomery and Minisink Turnpike). It was the second school for this district. The first was known as Rat Town School, because of rats that infested the old tannery nearby. The name followed the new school until 1876 when each taxpayer brought a maple tree to be planted at the site. The name was officially changed to Maple Dale in 1881.

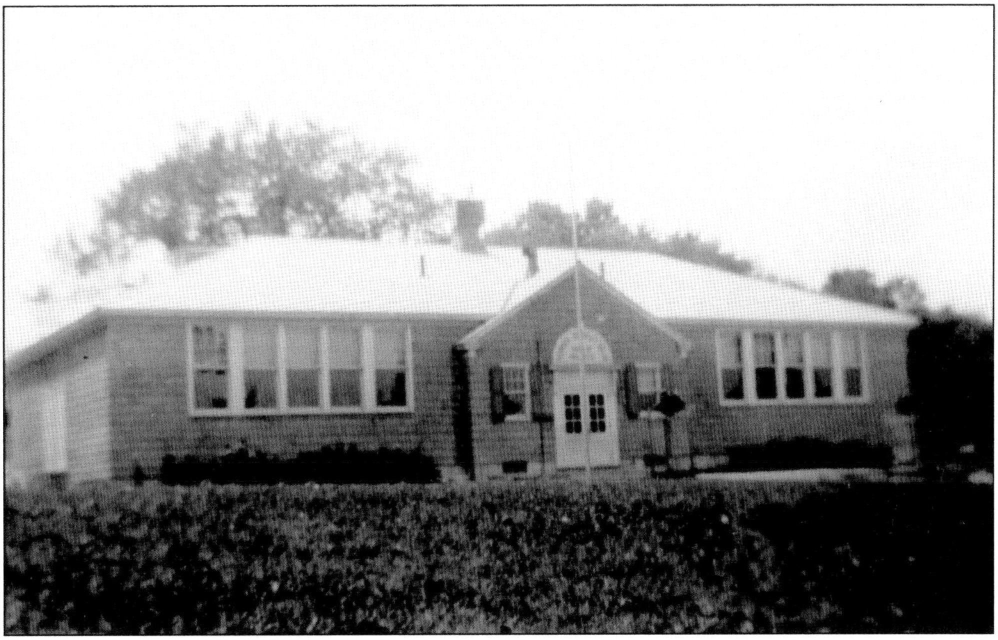

Pilgrim Grammar School, District No. 18, built in 1870, was located on Route 211 West. The building still stands.

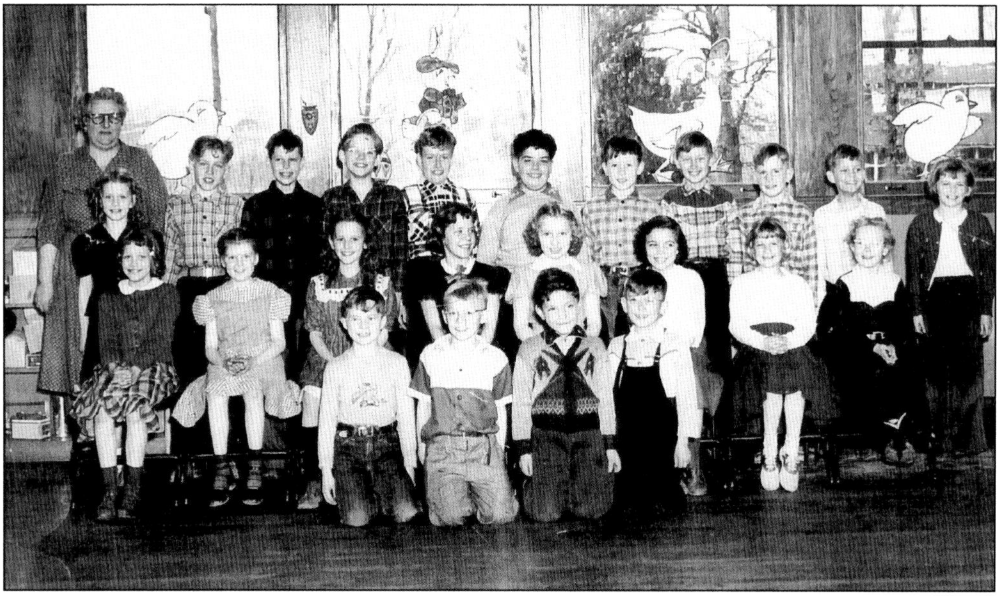

In this 1949 school photograph are, from left to right (first row) Mervin Lewis, Robert Wells, Jim Kurtz, and Bobby Zwart; (second row) Carol Kurtz, Francis Smith, Nancy Zwart, Dorothy Kurtz, Barbara Wells, Rosanna Orrio, Virginia Bender, Midge Boorman, and Linda McGinn; (third row) Judith Skidmore, Glenn Francisco, Bruce Abramson, Thomas Dempsey, Donald Dunlap, Leonard Ander, Daniel Hulseapple, Richard Lundren, Douglas Adamson, and Billy Dempsey; (fourth row) teacher Gertrude Chambers. (Courtesy of Judy Harms.)

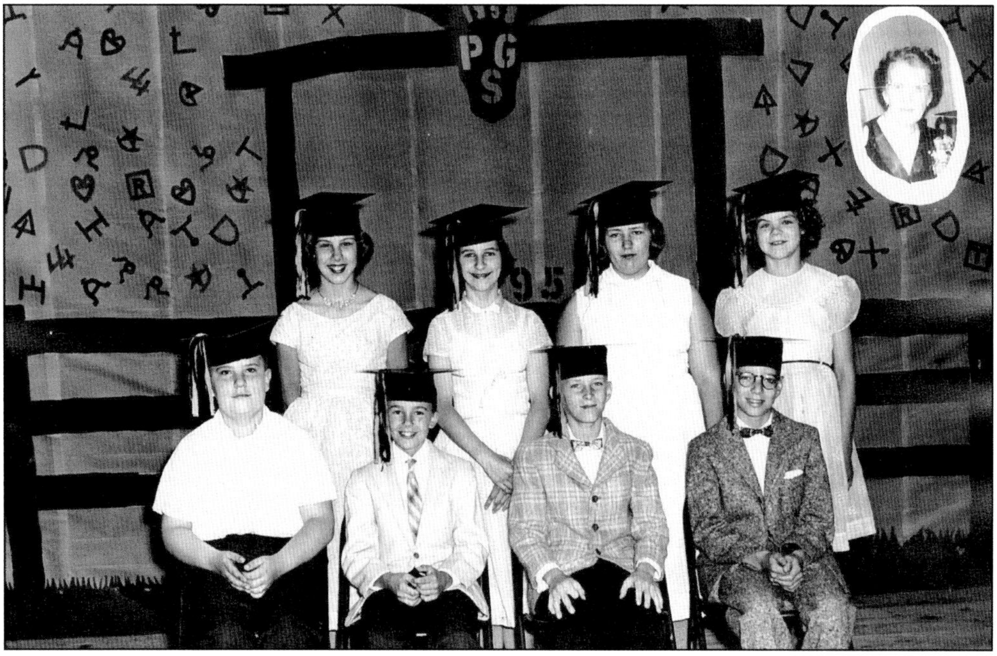

The 1958 graduating class poses for a photograph. From left to right are (first row) Steven Shock, Dennis Harms, John Unger, and Alan Lewis; (second row) Phyllis Fagen, Lois Anglymeyer, Kathy Joly, and Corrine Edwards. The teacher was Mrs. Carr. (Courtesy of Alan Lewis.)

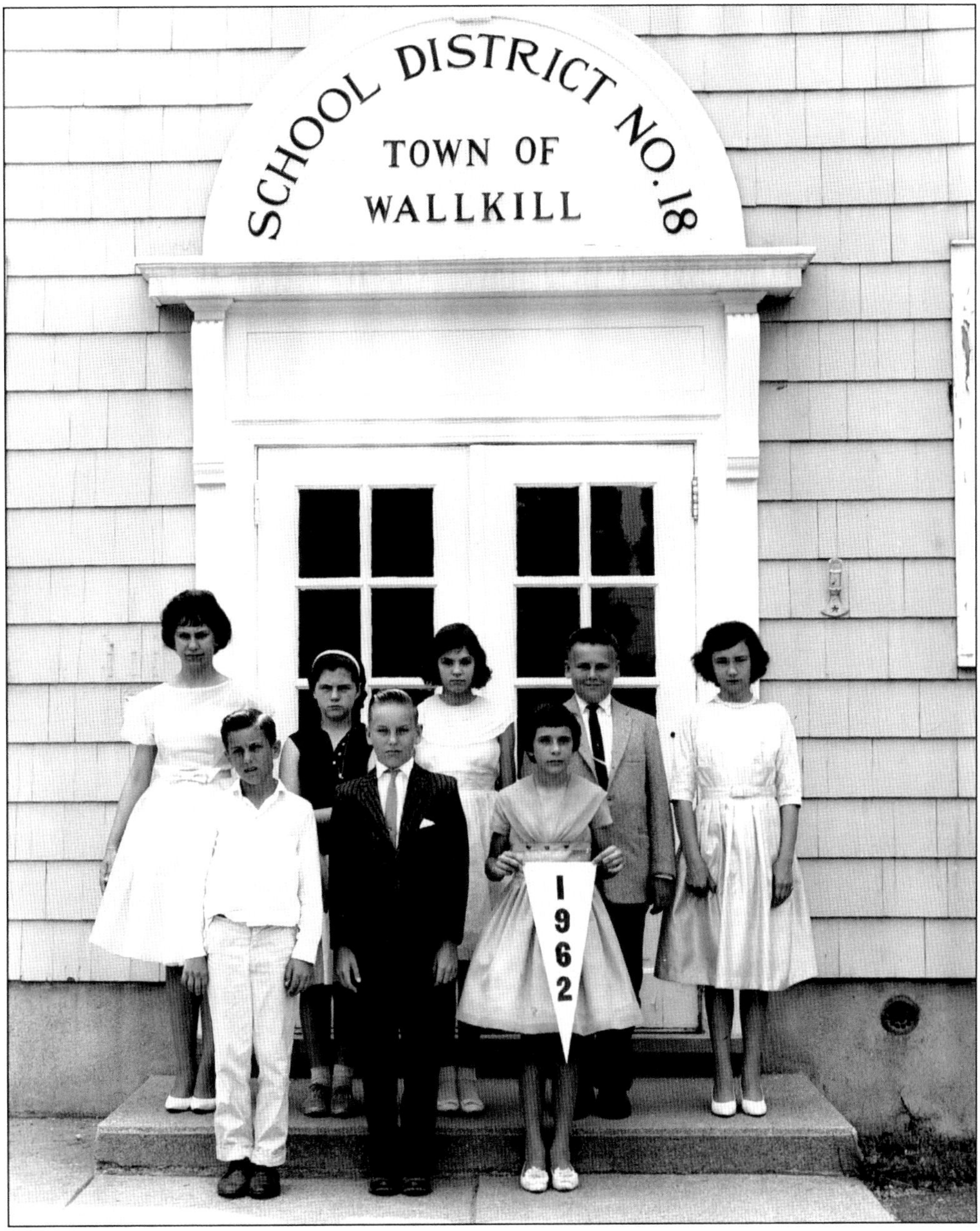

This photograph shows the 1962 graduating class at Pilgrim Grammar School. The young woman holding the date flag is Susan DeLito. The young man to her left is Phillip Adamson. (Courtesy of Phillip Adamson.)

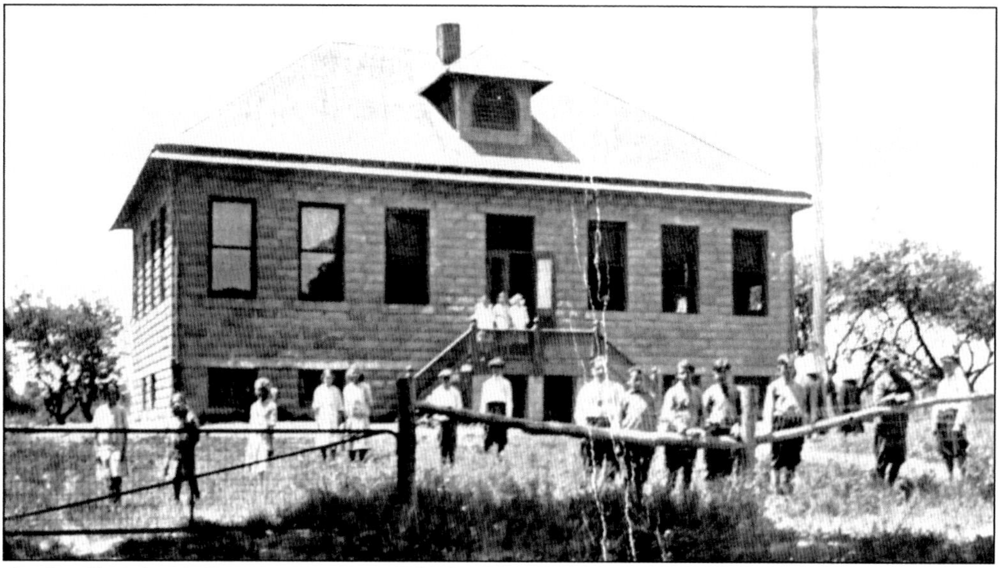

Circleville School, District No. 19, was built around 1907. Residents disagreed on where a new school should be located, and for a time the district had two schools: one at Bull's Hall in Circleville and the other at the White School. The new school built at Circleville served the area for 57 years until it was ordered to shut down in 1964. At the time 12 students were in attendance in this three-room schoolhouse.

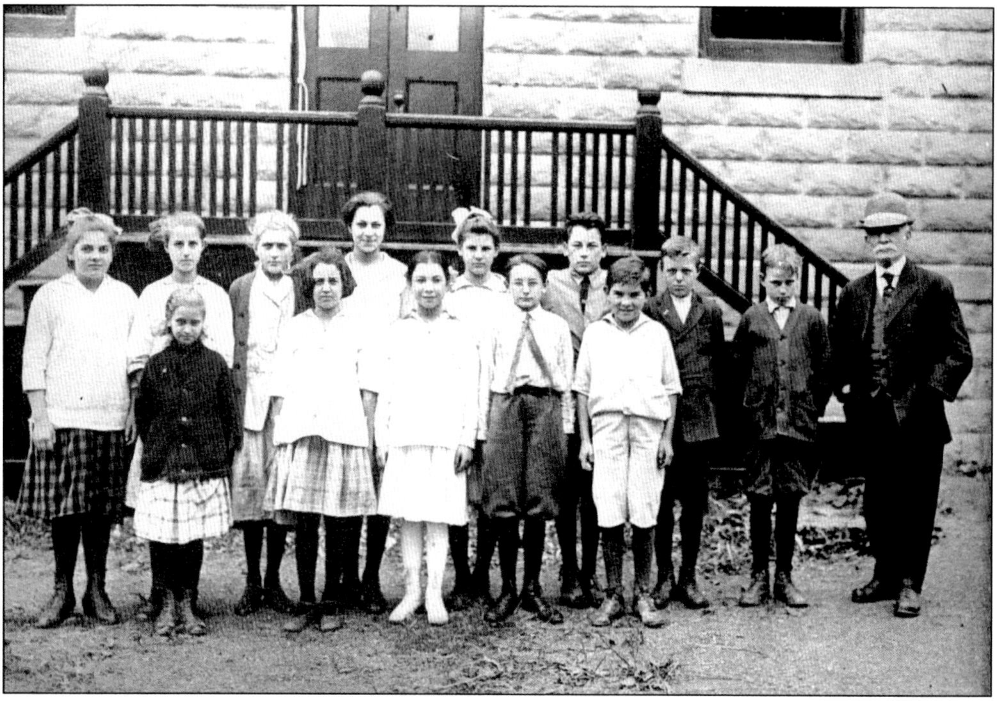

Included in this c. 1914 photograph of Circleville School students is teacher Mr. Wyant (far right). (Courtesy of the Paul Weisshaar collection.)

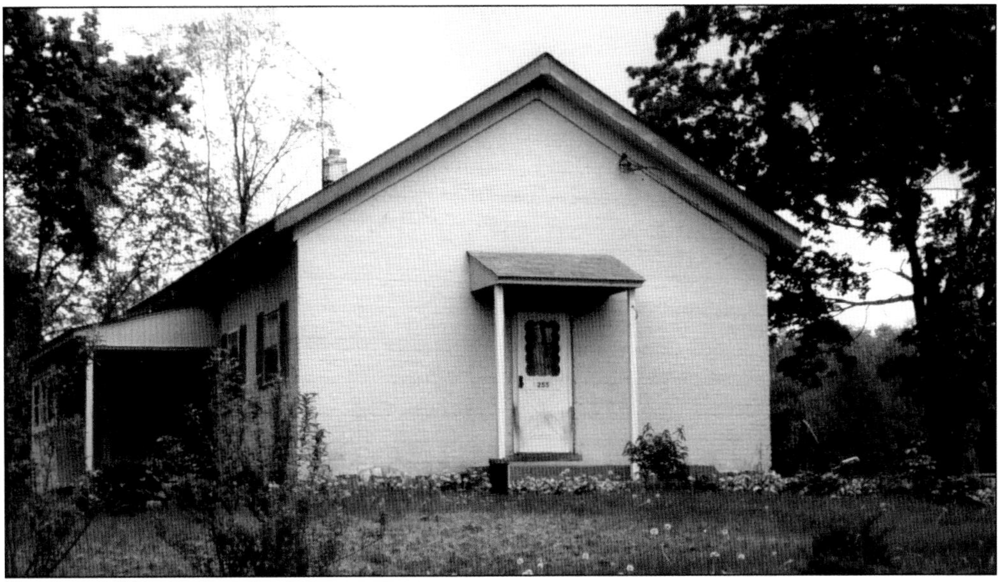

Mount Joy Union School, District No. 20, was the second schoolhouse for that district. The first one, built of wood, was destroyed by fire in the mid 1800s. The second, built of brick in 1866, remains. Before the Revolutionary War, a group of men became temporarily lost in the wilderness and could not determine their whereabouts. As they came to an elevation, they climbed to the summit, saw the Wallkill River, and immediately knew where they were. They named this hill Mount Joy to express their feelings.

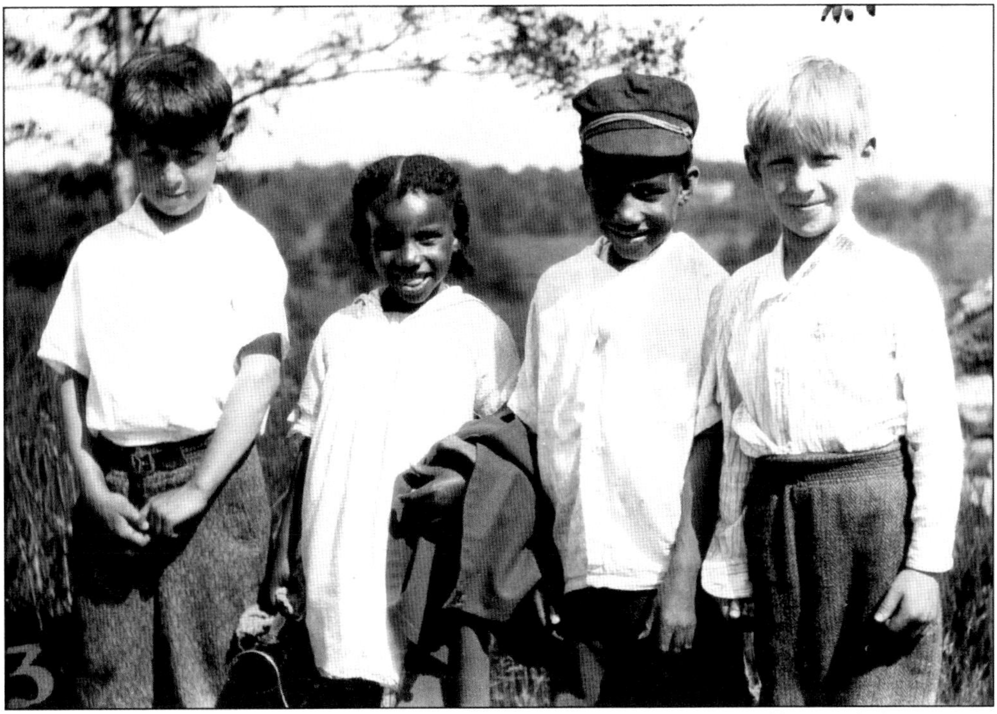

In this 1931 Mount Joy School photograph are, from left to right, John Hoffman, Thelma Dixon, John "Top" Dixon, and Charles Hoffman.

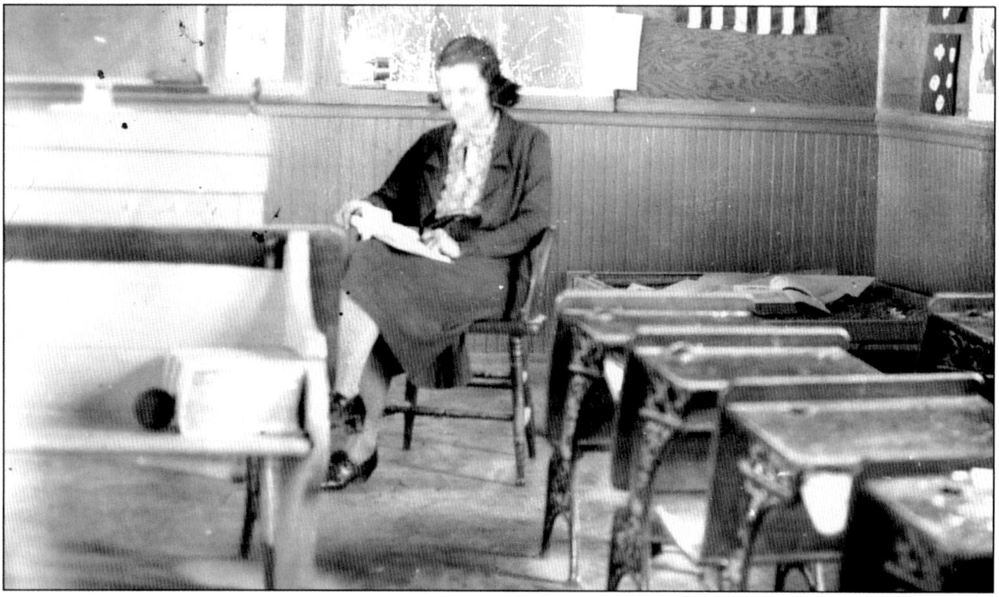

Catherine MacGowan Cutler taught at Mount Joy from 1930 to 1940. (Cutler gave her collection of Mount Joy photographs to former student, Robert N. Clauson who graciously donated them to town historian Dorothy Hunt-Ingrassia.)

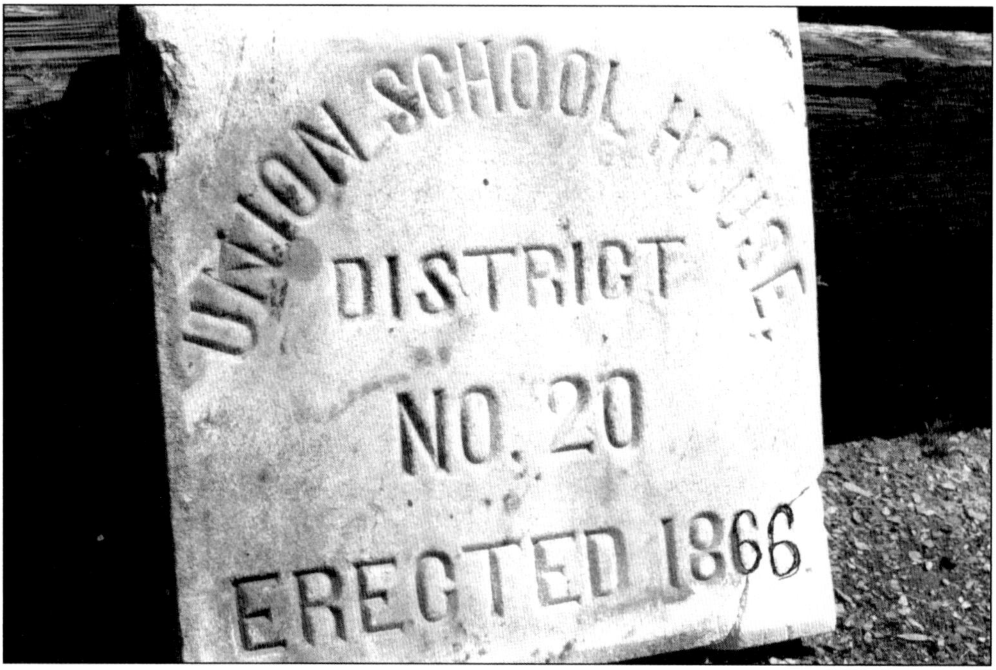

This stone plaque was located over the entrance doorway for 74 years. The engraving on the other side indicates it was a gravestone of Mrs. Robert Burton, who died in 1861. Why the gravestone was used remains a mystery.

Nine

Fire Companies

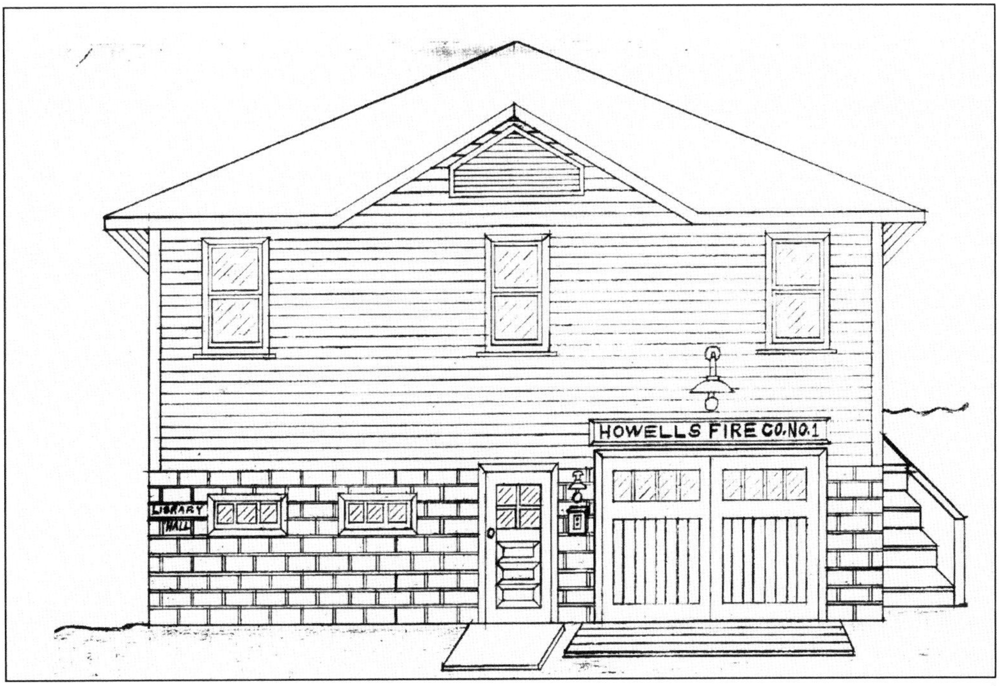

The first fire company formed in the Town of Wallkill was the Howells Fire Company organized at Library Hall, Howells, on July 14, 1924. The first chief of the company was Frank Vail, who served from 1924 to 1927. The Howells Fire District was established in 1925, and it contracted with the Buffalo Fire Appliance Company for a triple combination apparatus on a Larrabee chassis for the sum of $6,758. In 1941, the Wallace Feed Store building was purchased for the sum of $1,000 and remodeled. The Barn, as it is known, has been the scene of numerous fund-raising events and dinners. In 1969, a new four-bay firehouse was constructed, and today, the district owns a 1992 Pierce Arrow pumper, a 1999 Pierce Saber pumper, a 2001 Ford Danko brush truck, and a 2005 Crimson tanker. This drawing of the firehouse was done by Bob Howell.

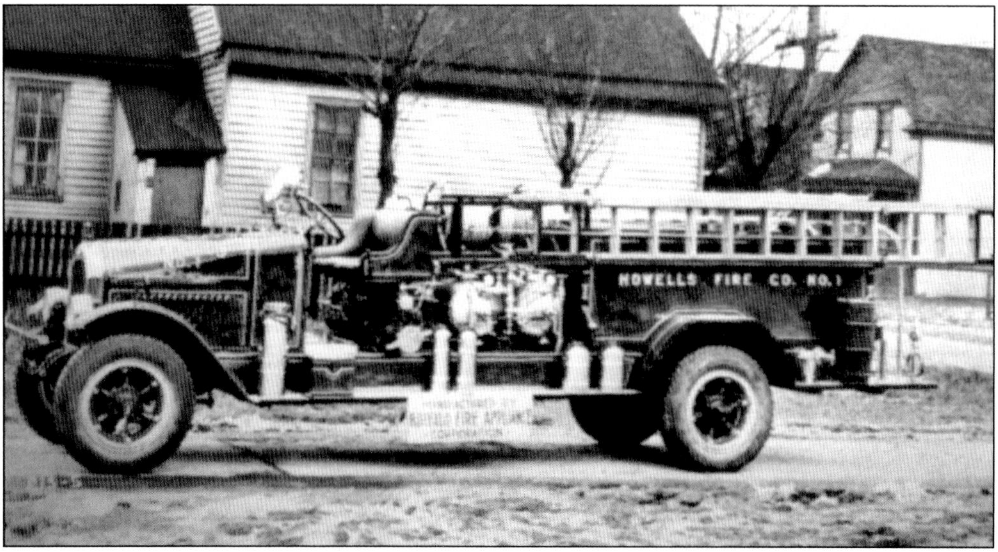

Shown is a 1925 Larrabee pumper. (Courtesy of Howells Fire Company.)

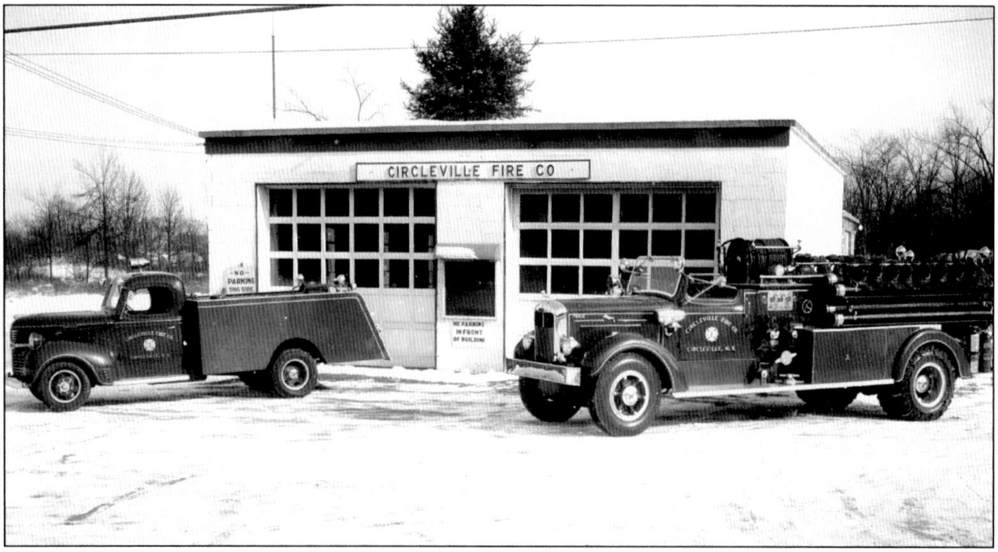

Circleville Fire Company was organized in early 1947. Ground was broken for the construction of a truck house in September 1947. Circleville Fire District was approved by the Wallkill Town Board on November 6, 1947. The first truck purchased was a 1928 American LaFrance 650-gallon-per-minute pumper for $1,150. The first elected chief was Clarence Bergman. In the late 1960s, great growth developed in the eastern end of the fire district. Land was purchased, a substation was built, and in December 1975, Station No. 2 was officially occupied on Goshen Turnpike. In 1994, a new four-bay firehouse was dedicated at Station No. 1, Circleville. The district now has at Station No. 1 a 1997 Freightliner rescue truck, a 2005 KME pumper, a 2000 KME tanker, and a 1997 Ford fire police van. At Station No. 2 are a 2000 Ford rescue truck and a KME pumper. Shown in 1955 is the Circleville Volunteer Fire Company's early two-bay firehouse, with a Dodge tank truck (left) and a Mack pumper. (Courtesy of the Paul Weisshaar collection.)

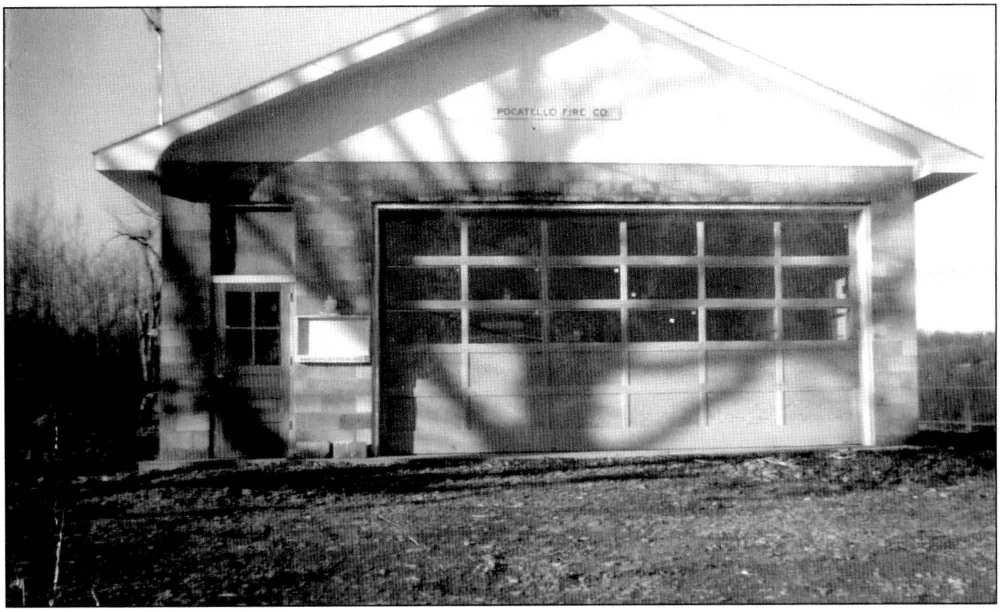

This photograph is of the Pocatello Firehouse, which was completed in 1965. (Courtesy of Pocatello Fire Company.)

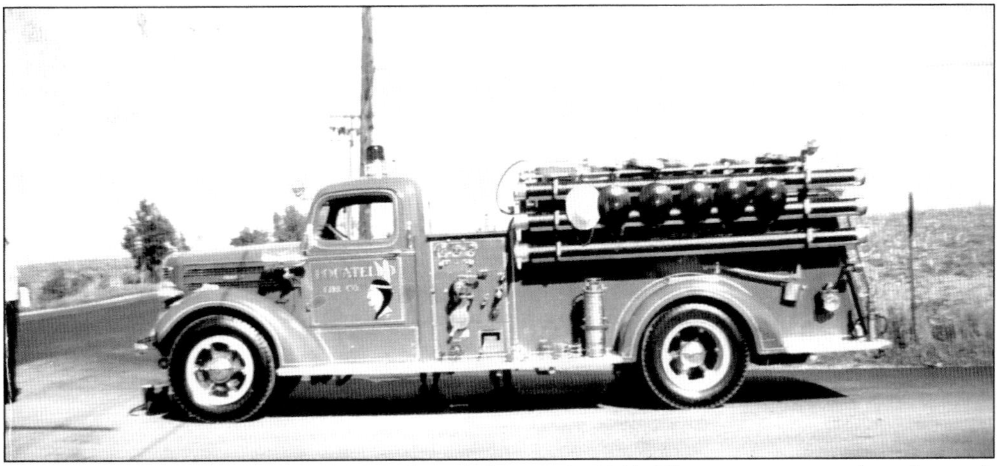

Pocatello Fire Company was organized on February 8, 1963. The company purchased a tank truck on August 23, 1963, and refurbished it, and the 1,350-gallon truck was ready for firefighting status by August 31, 1963. The first elected chief was Howard Myers. Groundbreaking for the permanent firehouse began on October 21, 1964, and the building was completed in early 1965. The town board granted Pocatello Fire Company status as a fire district effective January 1, 1965. The second piece of apparatus, formerly owned by the Highland Mills Fire Company and delivered on February 1, 1964, was a Mack truck, which had a 350-gallon water tank and a 500-gallon-per-minute midship rotary-geared pump. On April 2, 1966, a new truck with a 750-gallon-per-minute front-mounted pump and 1,200-gallon booster tank was put into service. The district now owns a Sutphen 1,300-gallon-per-minute pumper, a Sutphen tanker with a 2,800-gallon capacity and 1,600-gallon-per-minute pump, and a light rescue truck. Shown is Pocatello's Mack pumper. (Courtesy of Pocatello Fire Company.)

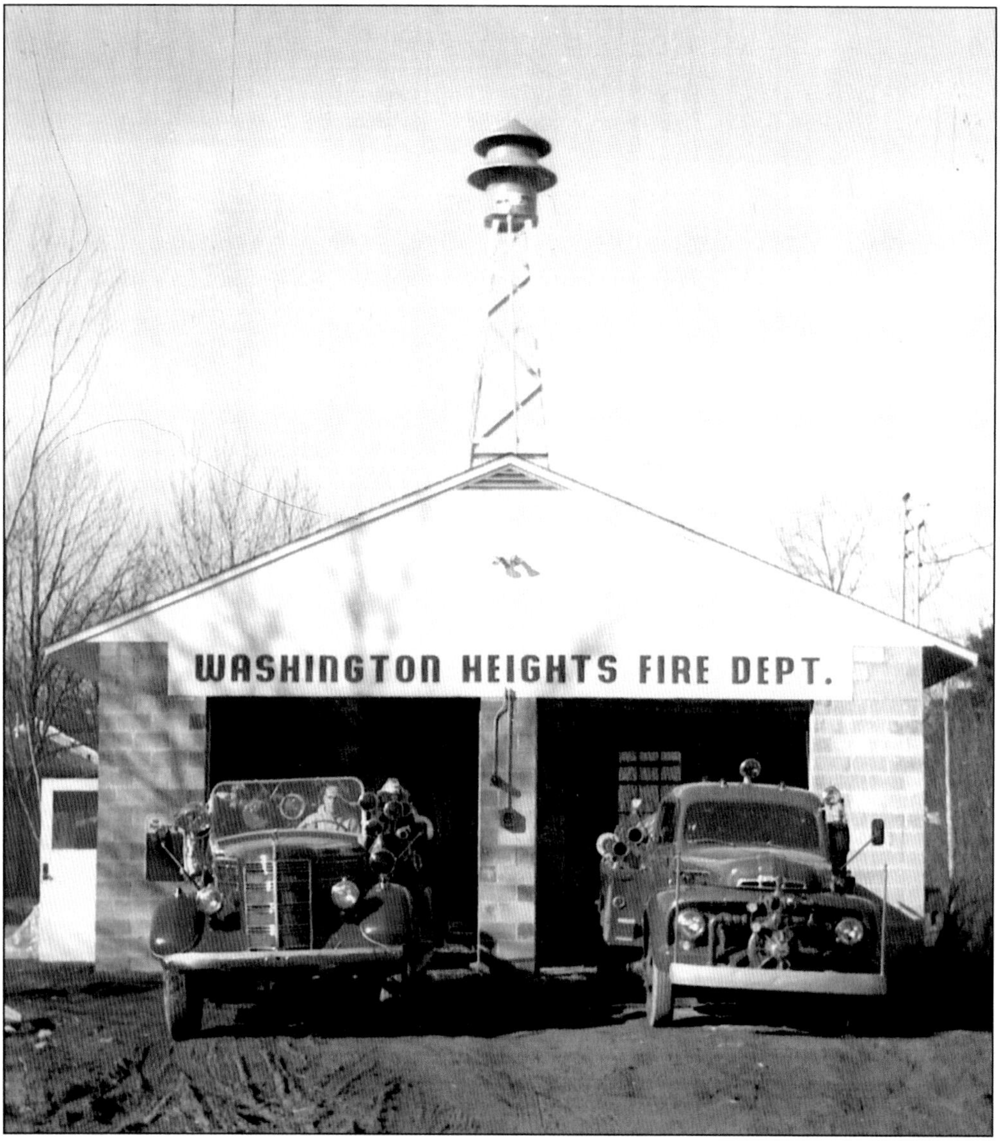

On May 3, 1962, area residents voted unanimously to form the Washington Heights Volunteer Fire Company. Richard Carey, a Town of Wallkill garage owner, donated a truck chassis, and Sam E. Fast, Wallkill oil dealer, donated an 860-gallon tank. The first elected chief was Richard Worden. In June 1962, the Wallkill Town Board voted to approve the establishment of the fire company and voted to award a fire protection contract to the company. In August 1962, a 1948 Mack open cab pumper was purchased from the Collingdale, Pennsylvania, Fire Company for $3,250. Footings were poured for a two-bay firehouse on Alabama Avenue and Ohio Place, and by October 1962, the firehouse was 60 percent complete. Formal approval by the Town of Wallkill Town Board for the Washington Heights Fire District was given on June 23, 1963. The firehouse was increased in size, and a 250-seat hall was completed in 1968 and dedicated in memory of Fred Heater, one of the first elected fire commissioners of the district. Today the District has a 1988 Young Duplex 1,000-gallon pumper, 1998 Central States Freightliner 1,000-gallon pumper and a 1990 Dodge 4-wheel drive utility truck.Pictured is the original Washington Heights firehouse, with a Mack truck (left) and tanker. (Courtesy of Washington Heights Fire Company.)

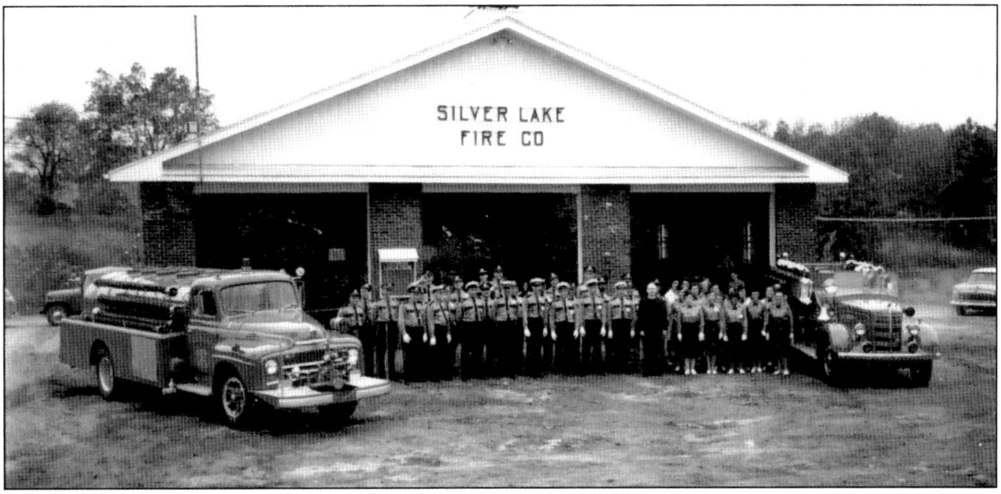

The Silver Lake Fire Company was organized in January 1963. The firemen met at their temporary headquarters, a barn on Route 84 (now Route 211). A 1,200-gallon 1952 International tank truck was purchased June 26, 1963, refurbished in two months, and put into service. Property was purchased on what is now Maltese Drive, and a three-bay firehouse was built by the volunteers. In February 1964, a 1946 Mack pumper was purchased. The first elected chief of the Silver Lake Company was Carl Schumacher. The firehouse has been enlarged to five bays and the district now owns a 1990 Sutphen aerial ladder tower, a 1993 Pierce engine, a 1996 heavy rescue truck, a 2004 American LaFrance engine, and a 2006 Ford F550 support vehicle. Pictured in 1964 are the firehouse, apparatus, firemen, and auxiliary. (Courtesy of Silver Lake Fire Company.)

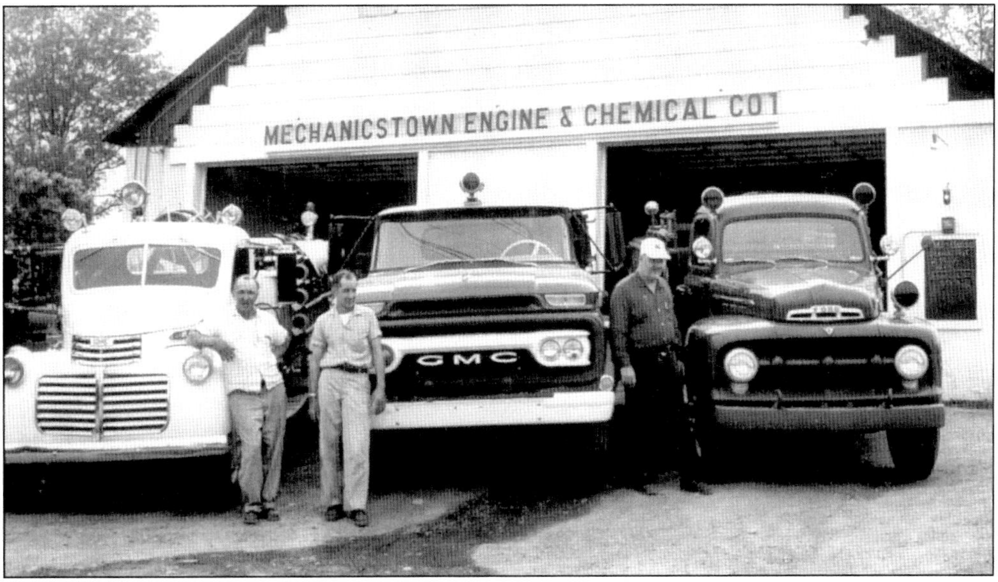

Mechanicstown Engine and Chemical Company No. 1 was chartered in 1927 and reorganized in 1953. In 1954, the company built a fire station at Ridgewood Avenue and Victory Street in Mechanicstown. The first elected chief was Warren Bullis in 1957. The Wallkill Town Board voted to establish the Mechanicstown Fire District in 1964. The 1954 Mechanicstown Fire Station is shown with, from left to right, Peter Pulos, Everett Garrison, and William Bohm standing in front of the apparatus. (Courtesy of Mechanicstown Engine and Chemical Company No. 1.)

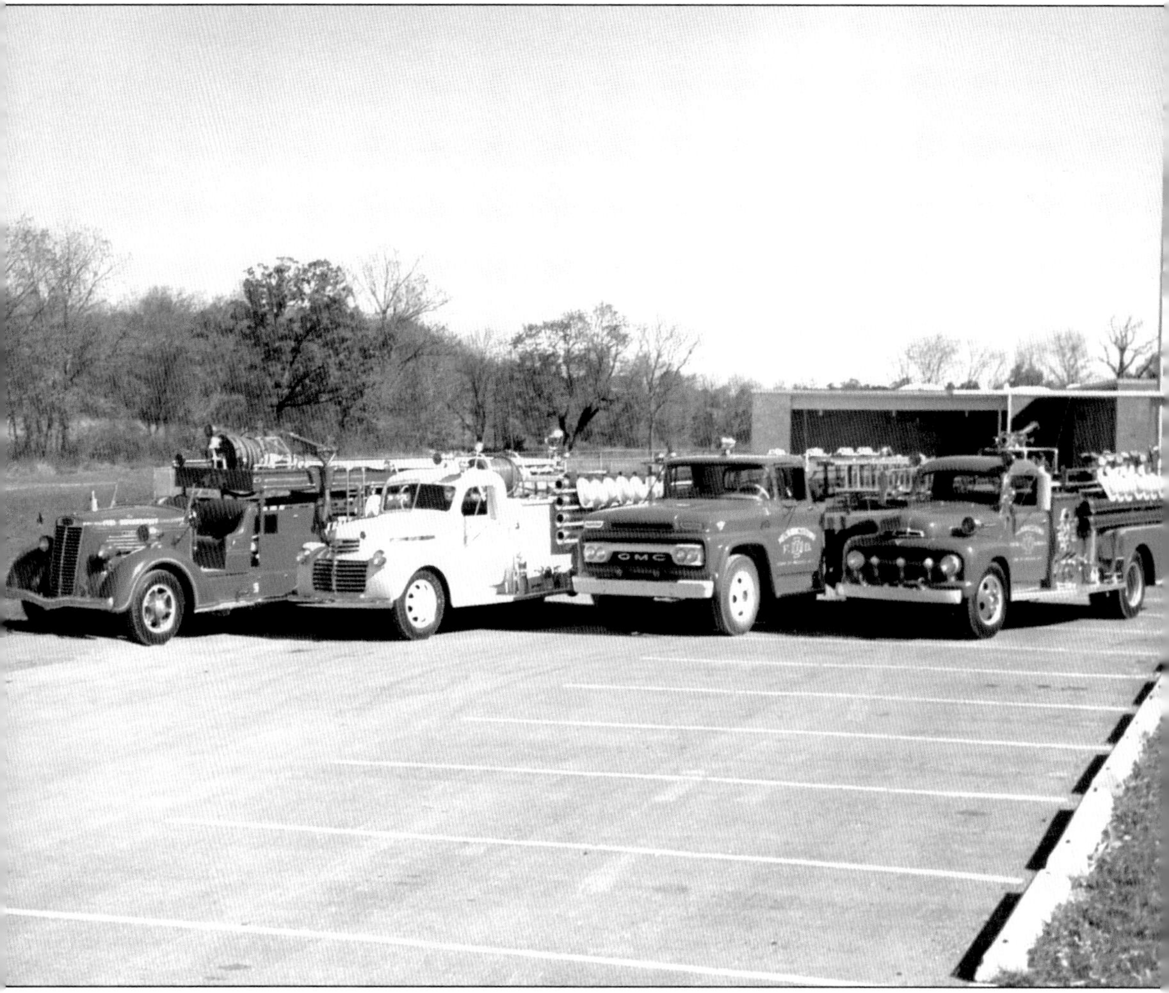

In 1963, Mechanicstown Fire Company owned a 1941 Autocar City Service, a 1941 GMC Sanford 500-gallon-per-minute pumper, a 1962 GMC tanker, and a 1951 Ford Seagrave 500-gallon-per-minute pumper. In 1993, the original fire station on Ridgewood Avenue was demolished and a modern five-bay firehouse was built on the site. Current apparatus at Station No. 1 are a 1994 Spartan Saulsbury Heavy Rescue, a 2001 KME 100-foot aerial, a 2004 KME 2,000-gallon-per-minute pumper, a 2004 KME minipumper, a 1997 Dodge van fire police vehicle, and a 1997 Spartan Saulsbury 900-gallon and 2,000-gallon-per-minute pumper. A substation on Stony Ford Road was later erected to serve that part of the district. The apparatus at Station No. 2 consists of a 1990 KME 1,500-gallon and 2,000-gallon-per-minute pumper, a 1985 GMC brush truck, and two 2003 Sportsman 700s with trailers. (Photograph courtesy of Art Bartow; information courtesy of Mechanicstown Engine and Chemical Company No. 1.)

Ten

RAILROADS

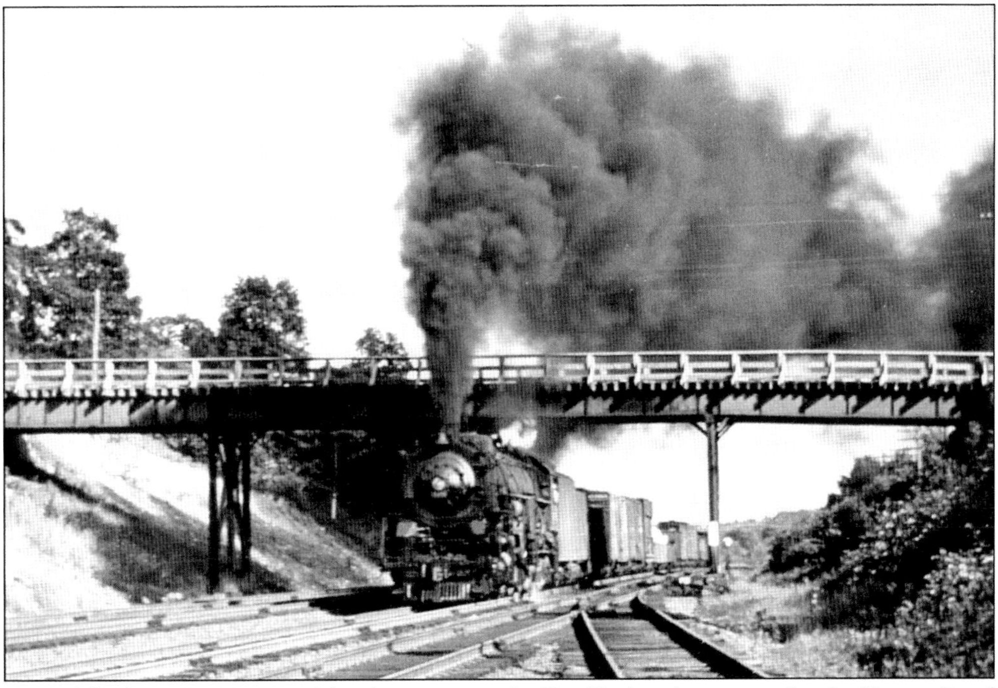

One of the last steam-powered freight trains on the Erie Railroad passes under the Bowser Road Bridge, headed for Port Jervis in 1952. (Photograph by Marvin H. Cohen)

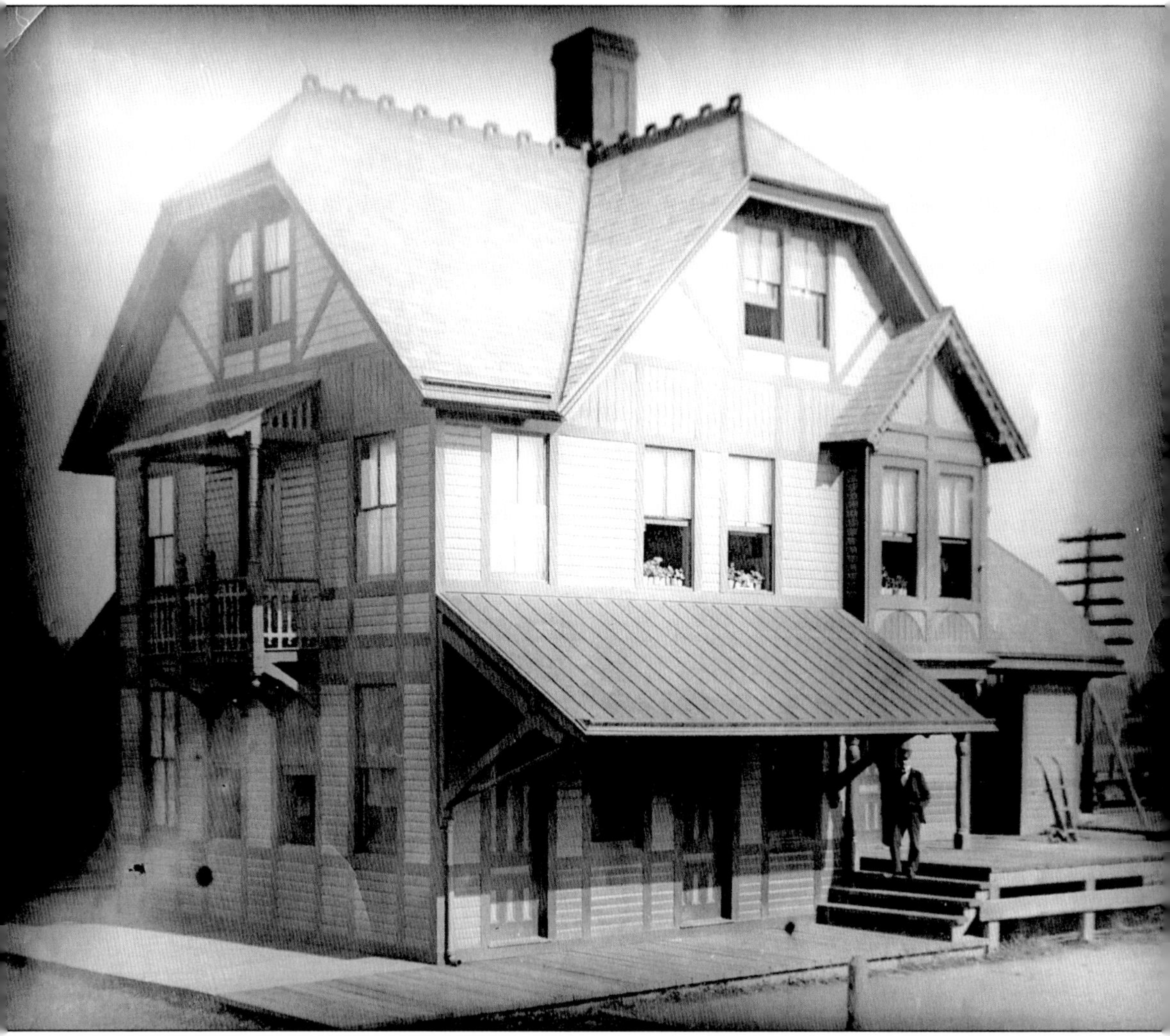

This is the Mechanicstown station of the New York, Ontario and Western Railway. The building, located on Dunning Road, still stands. Its last use was as a restaurant called the Rusty Nail.

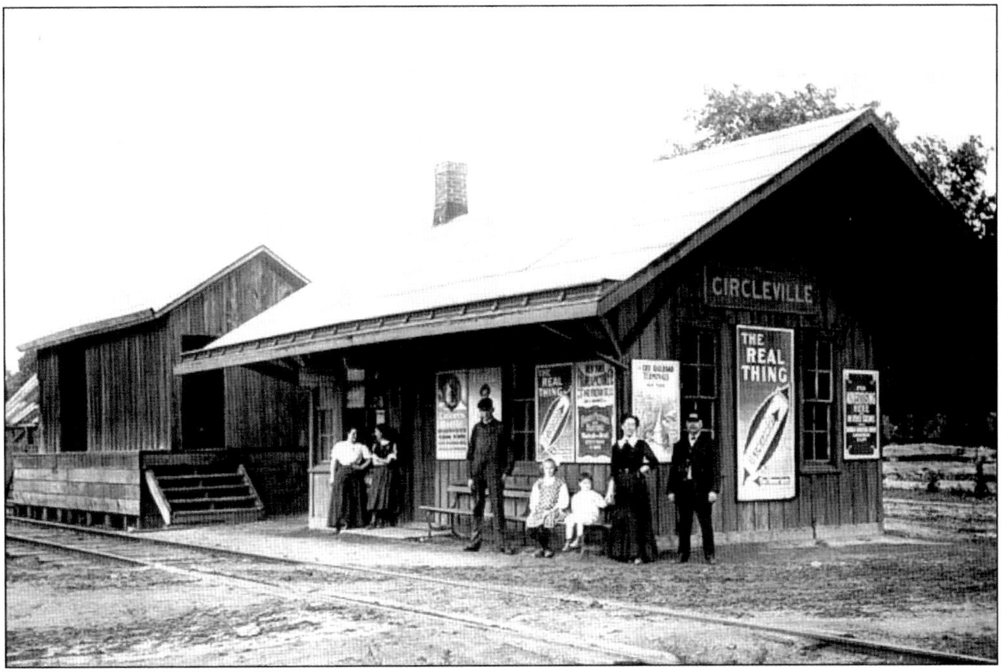

This 1910 scene shows the Erie Railroad's station at Circleville. The station was on the Erie Railroad's Crawford Branch, which served the communities of Circleville, Bullville, Thompson Ridge, and Pine Bush.

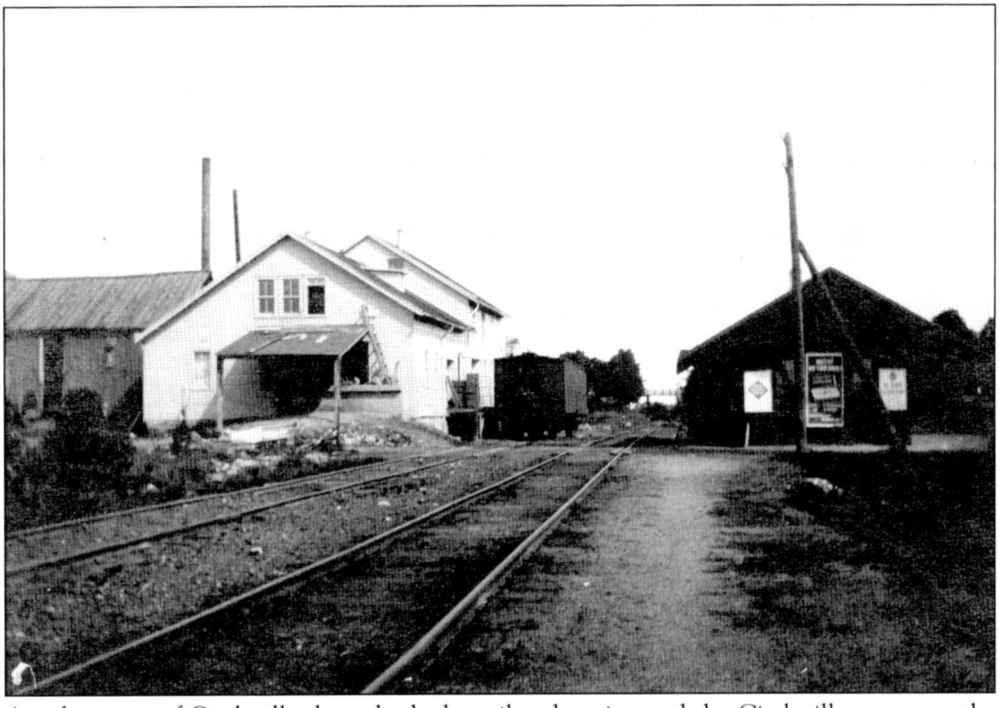

Another view of Circleville shows both the railroad station and the Circleville creamery, the source of much of the milk traffic on the branch.

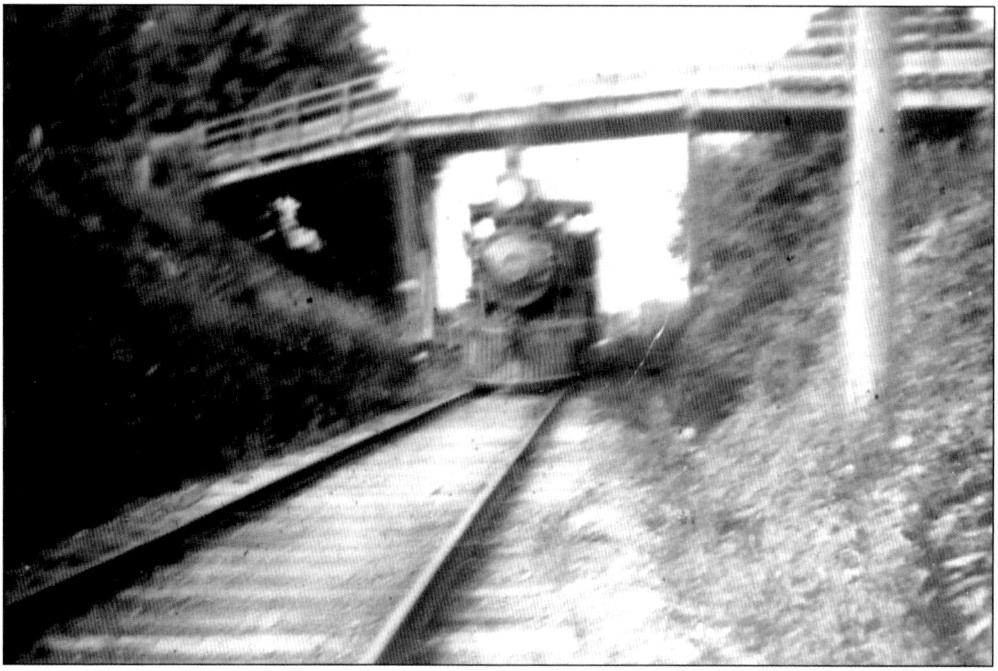

A vintage photograph shows a train passing under the Goshen Turnpike Bridge at Circleville around 1910.

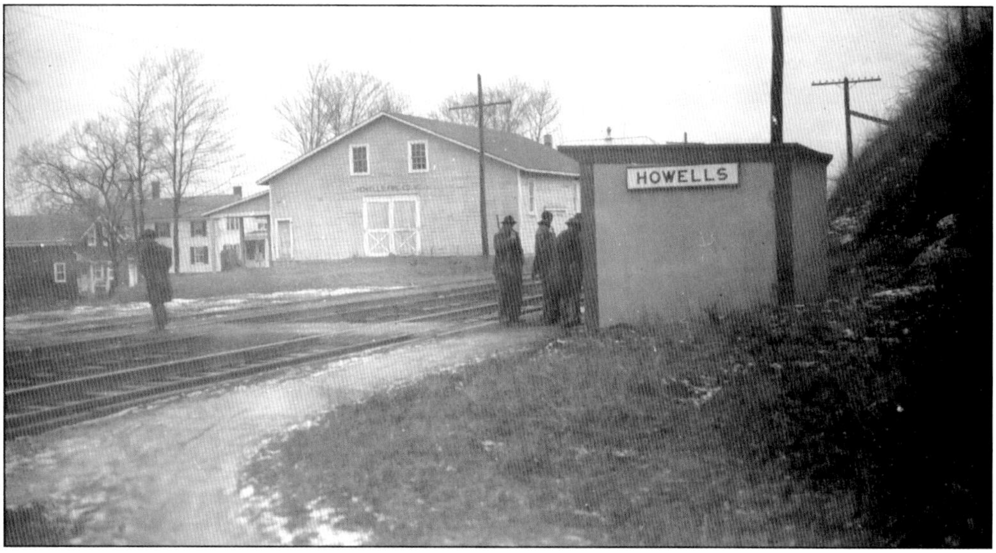

This picture shows the rudimentary passenger shelter on the old main line in Howells around 1950. The building in the background is now the fire department barn. The tracks shown here were removed in 1954 when all trains were routed through the mile-long Otisville tunnel.